# HE HOT TOPIC

**ABRIELLE WALKER** is the author of *Snowball Earth* and *An Ocean of Air*, and a journalist and broadcaster. Her recent radio series *Planet Earth under Threat* was a major success for the BC.

**IR DAVID KING**, until the end of 2007 the UK's chief scientific adviser, is widely credited with persuading the British government to take the lead on climate change. He is currently Professor of Chemistry at Cambridge University and Director of the New School for Enterprise and the Environment at Oxford University.

# THE HOT TOPIC

## HOW TO TACKLE GLOBAL WARMING AND STILL KEEP THE LIGHTS ON

Gabrielle Walker and Sir David King

BLOOMSBURY
LONDON · BERLIN · NEW YORK

First published in Great Britain 2008
This paperback edition published 2009
Copyright © by Gabrielle Walker and Sir David King 2008

Diagrams by John Gilkes

Bloomsbury Publishing Plc
36 Soho Square
London W1D 3QY

www.bloomsbury.com

Bloomsbury Publishing, London, New York and Berlin

A CIP catalogue record for this book is available from the British Library

ISBN 9780747596301

10 9 8 7 6 5 4 3 2 1

Typeset by Hewer Text UK Ltd, Edinburgh
Printed in Great Britain by Clays Ltd, St Ives plc

The paper this book is printed on is certified independently in accordance with the
rules of the FSC. It is ancient-forest friendly. The printer holds chain of custody

**FSC**
**Mixed Sources**
Product group from well-managed
forests and other controlled sources
www.fsc.org
Cert no. SGS - COC - 2061
www.fsc.org
© 1996 Forest Stewardship Council

For Rosa Malloy and Jane Lichtenstein

# Contents

# Part III: POLITICAL SOLUTIONS

# Preface

The North Pole of planet Earth is an extraordinary place. It's a smudgy circle of frozen ocean, hemmed in by the surrounding land masses of Siberia, North America and Europe. Cracks occasionally appear in its surface, where the ice has been torn apart by winds above and currents below. But for the most part, its grey-white façade is as unyielding as rock. You can walk on it, stamp on it, even land planes on it. When you're there, the Arctic sea ice doesn't seem remotely fragile, just motionless, silent and strong, as if water had been turned irreparably to stone.

And yet, photographs taken from satellites have now shown conclusively what scientists have been fearing for decades: the North Pole is melting. Each summer, the spread of the sea ice shrinks a little further. It is vanishing from beneath the feet of the Arctic's polar bears. If we do nothing to stop it, by the end of the century the ice, polar bears, and all, could be gone.

The story of global warming has progressed in the past few years from conjecture, to suspicion, to cold, hard fact. We now know for certain that in every inhabited continent on Earth, year by year and decade by decade, the world's temperature is rising. Something, or someone, is turning up the heat.

Should we care? After all, over the billions of years our planet has been around its climate has changed many times. In the geological past there have been ice ages, global floods and heatwaves. There have also been winners and losers throughout Earth's history – some species that have become extinct and others that have gone forth and multiplied.

But this time is different. If the current wave of change has its way with us, the polar bears will not be the only ones to suffer. Human civilisation has never before been faced with a climate that is changing this fast or this furiously. The threat has become urgent. In 2004, one of us (David King) caused a furore by describing climate change as 'the most severe problem we are facing today, more serious even than the threat of terrorism'.[1] Since then, the scale of the problem has become even clearer.

Also, of course, the amount of material focusing on the problem has multiplied almost uncontrollably. Books, newspapers, TV, radio – another day, another headline. It has become almost impossible to sort out what really matters.

Amid this cacophony there are a handful of voices that persist in arguing that warming isn't happening, or that it's not caused by humans, while others see disaster around every corner and indulge in gory scenarios that have been labelled 'climate porn'. We don't agree with either of these approaches. Climate change is happening, and humans are very largely to blame. However, we do not believe that disaster is inevitable. A few shiny new Priuses won't get humans out of this mess, and nor will sticking our collective heads in the sand. But we do still have time to tackle the worst aspects of climate change if we act fast and work hard.

In the course of this book we will pick our way through the blizzard of information and misinformation about global warming, explaining each point in the most straightforward way possible. We will discuss the scientific basis for the problem, the possible technological solutions – and the political sticking points. We are both trained scientists, and our approach will be a scientific one – to examine the evidence, giving most weight to rigorous research that has been tested by peer review.

Though between us we have considerable experience in the worlds of media and politics, we are neither lobbyists nor politicians, and we have no personal axes to grind. We will unpick the entire essential story of global warming – what we humans have done, how we have done it, how we will need to prepare for the changes we can't stop and how we can prevent the even worse effects that will otherwise follow. We aim to tell you everything you wanted to know about global warming but were too depressed to ask.

However, this is not a book about generic 'green' issues. Most measures that increase efficiency and reduce waste will also help – at least, a little – with global warming. But this book is not a general environmental call to arms. It proposes a very specific set of solutions to a very specific, though wide-ranging, problem.

In particular it seeks to show that the story need not necessarily have an unhappy ending. Global warming is a serious problem, probably the most serious that the human race has, collectively, ever faced. But we can still do something about it. This is neither a time for pessimism nor for denial. It is a time for constructive, determined action.

# Part I: THE PROBLEM

Before we can start discussing how to get ourselves out of the climate mess, we first need to set out the problem. There has been an extraordinary amount of confusion and misinformation about the science of climate change – which is surprising since it is one of the few areas of complex science for which researchers are in almost unanimous agreement. In the next few chapters we will explain the science of global warming – what is happening, how we know the cause, the future changes that are now inevitable and the ones that we still have a chance of avoiding.

# 1

# WARMING WORLD

Climate change isn't new. Our planet is restless and its environment rarely stays still for long. There have been times in the distant past when carbon dioxide levels were very much higher than they are today, and Antarctica was a tropical paradise. There have been others when carbon dioxide levels were much lower, and even the equator was encrusted with ice.

But over the past 10,000 years, which is all the time that human civilisation has existed, the Earth's climate has been unusually steady. We humans have become used to a world where the way things are is more or less the way they will be, at least when it comes to temperature. In other words, we have been lucky.

Now, our steady reliable climate is changing, and this time Nature isn't to blame. But how do we know for certain that the world is warming, and how can we identify the culprit?

## The heat is on

When you're trying to measure if the world's temperature is rising, the biggest problem is picking out a signal from the background 'noise'. Even in our relatively stable times, temperatures lurch up and down from one day to another, from season to season, from year to year and from place to place. To be sure that the underlying trend is changing, you need to take precise measurements from many different places around the world, and do so for an extremely long time.

We do have a few long temperature records, thanks to certain individuals who decided to make the measurements just in case they ever proved useful. The world's longest is the Central England Temperature Record, which is a tribute to the obsessive data-collecting habits of British seventeenth-century natural scientists. It covers a triangular region of England from London to Bristol to Lancashire and stretches back to 1659. This impressive record does show clear signs of warming, especially towards the end of the twentieth century.

However, the record covers only a tiny part of the globe. Changes in England don't necessarily reflect changes in Australia, say, or Brazil. It also doesn't go back far enough to reveal just how unusual our recent warm temperatures really are. How do they compare, for instance, to the apparent warm period in medieval times when the Vikings settled a verdant, pleasant 'Greenland' and there were vineyards in northern England? Or the so-called Little Ice Age in the mid-centuries of the last millennium, when the River Thames in London froze over completely so that frost fairs were held on its solid surface?

To answer these questions, scientists have come up with ingenious ways to expand the records geographically and extend them backwards in time. Some people have tried to interpret written archives that didn't quote actual temperatures,[1] but the best way is to look at records written not by humans, but by Nature.

Every year, the average tree grows a ring of new wood around its trunk. In a good year the ring will be thicker, in a bad year thinner.[2] Researchers drill a small core into the side of the tree, about the diameter of a wine cork, extract the wood, and then count and measure. By going to trees that are different ages, and even some trees that are long dead but have been preserved in peaty bogs, they have come up with a temperature record spanning more than a thousand years and from regions across northern Europe, Russia and North America.

For more tropical regions, corals can play a similar role since they, like trees, grow a new ring every year. And in the frozen north and south (and the snow-capped peaks of tropical mountains), ice also contains a record book of past climate. Each year's snowfall buries the previous one. If temperatures are cold enough, the snow stays around long enough to be squeezed into ice, clearly marking out the annual layers because summer's snow crystals are larger than winter's, or because more dust blows in each year with the winter winds. The amount of snow that fell in a given year, and especially the changing nature of the oxygen atoms bound up in the ice,[3] give clues as to how warm it was then.

Another clue comes from changing plant life, as written into the record of mud at the bottom of lakes. As temperature rises and falls, different plants flourish and each one sheds its pollen into passing currents of air. Some of this might land on the surface of a nearby lake, before slowly sinking into the mud beneath. Drill a hole in this mud, collect and analyse the pollen grains each layer contains, and you have yet another record of temperature changes over time.

Researchers have now used a host of different ways like these to analyse and splice together these different measures,

Changes in northern hemisphere temperature relative to the average value from 1961–90 in °C for the past 1,000 years. The different lines reflect data that come from different sources and methods, but all show the same dramatic increase in temperature in the last few decades.

and all come to strikingly similar conclusions for temperatures over the last 1,000 years.[4] The eleventh century was indeed relatively warm, corresponding to the Medieval Warm Period. ('Verdant' Greenland turned out to be more of a marketing exercise than the truth. Ice cores drilled into the heart of Greenland's ice cap show that a substantial quantity of ice has been present on the island for hundreds of thousands of years. Any Vikings who fell for the hype must have had an unpleasant shock when they arrived.)

Temperatures were also cooler in the seventeenth century, corresponding to the Little Ice Age, and again in the early nineteenth century. These warm and cool periods were apparently also fairly widespread, though they may have been less prevalent in the southern hemisphere.[5]

Year

(Source: P. D. Jones, T. J. Osborn and K. R. Briffa, 'The Evolution of Climate over the last Millennium', *Science*, vol. 292 (5517), pp. 662–7, 27 April 2001)

However, it was only in the twentieth century that temperatures really began to take off. The warming didn't happen regularly, but in two bursts – which turns out to be important. The first one occurred during the early years of the twentieth century and was marked enough that it made itself clearly felt. In 1939, *Time* magazine wrote: 'Gaffers who claim that winters were harder when they were boys are quite right . . . Weather men have no doubt that the world at least for the time being is growing warmer.'[6] But the following few decades brought slightly cooler temperatures, at least in the northern hemisphere, and public interest waned.

The second burst of warming began in the 1970s and has been gathering pace ever since. And, crucially, the temperatures we are experiencing now are hotter than they have been for the entire last millennium. Even the Medieval Warm Period was cooler than it is today.[7]

Let's put some numbers in. Globally averaged, from the 1910s to the 1940s temperatures rose by about 0.35°C. After that there was a cooling of about 0.1°C, and since 1970 the world has warmed by a further 0.55°C.[8] These numbers might not sound like much, but they are nonetheless very significant. Although the temperature where you live can change by much more than this within the space of a few hours or days, it is much more worrying when global annual averages show an inexorable upward trend. Averaging in this way smoothes out short-term flurries and shows what's really happening. That's why a small change in global average temperature can reflect a very big shift in climate. Speaking in global averages, only a few degrees separate us from the frigid world of the last ice age.[9]

Though the proxy records of tree rings, ice cores and the like give a good indication of average temperatures over a timescale of decades, they're not so hot on temperatures for individual years. Thus, although we can say that the temperature is now greater than it has been in the past 1,000 years, it's harder to say how 2005 compared with, say, 1105. For that sort of pinpoint accuracy only a human record will do.

Good widespread records started to become available by about 1850, so we can put the past few individual years into the perspective of the past 160 or so. Once again, the message is stark. The hottest years in the entire instrumental record were in 1998 and 2005. (They were very close, and opinion is divided as to which one takes the warming crown.) The years 2002, 2003 and 2004 were, respectively, the third, fourth and fifth warmest on record. In fact, eleven of the past twelve years have been in the top twelve on record.[10]

Temperature change over the past 150 years in °C compared to the 1961–90 average. (Source: IPCC)

The Intergovernmental Panel on Climate Change (IPCC) is an international body made up of leading climate scientists and government advisers from around the world. Because its reports must reflect the consensus view of all its many contributors, it has a reputation for being conservative. It is also widely considered to be the definitive authority on the science of climate change and in 2007 it won the Nobel Peace Prize.

The latest report from the IPCC, published in 2007, described the warming of the past few decades as 'unequivocal'.[11] There is no longer any room for doubt. The world is certainly heating up. What we need to know next is why.

## People who live in greenhouses

The prime suspect for causing this heating is, of course, the infamous 'greenhouse effect'. It is this that gives us our capacity to affect the climate; without it, we could burn fuel to our heart's content, and the planet wouldn't feel a thing. Because of this, the greenhouse effect is often portrayed as the villain of the piece. But it may come as a surprise to learn that the effect itself is a very good thing. Without it, the Earth would be completely frozen.

Looking at our nearest planetary neighbours, Mars and Venus, it's tempting to think that our planet has the best location in the solar system. Venus is closer than we are to the Sun, and so hot that its surface would melt lead. Mars is further from the Sun and its winters are so cold that steel on its surface would shatter. Earth, the in-between 'Goldilocks' planet, is supposed to be just right.

However, that's not quite correct. In fact, we're a little too far away from the Sun for comfort. Just going by our location the Earth should, by rights, be frozen over. This was discovered back in 1827 by French scientist Joseph Fourier, who had decided to try balancing the Earth's energy books.

Our planet's central heating system ought to be fairly simple: energy comes to us from the Sun, in the form of sunlight. The Earth soaks up this sunlight. It then glows with warmth, pouring out another form of light, which is too far beyond the red end of the rainbow for our eyes to see, and hence is called 'infrared'. (All warm bodies give off this invisible infrared glow – including humans. Night-vision goggles work by detecting it, as do heat-seeking missiles.)

Fourier thought that the infrared light given off by the invisibly glowing Earth would pour back out into space to balance the energy budget and set our global average temperature at a comfortable plus 15°C. But when he calculated the heat energy coming in from the Sun and going out from infrared radiation he was astonished. By rights, our global average temperature should be *minus* 15°C. In other words, the entire planet should be frozen. Fourier also realised that each night, when incoming sunlight was temporarily switched off, the outgoing radiation would continue to pour into space, which should have cooled the Earth's surface even more. In other words, there should also be much bigger differences between the temperatures of day and night than we see today.

Clearly something else is keeping us warmer than we deserve. Fourier realised that the atmosphere was the key. However, he didn't know which part of our air was acting as a warming blanket. This missing ingredient was discovered by a flamboyant Irishman named John Tyndall. Tyndall worked at London's Royal Institution and when he wasn't wowing the audiences of poets and politicians upstairs with his famously entertaining lectures about science, he was down in the basement tinkering with his experiments on the atmosphere. He was fascinated by Fourier's calculations, and wondered if something was blocking part of the invisible infrared glow, preventing it from escaping back to space.

To find out, Tyndall set up an artificial sky in a tube and started shining infrared light through it. He wanted his sky to be as clean as possible, so he took out all 'impurities' from the air. This left the two gases that make up more than 99 per cent of our atmosphere: oxygen and nitrogen. But to his bafflement, infrared light slipped through the air unhindered. In other words, the gases that make up most of our atmosphere –

nitrogen and oxygen – make no difference at all to its temperature.

On a slightly desperate hunch, Tyndall slipped a few of the 'impurities' back into his air. He added a whiff of methane, some water vapour and a soupçon of carbon dioxide, all of which exist in tiny amounts in the real atmosphere. And suddenly, everything changed. As far as infrared was concerned, Tyndall's artificial sky went black. These so-called impurities did indeed trap infrared and prevent at least some of it from escaping back to space. They were Fourier's mysterious warming ingredients.

Tyndall and Fourier had discovered what we now call the greenhouse effect. Water vapour, carbon dioxide, methane and the other so-called 'greenhouse gases' share a special skill that the more abundant oxygen and nitrogen don't possess. They act a bit like the glass windows of a greenhouse, which allow sunlight through to warm the air inside, but then prevent the hot air from escaping. The difference is that greenhouse gases don't block the air itself. Instead they're more like a one-way mirror. They let sunlight slip in through the atmosphere to heat the surface, but then block some of the outgoing glow of warmth that would otherwise carry heat back into space.

This discovery teaches two important lessons.

First, a little greenhouse effect is a very good thing. Without any intervention by greenhouse gases our planet would be frozen and lifeless. Or, as Tyndall put it, rather more poetically: 'The warmth of our fields and gardens would pour itself unrequited into space, and the sun would rise upon an island held fast in the iron grip of frost.'

★

Second, a little greenhouse gas goes a very long way. Watch out for people who say that greenhouse gases can't affect the Earth's temperature because they make up such a tiny part of the atmosphere. They are certainly scarce compared to oxygen and nitrogen, but that's not relevant. Thanks to their skills at trapping infrared radiation, a whiff of greenhouse gas can change the temperature of the entire atmosphere just as a few drops of ink can change the colour of an entire bathful of water.

The real atmosphere contains a host of greenhouses gases,[12] but the most important are the ones Tyndall tried: water, methane and carbon dioxide. Of these, gaseous water has by far the biggest effect on the temperature of the air. That's mainly because, compared to the other greenhouse gases, water is so abundant. It can make up anything from a fraction of a per cent to several per cent of the air, depending on the region, season and time of day.[13]

However, when it comes to the power to change the climate, carbon dioxide and methane (and to some extent those few other, scarcer, greenhouse gases) come into their own. Carbon dioxide makes up less than 0.04 per cent of the air, and methane even less than that. But they both punch considerably above their weight when it comes to global warming, for two important reasons.

First, there is already so much water vapour in the atmosphere that human activities make hardly any difference to the total, rather like adding a few bucketfuls of water to an ocean. But because there's relatively little carbon dioxide and methane, you don't have to add much to make a big proportional difference. It's like putting a few extra bucketfuls of water into a bath. Thus, humans have already almost managed to double the amount of greenhouse gases in the air.

And second, by trapping extra heat themselves, these green-house gases also have an indirect effect on the amount of water vapour in the air. Warmer air can soak up more water, and warmer lakes, rivers and seas can evaporate more easily into the atmosphere. The upshot of these two effects is that if you heat the air a little by adding extra carbon dioxide, it then takes up much more water vapour. This new water acts as a greenhouse gas in its own right and heats the air up even more, roughly doubling the effect the greenhouse gases would have had if they acted alone. Scientists call this a positive feedback – positive not because it's good, but because it amplifies the original effect rather than diminishes it.[14]

So, if you changed the quantities of the greenhouse gases in the air, you would expect the temperature to go up. And that's exactly what we have been doing for the past few hundred years. Since people began throwing coal on to their fires, or stoking up their steam engines, carbon dioxide levels have been rising. The discoveries of oil and natural gas have accelerated the process. Every gas-fired cooker or central heating boiler, every tank of petrol and every power station fuelled by coal, gas or oil has added a little more carbon dioxide to the air. Oil, coal and natural gas are the three wicked witches of the climate change story, because they are all dense repositories of carbon.[15]

## How are greenhouse gases changing?

Carbon is a wonder element, a supreme networker that can make chemical bonds with more or less anything else. Because of this extreme flexibility, carbon is the ultimate building block for all life on Earth. It forms the backbone for everything from carbohydrates, proteins and fats to leaves, wood, bones, skin and hair.

One consequence is that when you burn something that was once alive, you will release the carbon it contained, usually in the form of carbon dioxide.[16] That's what happens when you burn oil, coal and natural gas. These three are known as 'fossil fuels', because they are literally the fossilised remains of animals and plants that lived many millions of years ago, and had, until the beginning of the Industrial Revolution around 1850, remained safely buried in the ground.

To make coal, you need trees, swamps and plenty of time. Most of the world's black coal was created between 360 and 290 million years ago in a period known, appropriately, as the Carboniferous. This was a time when insects grew to astonishing, horror-movie sizes – millipedes were two metres long, spiders and dragonflies spanned up to a metre and even cockroaches could be as big as thirty centimetres. The coal itself came from the bodies of mighty trees growing in the swamps that covered the Carboniferous Earth.[17] When these trees toppled, the stagnant swamp protected them from rotting, and they were gradually compressed, dried out and cooked into the coal that we burn today.

Making crude oil is a more delicate process. Oil was formed, much of it also in the Carboniferous period, from the dead bodies of tiny sea creatures, but these bodies had to be trapped, preserved, and cooked to exactly the right temperatures and pressures. That's why oil is found in far fewer places than coal. If the cooking process went awry, the oil broke down and turned into methane, also known as natural gas. Almost all oil deposits come with some methane, but methane is often also found on its own.

Since all three of these fossil fuels used to be alive, they are all made up of forms of carbon. Thus, burning fossil fuels produces carbon dioxide.

There's an important point to make here about the natural balance of carbon dioxide. Burning formerly living things isn't the only way that carbon dioxide can appear in the air. When we and most other living things breathe, we are 'burning' our food to produce energy (which is one reason we talk about burning calories). And because our food used to be alive, the by-product is carbon dioxide. The carbon dioxide that we animals breathe out is taken up by plants, which use it to make their bodies, providing us with the food that completes the cycle. Vast quantities of $CO_2$ pass through the atmosphere perfectly naturally in this way every day. What's more, burning wood, crops and anything else that used to be alive will also put carbon dioxide into the air. So why the focus on fossil fuels?

The reason fossil fuels are so important to the climate change story is that they involve burning carbon that had been buried for hundreds of millions of years. By contrast, the carbon inside wood was in the air fairly recently, probably just a few decades ago, before the tree soaked it up and converted it into trunk and branches. When you burn the wood, you're putting that same carbon dioxide back again. In the long term, nothing changes.

Similarly, when you breathe, you release carbon dioxide that was probably taken up in the past year or two to make your food. Again, zero sum.[18]

But when you burn something that has been buried, and hence kept out of the air, for hundreds of millions of years, there's an important difference. By burning fossil fuels we are tapping into an old, deep reservoir that has long been locked away, and thus we are drastically changing the balance of the air.

Does that really matter? After all, as we hinted in the Preface, there have been times in the past when carbon dioxide levels have been much, much higher than they are today. The trouble is that these times were unimaginably long ago, before humans were even a glint in Nature's eye.

We know this because, thanks to a miraculous application of science and ingenuity, we actually have pieces of ancient air to study. These come from Antarctica where the year-round freezing temperatures mean that snow that fell hundreds of thousands of years ago is still there today. It has been buried by subsequent layers, so you have to dig deep to find the really old snow (which has since been squashed down into ice). Researchers at Russia's Vostok station have done just that, drilling a core whose ice stretches back some 400,000 years. A subsequent core drilled at a joint French–Italian base at Dome C produced ice that is even older, at some 800,000 years.[19] Inside this ancient ice are tiny bubbles of air that were trapped when the snow first fell.

Scientists have analysed these bubbles to check how much carbon dioxide and methane they contain. The results show that over long time periods carbon dioxide levels naturally rise and fall. During ice ages, carbon dioxide tends to be quite low. During warmer times the carbon dioxide rises. However, there is not a single moment in the past 650,000 years when carbon dioxide has been anything near as high as it is today.[20]

We know that carbon dioxide levels have recently taken an ugly turn, thanks to an extremely persistent American researcher named Charles David Keeling. Back in the 1950s, Keeling decided to find out how carbon dioxide in the atmosphere was changing. He chose a site in Hawaii, far away from industrial sources that might bias his results, and then he started measuring. In those early years he had constant trouble persuading funders that the study was worth doing, and more importantly worth continuing. But he succeeded, and his 'Keeling curve' has become an icon of the global warming story.[21]

That's because the curve shows a never-ending rise. As the century has progressed, and we have burned ever more fossil fuels, Keeling's carbon dioxide curve has reared up like a malevolent serpent.

Once again, let's talk numbers. Because there's so little carbon dioxide in the atmosphere to start with, it's messy to use percentages. Instead, for carbon dioxide and other gases that are scarce in the air, scientists use 'parts per million', or ppm. One ppm is 0.0001 per cent.

During ice ages, carbon dioxide reaches a low of around 180–190 ppm. For the warmer periods in between (of which our current climate is one), carbon dioxide typically rises to a high of around 290. From the coldest point of the last ice age, about 20,000 years ago, until 1900, the levels lay in a healthy range of 260 to 290 ppm.[22]

But over the time of the Keeling curve, the level has sky-rocketed to around 385 ppm in 2008. The planetary atmosphere now contains a level of carbon dioxide that is nearly 40 per cent higher than its 'natural' pre-industrial values, and it is still rising at between 2 and 3 ppm per year.

What's more, the levels of other greenhouse gases like methane have been rising, too. In the case of methane the reasons for the rise are more complicated – it comes from increasing the area of rice paddy fields, from gas that escapes when you're drilling for oil and even from belching cows.[23] In addition, there are the artificial chemicals, the so-called 'CFCs', which nearly destroyed the ozone layer and happen to be excellent greenhouse gases in their own right. Putting all these together and calculating how much they add to the carbon dioxide effect, we now have a 'carbon dioxide equivalent' ($CO_2$eq) level of about 430 ppm. In other words, we have effectively added about 60 per cent to the greenhouses gases that were there before. And counting.

In summary, we know the world is warming. The physics first discovered by John Tyndall tells us that carbon dioxide is a greenhouse gas which heats the Earth. The ice cores also show that, when carbon dioxide goes up, temperature goes up. And carbon dioxide is higher now than it has been for hundreds of thousands of years. When you're looking for an explanation for the recent heating up of the Earth, carbon dioxide and its sister greenhouse gases are clearly the likeliest culprits.

But did they really do it?

# 2

# WHODUNNIT?

For the reasons already given in Chapter 1, the prime suspect for the warming of our climate is, of course, the greenhouse effect. But there are still other, perfectly natural ways to change the climate. How do we know that this recent warming isn't just part of a normal cycle?

The best way to tell is to look at the characteristics of the heating, a fingerprint that identifies which mechanism is responsible. For instance, some warming mechanisms work geographically very widely whereas others are more regionally focused. And some cause the atmosphere to heat through at every level, while others heat only closer to the ground. It's by looking at which possible mechanisms have changed in the 'right' direction, and then using these sorts of arguments to choose between them, that scientists have reliably identified the culprit.

As we mentioned in Chapter 1, the Earth's temperature is set by the balance between the sunlight it receives, and the infrared 'heat glow' that it radiates back to space. So, in principle, there are four possible ways to turn up the heat:

## Increase the amount of sunlight

Sunlight does indeed vary. Roughly every eleven years our parent star experiences bursts of energy followed by periods of sloth, and the strength and length of this cycle also change. For instance, during the so-called Maunder Minimum, between about 1645 and 1715, there were many fewer sunspots than usual, and this coincided with the coldest part of the Little Ice Age. Also, the Sun was a little more active during the early parts of the twentieth century, and this probably contributed to that first burst of warming.

However, the Sun has not been getting brighter in the past several decades. In fact, since 1970 the Sun has actually been cooling off slightly.[1]

Some researchers have suggested that the mechanism might be more subtle than this. Tiny, high-energy particles called cosmic rays constantly rain down on to the Earth from outer space. It's possible that when some of these particles hit the air, they encourage the formation of a cloud droplet. Thus fewer cosmic rays might equal fewer clouds, which – depending on the height of the clouds – might in turn mean that less sunlight is blocked.

The Sun itself could conceivably help to bring this situation about. When the Sun becomes more active, its magnetic field strengthens. This field stretches throughout the solar system and acts like a giant force field, blocking cosmic rays from entering our air space. Thus, a more active Sun would mean fewer cosmic rays, which might mean fewer clouds and a warmer climate.

This idea is intriguing, but it contains a lot of 'mights', which troubles many researchers. But a worse problem for its proponents is that recent evidence shows that numbers of cosmic rays haven't been falling lately, even though the temperature has certainly risen. In fact, like the Sun's total output, cosmic rays have gone in exactly the wrong direction. If anything, they should have caused cooling.[2]

In other words, by whatever mechanism you choose, solar changes cannot explain the dramatic rise in temperature over the past few decades.

## Reflect less sunlight directly back again

The way to do this would be to change the planet's shininess. Some of the sunlight that arrives on Earth reflects straight back into space before it can do any warming. For instance, it can bounce back off the top side of clouds, which is why it feels cooler when a cloud passes between you and the Sun.[3]

There's no obvious reason why clouds should have naturally changed in number during the last century. But sunlight can also bounce back if it encounters a haze of tiny particles, known collectively as aerosols because they float in the air.[4] If these have decreased in number in recent years, that could explain why the planet started to warm.

Natural versions of aerosols include bits of dirt, sand or dust, volcanic ash, soot, or liquid droplets of sea salt, and even the largest particles are still smaller than the full stop at the end of this sentence. Most of these are whipped up briefly by the wind and last only a short time in the air before falling back to Earth. But the ash and droplets of sulphate put out by volcanoes are thrown up higher into the air, and can sometimes live long enough to cause significant cooling.

In 1991 Mount Pinatubo in the Philippines erupted to dramatic effect. As well as the vast quantities of ash that rained down on to the land around, it also spurted a huge mass of aerosols thirty kilometres up into the air. This was so high that the aerosols lingered far above the weather systems that could otherwise have rained them back down to Earth. Over the next eighteen months they spread around the world, and global temperatures cooled by around 0.5°C. Dramatic eruptions like these cause aerosols to go high enough, and live long enough, to affect the climate. If such eruptions temporarily waned, that could cause the world to heat up.

It's a nice idea, but unfortunately it turns out to be wrong. There was a temporary lull in volcanic activity between about 1915 and 1956, but since then the world's volcanoes have been enthusiastically blowing their tops. In fact they resumed their activity just before the warming took off.[5] If anything, volcanic aerosols have been keeping a slight check on the temperatures in recent years. To find the reason for the warming itself, we have to look elsewhere.

## Spread the sunlight around differently as part of a short-term natural cycle

It's always possible that we're just going through a warm phase of some perfectly normal cycle that spreads the heat out differently, sometimes warming, sometimes cooling the Earth. We know that our planet has several of these cycles, most of which are not fully understood. Perhaps the most famous are the so-called Milankovitch cycles. These are slight wobbles in the orbit of the Earth around the Sun, which affect how much sunlight arrives in the northern hemisphere in summertime on a timescale of 100,000 years or so.

Scientists believe that this is what triggers the planet to cycle in and out of ice ages. It works because the northern hemisphere contains most of the Earth's land, and you need land to make glaciers. Slightly cooler northern hemisphere summers means that snow from the previous winter can stay around on the ground. Gradually, the snow turns to ice and giant glaciers begin to build up.

The change in the amount of sunlight in itself isn't large enough to explain the ice age. But other feedbacks quickly start to kick in. White ice reflects more sunlight than dark land, so the Earth itself begins to cool. Then, as the planet cools, various other mechanisms start to suck carbon dioxide out of the air – which makes for even more cooling. The upshot is that a small shift in the amount of energy falling on one part of the planet causes a massive change in the climate all over the world.

(Incidentally, this is why the temperature starts to drop a little in the ice core records before carbon dioxide levels change. Many sceptics argue that this time lag means that carbon dioxide can't ever be responsible for temperature changes. In fact, that's just to misread the record. In ice ages, what happens first comes from outside. But it's only when this triggers changes in carbon dioxide that the real temperature rises and falls start to kick in. After that, the ice core record shows remarkably well how tightly changing carbon dioxide is coupled to changing temperature. Once the change in $CO_2$ has been triggered, the two march in impressive lockstep.)

The likeliest candidate for warming on the timescale of years, rather than millenia, would be the so-called 'El Niño/ Southern Oscillation'. Roughly speaking, El Niño occurs when a warm pool of water that usually resides in Indonesia heads east towards the west coast of South America. Through a complex series of atmospheric connections, this process tends to warm the world a little. When the pool moves back west, the world correspondingly cools.

However, the warming effect of changing El Niño lasts only a few years. It also tends to have a very specific spatial effect; though the globe as a whole warms, the North and South Pacific tend to cool down. Our recent warming, by contrast, has been felt everywhere.

In fact the same sorts of arguments apply to any form of internal cycle you can think of. As the IPCC report put it: 'No known mode of internal variability leads to such widespread, near universal warming as has been observed in the past few decades.'[6] Moreover as we discussed in Chapter 1, Nature's temperature records show that we haven't seen warming like this for at least 1,000 years, which makes it even less likely that we are on the up phase of some natural cycle.

Which leaves us with . . .

## Trapping more infrared radiation as it tries to leave, otherwise known as the greenhouse effect

Chapter 1 describes the evidence that greenhouse gases affect temperature, and also the evidence that their concentrations have been rising. But there are extra reasons to believe that greenhouse gases are indeed the cause of the recent warming.

For one thing, unlike aerosols, which are rained out of the atmosphere relatively quickly, greenhouse gases are long-lived. Methane stays in the atmosphere some twelve years. Carbon dioxide remains in place for more than a century. Since both of these gases have plenty of time to spread right around the globe, their effect should be felt everywhere. And it is. The warming we have experienced since 1970 has shown up clearly on every inhabited continent.

Also, the heating effect from carbon dioxide tends to hug the ground. Normally, upper parts of the atmosphere soak up some of the outgoing heat and get a little warmer. But when carbon dioxide traps the heat below, like a blanket, the lowest part of the next layer up, the stratosphere, should begin to cool. This is one of the characteristic signatures of the greenhouse effect in action, and it's exactly what's been happening. Satellites and balloon-borne measurements show that the lower stratosphere has cooled by between 0.3°C and 0.6°C per decade since 1979, which is just what you'd expect if greenhouse gases were trapping radiation.[7]

The final proof that greenhouse gases really are the problem comes from atmospheric models of how the air works. Models have come a very long way in the past few decades. The most sophisticated ones, called Global Climate Models,[8] or GCMs, use large, fast (and expensive) computers to calculate the behaviour of the air. They envisage the atmosphere as adjoining towers of boxes, all of which obey the basic laws of physics. Air, heat and moisture pass between the boxes, radiation goes in and comes out. The air can also interact with the ocean, and in many cases with vegetation on the Earth's surface.

GCMs have been criticised because it's not always easy to tell how realistic they are. Even if they do an excellent job of simulating the world we see, that could just be because their operators have tweaked them to make sure they fit. Fortunately, though, we have plenty of information about how climate has changed in the past, often from the same sort of proxy measurements that we described in Chapter 1: ice cores, tree rings, corals, etc. So it's possible to test how good GCMs are by looking at how well they can reproduce the past. And, generally, the best ones do pretty well.

The models are not perfect. For instance, they still can't get down to the sort of regional detail we need to predict the events that will affect individual communities – such as storms and local shifts in rainfall patterns; they're not yet very good at simulating clouds; aerosols provide a particular challenge, and for this and other reasons different models still give a spread of answers about exactly how much temperature rise will come from a given rise in carbon dioxide. We address this further in Chapter 6.

But there is one thing that models can do that nothing else can manage, and that's experiments involving the entire planet. Normally, if scientists want to establish the cause of a particular effect, they try it in different ways. What happens if I add this? Let's try again taking away that. But with the climate problem they are stymied – there is after all only one Earth.

Models can help to fill in this gap. You can let a model run with different inputs – only solar activity, say, and volcanoes, or only greenhouse gases, and then see what the result looks like. Comparing that to the real world gives us clues about what was really to blame.

And when the GCMs do that, they all come to the same conclusion. There is no way to explain the warming of the past few decades unless you include the rise in greenhouse gases. But when you do put the gases in, you see exactly what happened in the real world. The same story applies individually to every inhabited continent on Earth. Each one has seen dramatic warming in the past few decades, and in every case the models can account for the warming only if greenhouse gases are added to the mix.

In fact, the models generally do a good job of explaining all the changes that have taken place in the twentieth century, including the fact that temperatures apparently dropped a little during the middle part of it – something of which climate change sceptics like to make great play. It turns out that the cooling came from something we've already discussed in this chapter: aerosols. They did in fact have a marked effect on the temperature of the twentieth century. It was anything but natural, however. Burning dirty coal produces plenty of

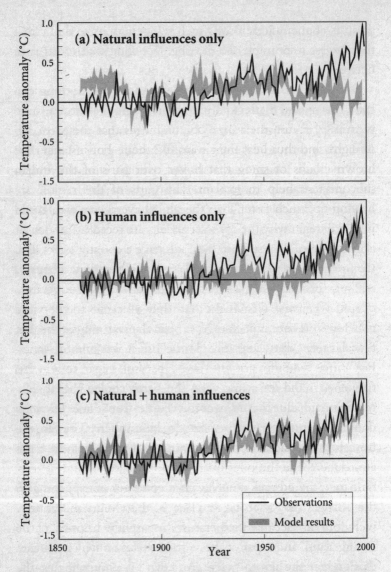

Temperature changes over the past 150 years in °C compared to the 1961–90 average. The models cannot reproduce this unless they incorporate both natural and human influences. (Source: IPCC)

sulphur-containing aerosols, and researchers now think that these were responsible for the slight cooling that took place between about 1940 and the late 1960s.

Some darker forms of aerosols formed from burning can have the opposite effect. Black or brown soot particles cause warming because their dark colour means that they soak up sunlight, and thus heat the air around them. For instance, the brown clouds of smog that hover over parts of the Indian subcontinent help to explain why parts of this region are heating up much faster than the global average, which could in turn explain why the Tibetan glaciers are receding at such an alarming rate.[9] But sulphate aerosols have a cooling effect, and they dominated during the middle of the twentieth century.

The early part of that century was hit by the cooperative effects of increased sunlight, reduced volcanic activity and increased greenhouse gases, counterbalanced a little by the aerosols from dirty coal. The overall effect was one of warming. But as the Sun's activity waned, aerosols began to win this tug of war, and for a few years the Earth cooled slightly.[10]

One major clue that this is correct comes from the fact that the cooling was only seen in the northern hemisphere. The aerosols from fires and factory chimneys are not thrown high into the atmosphere like the ones from Mount Pinatubo, and so they tend to be rained back down again after a week or so. Thus they don't have time to spread, and they have to linger where they were formed. Because the northern hemisphere has most of the world's land, and most of the world's industrialised countries, that's where the aerosols were. And that's why only the northern hemisphere witnessed this mid-century cooling.

But then many industrialised nations cleaned up their act. Nobody wanted to live in choking, filthy cities any more and a series of Clean Air Acts were passed. Ironically, in cleaning

The temperature is rising on every inhabited continent. Model simulations cannot explain this rise unless they incorporate the effects of human-induced changes in greenhouse gases. (Source: IPCC)

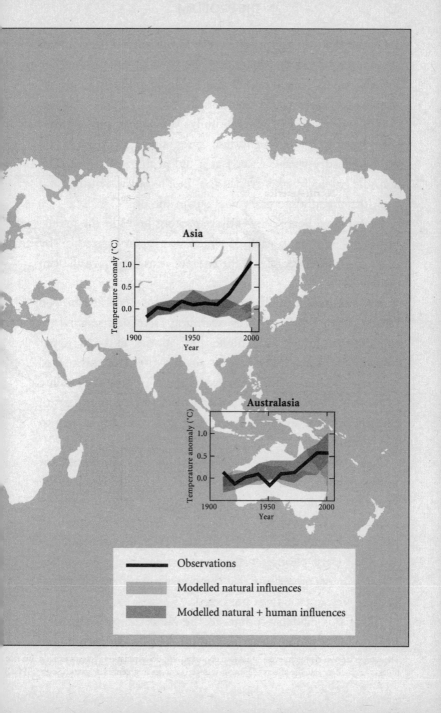

Asia

Temperature anomaly (°C)

Year

Australasia

Temperature anomaly (°C)

Year

Observations

Modelled natural influences

Modelled natural + human influences

away the obvious signs of pollution in our air, we lost some of the cooling effect that these particles were giving us. And we left the invisible and much more deadly pollutants, green-houses gases, free to do their worst.

The models show this beautifully. When they put together solar warming and greenhouse gases, the early part of the model century warms exactly as it did in the real world. The aerosols gradually take over in the middle of the century, and then the greenhouse gases win out in the end.[11]

There have been a few other apparent holes in the green-house gas argument, each of which was eagerly seized on by sceptics. But remarkably, in the last few years they have all been resolved.

For instance, though ground-based measurements showed clearly that the Earth was warming, satellites seemed to suggest that just a little higher up, in the mid- to upper troposphere, temperatures were not moving. But this turned out to be because of straightforward errors in how the satellite data were analysed. Proper analysis reveals that upper parts of the troposphere are indeed warming at a very similar rate to the ground.

Also, some people suggested that carbon dioxide would not increase the amount of water vapour in the air, because the upper part of the troposphere would dry out as the lower part moistened. Without the power of the extra water vapour to boost the carbon dioxide's greenhouse effect, they suggested, it wouldn't cause enough warming to matter. However, satellite measurements now show that the upper troposphere is indeed getting wetter exactly as predicted.[12]

All of this evidence points to the same thing. The recent heating up of planet Earth has carbon dioxide's fingerprints all over it. Or, to put it more succinctly, and to answer the question posed in the title of this chapter: Wedunnit. Human activity is to blame for the rise in temperature over recent decades, and will be responsible for more changes in the future. There are plenty of areas for debate in the global warming story but this is not one of them. If anybody tells you differently they either have a vested interest in ignoring the scientific arguments or they are fools.

Until now, we have focused on the changes in temperature that planet Earth has experienced in the past few decades. But these changes have also affected many other aspects of the climate, with corresponding trouble for its inhabitants. We'll talk about this in the next chapter.

# 3

# FEELING THE HEAT

So far we have experienced only a relatively small amount of global warming – about three-quarters of a degree centigrade. But that has still been enough to throw a substantial spanner into Nature's workings. It's not just that animals and plants can't take the heat, and simply keel over and die. Rather, their lives were carefully tuned to a climate that no longer exists.

The essence of the problem is timing. Animals use very specific cues to make decisions about when to emerge from hibernation, have sex or set out on a journey that will take them to the other side of the world. And cues that used to be ultra-reliable are now beginning to fall short. Around the world, spring is coming progressively earlier, and autumn ever later. Though some animals and plants are managing to cope, the natural world is like an orchestra. If the timing is off, you don't get beautiful harmonies – you get a mess.

Take the yellow-bellied marmot, a ground squirrel that lives in the mountains of western USA and Canada. Each year, these creatures decide when to emerge from their underground dens by testing the air temperature. Warm air ought to mean that the snow will soon be melting and food is on its way. But of late the warm air has come much earlier, when snow is still thick on the ground. Marmots have started coming out more than a month before they should, and are vulnerable both to lack of food and the tell-tale tracks in the snow that lead predators to their door.[1]

The Edith's checkerspot butterfly uses snow cover, rather than temperature, to decide when to emerge from its chrysalis and make its dash for reproduction. But in its own Rocky Mountain habitat, snow has been failing, tempting the butterflies out in April instead of May or June. In one year, there were no plants to feed them, and the butterflies' bodies littered the surrounding hillsides with a bright orange carpet of fresh, soft wings. After several more abortive attempts to reproduce, they have now vanished from this part of the world.

Changes in rainfall are also having their insidious, subtle effect. Generally speaking, northern parts of the world have been getting wetter but the tropics have been drying out. More rain has come to the eastern states of the Americas, northern Europe and northern and central Asia, whereas North Africa, southern Africa, the Mediterranean, and parts of southern Asia have all begun to lose water. But even in places where the annual rainfall has stayed more or less the same, the pattern has begun to change – with more intense rainstorms, and longer, drier periods in between.

The lemurs of Madagascar are a case in point when it comes to the subtlety of climate effects. These remarkable primates range from the minuscule mouse lemur, which is small enough to curl up in the palm of your hand, to the indri, which is famous for its haunting song and is about the size of (and looks rather like) a four-year-old child dressed in a baggy panda suit. A host of other species fit in between these two size extremes and each has its own individual calendar for mating. But what's really remarkable is that they all aim to wean their offspring at more or less the same time – when the fruits of the forest are at their most plentiful.

Lemurs, like many other animals, know the date from the length of time they see daylight. This is the one constant in a shifting world. At any point on the Earth's surface, the length of daylight is a function of where we are in our orbit around the Sun; it doesn't depend on temperature or rainfall or other capricious measures. Thus, the amount of daylight tells lemurs the date as surely as if they had a red ring scrawled on a calendar.

This approach works beautifully as long as the fruits play along. But if rainfall patterns change, even though the calendar may be right the availability of food can be very wrong. And there are already signs that this could be happening in Madagascar. The effect can be subtle: a little less nourishment, fewer young that survive the year, and a group that is just that much smaller. But with animals that have already been driven to the edge of extinction by the chainsaws that have destroyed most of their natural habitat, the subtle effects of climate change could easily be enough to tip them over.

The pied flycatcher has also begun to lose faith in its internal calendar. Each year these birds make an incredible journey of 5,000 kilometres from West Africa to their breeding grounds in Holland. Their starting date is strictly marked and for the past twenty years they have been arriving at the same time. But local temperatures in Holland have begun to change. Spring is coming earlier to Europe, and the caterpillars that the flycatchers' chicks are supposed to eat are past their peak by the time the chicks hatch. If they don't evolve a new starting date, they will die.

Some species are managing to adapt.[2] However, human-induced climate change is happening much faster than it does from natural causes. The result is that the creatures that can evolve with it tend to be the ones that are quickest on their evolutionary feet – which means flies and mosquitoes and other insects with short reproduction times rather than the bigger, more photogenic animals.

There are many other signs that the natural world is already feeling the heat. The tree lines are marching further towards the poles and up the sides of mountains. Animals are following their plant food up into the hills. Carefully sited national parks, designed to protect key habitats, are looking increasingly vulnerable, and conservationists are beginning to realise that climate change could be the final straw for many of the world's hard-pressed species.

No single species has yet earned the dubious honour of being the first undisputed victim of climate change. The best candidate to date has been Costa Rica's exquisite golden toad, which disappeared for ever in the mid-1980s from a rainforest that was apparently untouched by humans. At first, researchers suggested that it had died out as changing temperatures removed the mist that wreathed its cloud-forest home. But it later seemed more likely that disease had played a significant part in the loss of this and a large number of other Costa Rican frogs in the 1980s and 1990s. Still, in 2006 the original researchers published a paper making a very convincing case that climate change had created the perfect conditions for the disease to spread.[3]

Though many feel sad at the thought that the golden toad has hopped its last on Earth, it's easy to think that, with so very many species, we can probably spare a few without suffering much worse than a twinge of conscience. But that doesn't give enough credit to the sheer potential scale of the losses. The IPCC report predicts that between a fifth and a third of all species on Earth could be at risk of extinction by the end of this century,[4] and other researchers have even suggested it could be more than 50 per cent. That is enough to qualify for a mass extinction on the scale of the dinosaurs.

For now, what's perhaps more alarming is that global warming isn't only affecting individual species. It's also changing entire ecosystems. The two most dramatic examples are coral reefs that are turning white, and the north polar ice cap that is turning black.

## The case of the disappearing pole

Antarctica is an ice-covered continent surrounded by water, and the ice on its land can be several kilometres thick. The Arctic, on the other hand, is an ocean surrounded by a ring of land. The ice at the North Pole floats on sea water, and is just a few metres thick. Because of this, the ice there is much easier to melt.

Over the past thirty years, as temperatures have begun to soar, the area of summer sea ice has shrunk by nearly 8 per cent per decade.[5] It's shocking to watch a satellite sequence of the disappearing ice. Each year, the area of whiteness shrinks perceptibly, to be replaced by dark ocean.

The past five years have seen record low areas of sea ice, with 2005 providing what one researcher calls the 'exclamation point' in the record. That year had 20 per cent less ice cover than the average, a loss of about 1.3 million square kilometres.[6] In 2007 there was a new all-time record in which fully half the sea ice vanished. And 2008 was nearly as bad. Meanwhile, springtime temperatures began rising throughout the Arctic basin in the 1990s[7] and many parts of the Arctic have begun to experience unprecedented heatwaves.

Models predict that if greenhouse emissions continue the way they are going, by the end of the century the summer Arctic will be completely ice-free.[8] A planet that used to boast two polar ice caps will then have only one.

Already, the ecosystem is beginning to change. For instance, there are signs that the loss has begun to hurt polar bears, the poster child of the global warming story. Polar bears are specialist predators that feed almost exclusively on seals. The seals, in turn, breed on sea ice. So access to sea ice is vital for the bears, especially for the females that emerge from land-based dens with their cubs in the summer after a fast that has lasted six or seven months. If, on emerging, they face nothing but dark ocean water they must swim or starve. One group in Western Hudson Bay has already declined from 1,200 bears in 1987 to fewer than 950 in 2004.[9]

Losing the sea ice is bad not just for the larger, more picturesque members of the Arctic ecosystem, but for many of their smaller prey – right down to the ice-dwelling phytoplankton that make up a considerable proportion of the food supply.[10] It's not yet clear exactly how the Arctic species will shift to adapt to this new wetter Arctic, but the entire ecosystem will certainly change beyond recognition.

## Bleaching corals

Coral reefs harbour so many colourful species that they're often called the 'rainforests' of the ocean. In spite of their hard appearance, they are actually jelly-like creatures that quiver inside a calcium home of their own making. With them in their shell they have house guests in the form of algae, which provide the corals with food. Normally, this is an arrangement that suits both parties, but when the coral becomes stressed, the first thing to go is the tenant. The algae are unceremoniously ejected, and the coral turns white. This is known as coral bleaching, and it occurs in particular if the sea water grows too hot.

That's what happened in 1998, which was the joint warmest year in the entire historical record. Bleaching began in the Eastern Pacific, in French Polynesia, before it headed out west. For some reason it skipped over many of the western South Pacific islands, but it wrought havoc on the Great Barrier Reef. The damage was so dramatic there that the gigantic scarring was visible from space. The bleaching went on to the Indian Ocean, where it destroyed 90 per cent of the corals in the Maldives. Then to Africa and then to the Caribbean. The sheer global scale of the attack took researchers by surprise. Nobody had seen anything like it.

The bleaching returned in 2000, this time wrecking large swathes of Fijian corals. In 2002, the Great Barrier Reef was hit again, and in 2005 the Caribbean suffered even worse losses than it had in 1998.

Corals can survive bleaching episodes and retrieve their algae when the temperature cools. But if the warming is too great, or lasts too long, the coral dies. That's not to say it goes extinct. Reefs can be recolonised, or corals can set up new colonies elsewhere. They play the numbers game. So many coral larvae are released at each spawning that millions of individuals can die without the species disappearing altogether. They can also migrate to places with more appropriate temperatures and some may be able to adapt quickly enough, evolving a way to tolerate the higher temperatures and greater acidity. But as a result of the bleaching, many of the world's existing coral reefs are already dying. And as ocean temperatures continue to rise, the bleaching will only get worse.

Increasing carbon dioxide has another side effect that will also be bad news for corals. To date, the oceans have soaked up around half of the carbon dioxide emissions from burning fossil fuels, making cement and land-use changes. That's just as well, otherwise there would be even more carbon dioxide in the air and hence even more warming than we have seen so far. But the benefit has come at a price. All that additional carbon dioxide is gradually acidifying the ocean.

This seems hard to believe and, indeed, many scientists initially discounted the possibility. The oceans, after all, are vast and are also expert at neutralising any material that threatens to acidify their waters. However, the problem is that the carbon dioxide is arriving too fast. It's overwhelming the ocean's natural capacity to compensate. A report produced by Britain's Royal Society in 2005 estimated that the world's oceans had already increased their acidity by 0.1 units, which translates to an increase in the ions that cause acidity of some 30 per cent.[11] And one study calculated that unfettered carbon dioxide increases over the next few centuries could make the oceans more acid than they have been for 300 million years.[12]

Nobody yet knows whether this is having an impact on the world's sea creatures, mainly because it is hard to measure. But most agree that the effects will be felt soon, if, indeed, they are not already with us. According to the Royal Society report, animals with a high metabolism, such as squid, are likely to suffer in more acidic waters. But the real danger is to any animal that makes itself a shell, or skeleton, out of the calcium carbonate (the same stuff as common chalk) dissolved in sea water. The more acidic the sea water, the harder it is to make your shell, and in the extreme the shells already made will begin to dissolve.

This danger applies to creatures that span a wide part of the food chain, from tiny plankton and pterapods – which feed cod, salmon and whales – to mussels, conch and sea urchins. It applies particularly to corals.

Sixty-five million years ago a meteor the size of New York

slammed into the Earth. The environmental chaos that ensued is widely believed to have put paid to the dinosaurs. But it also had another, less well-known effect. According to Ken Caldeira at the Carnegie Institute of Washington in California, the meteor also threw up vast amounts of sulphur which then rained down on the ocean as sulphuric acid. The upper ocean became acidified for a brief moment, perhaps just one or two years. But that was enough. More or less every sea creature that built shells or skeletons out of calcium carbonate became either rare or extinct. A handful of corals must have survived, or we would not still have them on Earth today. But they were nonetheless too scarce to leave their imprint; they did not reappear in the fossil record for a full two million years.[13]

In all, the IPCC report states that more than 29,000 observational data sets in seventy-five different studies show significant changes in physical and biological systems around the world.[14] And 90 per cent of these go in the direction you would expect because of warming. What's more, the regions where the changes are happening coincide with the regions where most warming has been seen. This can't just be a question of natural variability. The message from the natural world is that climate change is already here.

That sounds like bad news for lovers of wildlife, but it's actually more important than that. Our ecosystems work for us, in ways that we're so used to that – in Joni Mitchell's memorable words – 'we won't know what we've got till it's gone'.[15] These so-called ecosystem services account for more than providing an aesthetic backdrop for a walk in the woods. They also give us food and natural materials to work with, and do a host of other jobs that include soaking up our pollution, delivering water where we need it and holding it back where we don't.

Though it is always hard to pin any one occurrence on to

climate change, three recent dramatic events have helped to throw the human dangers of messing with the climate into stark relief.

## Climate wars

Until a few decades ago few westerners would have heard of Darfur, a region of western Sudan, just south of the Sahara. This was, after all, an essentially peaceful region where nomadic Arab herders grazed their animals amicably on the land of African farmers. Now, of course, Darfur is a place of almost unimaginable horror. Something happened to set those erstwhile peaceful neighbours at each other's throats. More than two million people have been 'displaced', their homes destroyed and their lives ruined. At least 400,000 civilians have been killed.

The origins of the conflict are complex, but they were triggered by an ongoing drought that took its first terrible hold in Sudan and the Horn of Africa in the mid-1980s. Life that was already on the edge was about to tip over it. People and cattle died in horrifying numbers. And the scarce resources of water and fertile land that remained became a breeding ground for conflict. In the late 1980s, the increasingly desperate Arab herders began to set themselves against their farming neighbours. The result we know only too well.

At first, it was assumed that the drought that triggered this war over resources had been caused by environmental degradation. Westerners tutted that irresponsible overcropping and overgrazing had turned the land into a dust bowl. But more recent models have shown that land use isn't the answer.

Instead, models suggest that the reason for the drought is tied to a cooling in the northern Atlantic relative to the southern.

This in turn changed the location of a set of air currents known to scientists as the Intertropical Convergence Zone, and to the farmers and herders of Darfur as the bringer of rain.[16]

The picture now becomes muddier. It is possible that cooling of the northern Atlantic is down to natural causes. But it's also possible that it happened because of the partner in crime of carbon dioxide: sulphate aerosols. As we explained in Chapter 2, these arise, among other reasons, from burning dirty coal. Because they reflect sunlight directly back out to space, they are engaged in a perpetual tug of war with carbon dioxide, causing cooling that partly balances the greenhouse heating. Although many of these aerosols have been cleaned up in the past few decades, they still billow out from power stations and factory chimneys in enough numbers to cast a pall over the oceans that abut the industrial centres of the world.

And the key effect with regard to Darfur was a purely regional one. One model suggests that over the North Atlantic clouds of aerosols may have bounced a little sunlight back to space, which cooled the local sea surface, which in turn sent the Intertropical Convergence Zone southward, and robbed the Sahel of its rain.[17]

Of course what followed the drought was politics – notably the neglect of the region and then unleashing of power-hungry warlords by Sudan's central government at Khartoum. But the violent, horrifying conflict might never have taken hold had the burning of fossil fuels not laid the groundwork. As one writer put it: 'In decades to come, Darfur may be seen as one of the first true climate change wars.'[18]

Whether or not this is true (and the models have yet to agree among themselves), Darfur remains a dramatic example of how a small shift in climate in just one region can have dramatic and horrifying human consequences.

# Katrina

The same sort of arguments apply to another recent disaster. On the morning of 29 August 2005, Hurricane Katrina struck south-east Louisiana. It was the sixth strongest Atlantic hurricane ever recorded, though it weakened considerably before it hit land. Nonetheless, it was also one of the deadliest Atlantic hurricanes. Katrina caused $80 billion damage and took more than 1,800 lives. It also, infamously, turned New Orleans – a major city in the world's richest country – into a hellhole, a place where bloated bodies floated through the streets, and where lawlessness and disease were rampant.

Though many people have suggested that Katrina was a direct consequence of climate change, we don't know if this is true. Think of a dice loaded so that it is twice as likely to throw a six. Half of the sixes that you throw afterwards would still be 'natural' ones. But the other half would come from the change you had deliberately made. We don't know, can't know, if Katrina was a 'natural' throw of the climate dice or one of the loaded ones. What we can say is that, thanks to climate change, more Katrinas are likely to be on their way.

Warming is unlikely to make a difference to the *number* of hurricanes around the world.[19] But it is very likely to make them more *intense*. The energy that feeds hurricanes comes from warm sea water, which is why they only form in the tropics, and then only in the hottest months. Global warming is already causing the sea surface to heat up,[20] and that in turn is increasing the hurricanes' chances of becoming truly destructive. More intense hurricanes also have more water to work with, as rising sea levels give them ever greater reach.

Sea temperature isn't the only influence on the ultimate power of a hurricane. If wind speeds change at different heights above the water surface, this can slice up the baby hurricanes before they can grow big and strong. However, historical evidence suggests that rising temperatures are already having an effect. Over the past thirty years, hurricanes have indeed become roughly 70 per cent more energetic.[21] Since 1970 the numbers of category 4 and 5 storms – the strongest and most destructive – have dramatically increased, with the areas worst hit being the North Pacific, Indian, and South-west Pacific Oceans. Hurricanes may even be expanding their historical boundaries: in March 2004 the first ever tropical cyclone in the South Atlantic smashed into the coast of Brazil. It took fore-casters so completely by surprise that they didn't even give it a name.

## Heatwave

In the summer of 2003 an intense wave of heat spread across Europe. While the most northerly countries basked in the unexpected warmth, the rest of Europe fried. Wilting crops cost farmers more than $12 billion. Forest fires in Portugal caused another $1.6 billion worth of damage.[22] And people died. The statistics for numbers of deaths per month across the Continent show an enormous spike in the first few weeks of August, the hottest month. They occurred among people in every age group from forty-five upwards. Most were already vulnerable: older people, asthmatics, people who literally couldn't stand the heat. And yet, they were not already close to death. If they had been, the abrupt rise in deaths in August would have been followed by a drop over the following few months as the statistics caught up. But this didn't happen. Instead, at least 35,000, and perhaps as many as 52,000, people died significantly before their time.[23]

So was this heatwave just a 'natural' blip or was global warming to blame? In this case, unlike the two previous ones, the evidence for the involvement of climate change is compelling. In 2004 several British researchers ran one of the world's top climate models with just natural variations in solar and volcanic activity and then ran it again with greenhouse gases added in. Then they calculated how much the greenhouse gases had increased the risk of a summer at the 2003 level. Their results showed that global warming had made such a summer very much more likely than before.[24]

One way to understand this is to think about the difference between climate and weather. Weather is what we experience month to month and year to year. It fluctuates constantly, and a graph of the changes in annual temperatures in central Europe over time shows a forest of small spikes, some going up, some down. Climate is the average of these fluctuations over time, a line drawn through the middle of the spikes.

Of late, our climate has been warming, so this steady average line drawn through the spikes that mark out our annual temperature has been rising. That means that any upward spike that is otherwise a fairly ordinary departure from the average is now starting from a higher baseline. It peaks at a much higher temperature than it would otherwise have managed.

In this way, fully half the excess temperature of 2003 came from the rising baseline. The rest came from what would otherwise have been a hot, but not especially unusual, temperature spike. By the way, the baseline has risen so much that the average summer temperature in central Europe is now close to the value for the hottest summer of the twentieth century. In the next few decades, the baseline looks likely to

Actual and smooth summer temperatures in Europe in °C (black lines) compared to the 1961–90 average, ending with the 2003 European heatwave (cross). According to the models (grey line), by 2040 the value for 2003 will have become typical. (Source: P. A. Stott, D. A. Stone and M. R. Allen, 'Human contribution to the European heatwave of 2003, *Nature*, vol. 432, pp. 610–14, 2 December 2004)

rise to match the temperatures of 2003. *Then*, when a hot summer spike comes along, the effect will be truly searing.

These are just a few examples of ways that relatively small changes in climate have already caused massive human suffering. Like it or not, insulated in cities or out on the prairie, or the steppe, or the savannah, we all depend fundamentally on the services the natural world brings to us – and suffer when these services are withheld.

However, that's not to say that we should just sit back and take what's coming to us. The human suffering in each of these cases would not have been inevitable if we had been properly prepared. The next part of the story is to figure out exactly what we should expect from climate change over the next few decades, and how we will have to prepare ourselves to cope.

# 4

# IN THE PIPELINE

## Change is inevitable

Most people have now realised that climate change is upon us. If pushed, most would probably also say that, if we don't do something to change the way we live, things are likely to get worse. But few seem to have noticed one of the most important points to emerge from the last few years of scientific projections. All the evidence suggests that the world will experience significant and potentially highly dangerous changes in climate over the next few decades *no matter what we do now*.

That's because the ocean has a built-in lag. It takes time to heat up, which is why the nicest time to swim is often the end of the summer rather than the middle. The same principle holds for global warming, but on a longer timescale: because the oceans gradually soak up heat generated by the extra greenhouse gases, the full effect won't be felt for decades to centuries.

This means that whatever we do now to change our carbon habits will take several decades to have any effect. In other words, according to the best that our most sophisticated models can tell us, the next twenty to thirty years will be more or less the same whether we quickly kick the carbon habit, or continue burning as many fossil fuels as we possibly can.[1] Whatever we do today to reduce emissions will matter for our children's generation and beyond, but not for our own. The problem of climate change is one of legacy.

We'll talk more about this later. For now, the important point is that a certain amount of climate change is already in the pipeline. Though some of the details are sketchy, scientists have a reasonable idea of what the next few decades will hold. Note that the descriptions that follow assume we do nothing to prepare for the changes that it's now too late to stop. Later in the chapter we will explain some of the ways in which we can learn to adapt.

## Storms

As we mentioned in Chapter 3, hurricanes will probably not increase in number, but are likely to get stronger and last longer. Outside the tropics the picture is more complicated. Storms there are much larger and more sprawling than hurricanes. They deliver unpredictable weather, but also essential rain to large swathes of the middle latitudes in both hemispheres. Whether they change in number or intensity depends on a complex set of variables including temperature, moisture levels and how quickly the temperature changes as you go from the warm tropics to the cold poles. As yet, the models don't agree. However, one thing that seems clear in all the models is that the storm tracks – the upper atmosphere 'guide rails' around which the storms roll – are likely to shift polewards, which would mean less rain in southern Australia, the northern US and parts of southern Europe. Most models also predict a strengthening of the fierce westerly winds in the Atlantic, which would mean stronger winter storms hitting northern Europe.[2]

## Water

There will be less snowfall, fewer glaciers, more variable rainfall patterns and more intense individual rainstorms. By the middle of the century, high latitudes and some wet tropical areas will become up to 40 per cent wetter – with more water flow from rivers and generally more water availability. But some regions in the middle latitudes (such as southern Europe and the south-western US) and in the dry tropics will become up to 30 per cent drier. Disappearing glaciers and snow cover will reduce the meltwater that normally flows from mountain ranges, which will affect more than a billion people.

In West Africa, twenty-five watercourses cross the boundaries of seventeen different countries and, as the region dries, there will be an increasing danger of the sort of conflict that has devastated Darfur. To the north, ten different countries share the resources of the River Nile. While the population in these nations is set to burgeon, many climate models are predicting that the waters will recede.[3] Even in places where the annual rainfall drops, individual storms are expected to dump more water in intense bursts. Nearly one and a half billion people live in river basins that are more likely to flood as a result.

## Heatwaves

In the next few decades, heatwaves such as the one that caused devastation in Europe in 2003 will become increasingly common. By the 2040s, for instance, at least half the European summers are likely to be just as hot.[4] Many other regions are likely to suffer the consequences of dry, hot summers, especially with increasing wildfires such as the ones that scarred mainland Greece in 2007. This will, however, come with a climate upside. There are also likely to be fewer seriously cold winters. Since deaths from the cold usually outnumber those from heat by a considerable margin, this means there could be an overall decrease in the number of temperature-related deaths. However, as the authors of one study put it: 'This offers little reassurance for those affected by the heat.'[5]

## Monsoons

There is considerable uncertainty about which way the monsoons will go. A combination of the local cooling effect of aerosols over the Atlantic and Indian oceans, and the possible weakening of the ocean circulation, suggests that monsoons may become drier, which would be potentially catastrophic for regions whose livelihoods are sensitively dependent on the annual rains.

On the other hand, many models predict that the Asian monsoon is likely to get gradually wetter. That sounds like good news, as it would bring more water to around two billion people in East and South Asia. However, this is likely to fall in even more intense bursts than normal, which could mean severe flooding. In August 2005, Mumbai experienced a record-breaking rainstorm. One metre of rain fell on the city in just hours. The resulting floods closed schools, banks, the stock exchange and the airport. More than 1,000 people died.[6]

## Food and forests

The good news is that global food production is set to increase over the next few decades. The devil, however, is in the regional detail. For middle to high latitudes, crop productivity is likely to go up. (Though if the temperature creeps up more than 2–3°C, productivity tumbles even there.) By contrast, at lower latitudes, especially tropical regions, even the small rise in temperature predicted for the next few decades will send crop production tumbling. That, of course, covers most of Africa and parts of Asia whose populations emit only a tiny amount of carbon dioxide per person relative to western countries. It's a nasty irony that the people least responsible for the problem will also be the ones to suffer first and most.

## Rising sea levels

As the oceans warm they expand. This effect, coupled with melting glaciers, is already raising sea levels all over the world. For the twentieth century, the rate of rise was about two millimetres per year, but of late it has risen to three millimetres a year and counting. Most researchers think that the rate will accelerate as warming temperatures eat further into the great ice sheets of Greenland and Antarctica. But even over the next few decades, the current rate is enough to produce a rise of up to ten centimetres.

That might not sound like much but it's also important to realise that the rise isn't uniform. The ocean is surprisingly lumpy, currents and the spinning Earth send water sloshing from one ocean basin to the next. Thus, in some places the rise in sea level will be greater, and in others sea level will even fall. (Despite what sceptics say, some regions of falling sea level are a perfectly normal consequence of the way the oceans behave, and emphatically not a counter-indicator of climate change.)

The rising ocean will bring erosion and flooding to many coastal regions, as well as turning coastal wetlands into salt marshes. More than three billion people, roughly half the world's population, live within 200 kilometres of a coast. Many of these are close enough to suffer from what will be increasingly deadly storm surges that bring the sea flooding inland. And many, too, live in developing countries where they have the least financial resources to adapt and are the most dependent on local food and water supplies. But the rising sea does not pick and choose, and it will equally come for the big coastal cities of industrialised countries – for instance London, New York, Tokyo and Sydney.

To some extent this is already happening. The Thames Barrier stretches across the mouth of the River Thames and can be raised to protect the city of London from flooding. When it began operating in the early 1980s it was used on average once every three years. Now it is being deployed up to six times a year.

## Corals
Within the next few decades, the world's coral reefs are going to be hit hard by the double whammy of a more acidic ocean and rising sea temperatures. Although individual coral species are unlikely to become extinct, many existing coral reefs will bleach and die, which will in turn affect the people who rely on the fish they shelter for subsistence, food and tourist income.

## Development
Many of the variations that climate change will bring over the next few decades will specifically exacerbate the development problems already faced by large parts of the world. For instance, even in today's world 800 million people are undernourished, and the projected drop in food production in low-latitude areas will only make this worse. Similarly, about two billion people currently lack access to clean water. The rural poor depend more than anyone on ecosystems for their livelihoods. Reduced water flow in some areas may make energy supplies from hydropower less reliable. And, of course, there is the danger that competition for dwindling resources will exacerbate problems of local, national and regional security.

Along with these general effects, different regions of the world will experience specific changes. Some will be beneficial. Most will not. The next few pages show what each part of the world can expect from the climate change already in the pipeline.

One final but important point concerns what we should expect over the next few years. A recent paper in *Nature*[7] suggested that a natural cooling cycle during the next decade might temporarily mask the world's warming. If they are right, a succession of relatively cool years might lull us into a false sense of safety. The trouble is that in the following decade the natural cycle would reinforce global warming and the temperatures would dramatically increase. By then, if we have done nothing to kick the carbon habit, it might well be too late.

## Learning to adapt

Four and a half kilometres above sea level, high on the Tibetan plateau, lies a lake called the Tsho Rolpa. Warmer temperatures have accelerated the melting of the region's glaciers that feed this lake, and between the 1950s and the 1990s the Tsho Rolpa's area grew by more than a factor of seven.[8] By now, 100 million square metres of water were straining at a flimsy moraine dam, threatening a hydropower plant downstream as well as many villages. Therefore, the Nepalese government cut a channel into the moraine wall and installed a gate to control the release of water and lower the lake level. The construction project took four years and cost US$3.2 million. Meanwhile, in case of flooding, an early warning system was established for nineteen villages downstream. The villagers themselves helped to design the scheme and carry out periodic drills to ensure that everyone knows exactly what to do when the warning sounds.

|  | Water shortage | Food production | Disease |
|---|---|---|---|
| Africa | 75–250 million people at risk by 2020s. | Reduced yields across the continent, in some countries as much as 50% by 2020. Hundreds of millions at increased risk of famine. | Malaria likely to reduce range in southern Africa but begin to extend range to Eastern Highlands. |
| Asia | 120 million–1.2 billion people at risk by 2020s. | 2.5–10% decrease in crop yield in 2020s. Up to 49 million at risk of hunger. | Flooding and high temperatures increase risk of infectious diseases especially cholera, typhoid. |
| Australia, New Zealand and small islands | Reduced water run-off in most of eastern and south-western Australia, with a fall of up to 20% in the south-east by 2030. Significantly less snow cover in the south-east. | Enhanced growing conditions for much of New Zealand and wetter parts of southern Australia. Possible reduced yields in parts of eastern New Zealand and southern/eastern Australia that are far from large rivers due to a combination of drought and fire. Risk to fish supply from corals around small tropical islands. | An additional 0.1–0.3 million exposed to the risk of dengue fever by 2020. |

| Flooding | Heatwaves and fire | Corals and ice |
|---|---|---|
| High risk to large coastal cities such as Lagos and Alexandria. | Combination of drying and rising temperatures brings increased threat of burning to many forests. | Red Sea and East African corals at risk of bleaching. |
| 2.5 million people flooded by 2050, mostly in the Ganges-Brahmaputra and Mekong mega-deltas. Many more at risk from increasingly intense typhoons, rising sea levels and storm surges. More variable monsoon might bring flash flooding. | Increased mortality from severe heatwaves for the southern and eastern parts of the continent, and possibly also Siberia. Reduced mortality from serious cold events. | Very substantial or complete loss of Himalayan glaciers by 2035, together with loss of 30% of coral reefs. |
| Rising sea levels and more intense cyclones increase risk of coastal flooding in Australia and New Zealand. Very substantial risk of increased flooding in low-lying small islands, as well as encroaching saltwater into coastal fields. | 4–25% increase in frequency of fire-danger days in south-eastern Australia by 2020; heat-related deaths to double in Adelaide, Melbourne, Perth, Sydney and Brisbane by 2020. | 58–81% of the Great Barrier Reef bleached every year by 2030. Also substantial bleaching of corals around small islands. |

|  | Water shortage | Food production | Disease |
|---|---|---|---|
| Europe | In southern Europe surface run-off decreases by 0–23% by the 2020s. Longer droughts and significantly increased fire risks, especially in the Mediterranean. | Higher crop yields for northern Europe but reduced yields for the south, especially in the Mediterranean, south-west Balkans and the south of European Russia. | No significant change expected |
| Central and South America | 7–77 million people at risk by the 2020s. | Soybean yields could rise but rice yields are likely to fall. Wheat and maize hard to predict but overall 5 million people at increased risk of hunger by 2020. | Possible reduction of malarial risk in Amazonia and Central America, but range could begin to extend beyond previous southern limit. |
| North America and polar regions | 41% of water supply to southern California vulnerable to loss of snowpack from Sierra Nevada and Colorado River basin. | Likely increases in crop yield of 5–20% over the next few decades, but crops currently near climate threshold, e.g. wine grapes in California, likely to suffer falls in yield, quality or both. | Boundary for tick-borne Lyme disease likely to shift 200 km northwards by the 2020s. |

| Flooding | Heatwaves and fire | Corals and ice |
|---|---|---|
| Increased storm intensity in the North Atlantic to 2030. Higher sea levels, more severe winter storms and more intense rainfall events threaten coastal and inland cities, especially in the north, where run-off is also projected to increase. | By 2030 heatwaves such as the one in 2003 that killed more than 30,000 people will become the rule rather than the exception. There will, however, be reduced deaths from serious cold events. | Substantial loss of alpine glaciers; decrease in area of seasonal snow cover, especially at lower elevations. |
| Danger of flooding in low-lying areas, especially El Salvador, Guyana and Argentine coast. More intense hurricanes in Caribbean. | More frequent wildfires in much of South America, including the Amazon rainforest, and in parts of Central America. | Substantial or complete melting of most tropical glaciers. Severe bleaching of Caribbean corals. |
| Coastal cities increasingly vulnerable to flooding, especially in Gulf of Mexico, as tropical storms grow more intense. | Storm tracks moving north will bring droughts and fires to parts of the northern and western US, where the average area burned each year has already almost doubled. Also increased fire risk in southern Canada. | Very substantial or complete melting of ice in Glacier National Park by 2030. Considerable loss of glaciers from Greenland, Alaska, northern Canada and the Antarctic peninsula. Very substantial loss of Arctic sea ice by 2030. |

We mention this story because it encapsulates several of the lessons we must learn in adapting to climate change. Part of the answer will come through engineering projects, part through warning systems and preparedness. The rest, perhaps the hardest part, will require changes in many of the ways that we currently make our living.

## Engineering projects

One of the most important roles that engineering projects will play in helping to adapt to climate change will be to provide protection against coastal flooding (through rising sea level and increasing storm surges) and inland flooding (because of more intense rainfall). The UK is now in the process of implementing a country-wide strategy for flood and coastal defences, based on a detailed Foresight report commissioned by one of us (David King) in 2002. We learned many useful lessons from this exercise.

First, there is the importance of accurate – and regionally detailed – model predictions. The Hadley Centre models that we were using had a resolution of 260 by 260 kilometres. In other words, the results came out as uniform squares with sides of 260 kilometres. On a global scale, that tells you a lot. But if you start to use boxes that size to try and draw conclusions about an individual country you end up with almost no regional detail. What we really need for good adaptation strategies for individual cities, counties and regions is global models that can make accurate climate predictions on a 60 by 60 kilometre scale, or even lower. That sort of resolution is in the pipeline but will require the world's largest computers to implement. It should be an urgent priority. Note that what's important is not so much a detailed prediction of where exactly more rain will fall. Instead, the models will identify the areas that are most vulnerable to likely changes and extreme events.

The next step is to design the barrier, levee or drainage systems to cope with the changes that the models predict. Though it sounds obvious, this is extremely important. Hurricane Katrina was certainly strong, but it wouldn't have had the same deadly impact had the levees only been higher and stronger. New Orleans' defences were designed to cope with an event that would be expected to occur once in every two hundred years, which wasn't nearly enough even before climate change started raising the baseline.

This illustrates an important aspect of the rhetoric about climate change. In spite of what you might hear from some of the more fervid doomsayers, the reason that hurricane damage has risen in the past few decades is not, in fact, because of more intense hurricanes. Even though hurricanes do seem to have been getting stronger, a much bigger factor to date has been the rush to the coast. There has been a massive increase in the numbers of people living on the world's coastlines, and a minimal amount of attention paid to protecting them. The increasing storm intensity and rising sea level that we can anticipate in the future will only make this situation worse.

Once the projects are designed, it's necessary to test whether they are likely to be effective. The UK's Foresight project designed a computer program called 'Floodranger' which was based on the computer game SimCity. The program allowed designers to 'build' their project, run the climate forwards and see how the defences coped. The value of this approach became clear when the model produced some surprising results. For instance, it suggested that the coasts weren't the only problem. Floodranger showed that inland cities could also suffer if flash floods from more intense rainfall overwhelmed their drainage systems. This is exactly what happened in the British floods of 2007, during which more than twenty people died and tens of thousands were washed out of their homes and businesses.

Finally, there need to be funds to pay for the adaptation. The British government is now putting £500 million per year into an urgent programme to upgrade coastal and drainage defences and this will rise to £700 million per year in 2011.

Similar national programmes will need to be put in place for vulnerable regions around the world. The UK is now working with China to transfer the lessons learned to Shanghai and the Yangtze basin. Many of the most vulnerable countries are also the ones least able to pay for national programmes on this scale, and we will talk more about how these can be paid for in Chapter 10.

Projects like these should also be constantly revisited as the models progress. In the case of the Foresight project, this will happen every five to ten years.

Meanwhile, the message is beginning to filter through to many parts of the world that any major new civil engineering project will need to take climate change into account. For instance, the 13-kilometre Confederation Bridge in Canada, which connects Prince Edward Island to the mainland, was built one metre higher than is currently needed, to take into account the possible rise in sea level over its hundred-year lifespan.[9] Similarly, Boston's Deer Island sewage treatment plant has been built on a high enough elevation to protect its output pipes from being inundated by rising sea water. Up on the Tibetan plateau, the Qinghai–Tibet railway is vulnerable to melting permafrost. Some 500 kilometres of the railway rests on permafrost that is within a few degrees of thawing, and engineers have incorporated into the design a combination of insulation and cooling systems to ensure that the trains will not tip the permafrost over its melting threshold.

The Konkan railway in western India, the Copenhagen metro in Denmark and the Thames Barrier in London are all currently undergoing assessment for incorporating climate change into their designs.

## Sound the alarm and know the drill

This approach will be necessary for the sort of sudden, dramatic events that can cause considerable loss of life and damage to property if they take us unawares. Tragic examples that we have already experienced include the 2003 heatwave in Europe, the deaths from Hurricane Katrina in New Orleans in 2005 and the wildfires that scorched Greece in 2007. A combination of effective warnings and preparedness for these events could have saved thousands of lives.

When it comes to early warnings of natural disasters, one of the best examples is the one in place in Bangladesh for an impending typhoon. The World Meteorological Organization (WMO) issues a warning that a severe storm is on the way. Men on bicycles with whistles transfer this information to the populace. The local people have been drilled to move immediately to higher ground or to high-rise shelters. Though typhoons in the region seem, if anything, to have been growing more severe, death rates have plummeted.

This illustrates the two important aspects of any effective warning system. First, the alarm has to be official, provided by one overseeing and reliable body that will vet any potential threat. Above all, we can't afford false alarms so that people become complacent.

The WMO has already agreed to work with the United

Nations to extend its warning system beyond hurricanes and typhoons to all physical natural disasters. We propose that it would be very natural to include extreme weather in this programme. The WMO would be the most effective body to oversee a global warning system for events linked to climate change.

Second, everybody has to be clear about exactly what to do. In central Europe in 2003, many people – including hospital staff – were on holiday when the heatwave struck. There was nobody to issue simple information to vulnerable older people, such as ensuring that they drank enough water to avoid dehydration, or that they changed their habits and went out only during the coolest parts of the day.

While we're talking about adapting to heatwaves, it's worth a comment about where the danger actually lies. We humans are already amazingly adaptable to the temperatures we happen to find ourselves in. One study discovered that the ideal temperature range in northern Finland to minimise heat-related deaths was 14.3°C to 17.3°C, while the temperature that the people of Athens coped best with was a much hotter 22.7°C to 25.7°C. The message here is that we survive best at the temperatures we're most used to.[10]

Much of how we adapt has to do with habits, such as what time of day we typically choose to do outdoor work, or whether we drink water before leaving the house. The rest depends on how our infrastructure is set up, such as the sorts of buildings we live in and the means of transport we use outside. Habits are easier to change than buildings, but neither of them typically changes very fast.

Thus the problem with a heatwave (or, indeed, a cold spell) is that it takes the temperature above (or below) our comfort zone more quickly than we can reasonably respond to. That's why so many people died in Europe in 2003. The challenge now is to adapt our habits and our buildings beforehand, so that we can be ready when the heatwaves come.

## Gradual loss of ecosystem services

In some ways, this is the hardest adaptation to quantify. In this category go different gradual changes in our capacity to extract a living from the land. We have already described many of these above – such as changes in water availability, temperature or a shift in the pattern of pests or illnesses. What's needed is a big improvement in the models to identify the regions that are most vulnerable to these changes, and come up with strategies to cope. These might include changing crops to varieties that are most resistant to drought, and perhaps using biotechnology to help develop new, more resistant strains; changing planting dates and irrigation methods; harvesting and storing rainwater more effectively; using controlled burning to reduce fire risks; planting mangroves to provide natural sea walls against the rising waves and to reduce loss of soil from the coast.

Approaches like these will need to be integrated into a national strategy for each country in the world. It's not enough to build up the sea walls and hope for the best. Every government will need to know exactly what climate change will mean for their country, and how they will need to respond.

Some climate changes might overwhelm our capacity to adapt. If your land is in one place, and your experience lies with the crops you have traditionally grown there, it won't neces-sarily be easy to switch to something different. Social, eco-nomic, political and cultural barriers all stand between the world we have now and the one that we will soon have as climate takes its toll. And in some cases, for instance the lowest lying atolls threatened by rising sea levels, the only recourse might be to move.

It is already too late to stop the changes that we describe in this chapter. These adaptations, and more, will be necessary no matter what we now do to reduce the impact of future warming. Part III will look more closely at how the adaptations will be paid for, and how they can be politically encouraged. But for now, it's worth noting that no part of the world can be treated in isolation. The climate change that is already in the pipeline will hit hardest those countries that are least equipped to deal with it – and that have been least responsible for releasing the emissions that caused the problem in the first place. Because of this, we believe that developed countries have a moral responsibility to help the developing world cope with the coming damage. But there's an even stronger reason why we need to pay serious, united, international attention to adaptation. From the security of our food and water supplies to the economic implications of massive environmental migration, when global warming affects anybody those effects can quickly lead to trouble elsewhere.

# 5

# CLIMATE WILD CARDS

If the world will now need to adapt to change regardless, can't we just keep on burning fossil fuels and simply prepare ourselves for the consequences? That would only work if we were completely confident of being able to take anything the Earth's climate can throw at us. The trouble is that there are many ways in which it can take us by surprise.

The opening scenes of the Hollywood climate disaster movie *The Day After Tomorrow* show the hero working in Antarctica. He is camping on a massive floating shelf of ice, called Larsen B, drilling ice cores through its surface. The first sign of impending doom comes when the ice shelf cracks, right across the research site. In trying to save his precious ice cores, our hero only just survives.

This scene is based, loosely, on a true story. Larsen B is a real ice shelf – or at least it was. It was more than 3,000 square kilometres in area, and 220 metres thick. In February 2002, over a period of just a few weeks, Larsen B unexpectedly shattered. By the beginning of March, 500 million tonnes of ice, covering an area bigger than the county of Somerset, had vanished.

Though scientists had already noticed that this part of the Antarctic was getting steadily warmer, the Larsen B break-up still happened more quickly than anyone had expected. In fact, it happened more quickly than even the Hollywood script-writers could handle. One scientist remarked after seeing the film that in real life the cracks would have been happening all around, and the hero would have had to run for his life. This was perhaps the only example of a Hollywood disaster film that underplayed reality.

However, many of the movie's subsequent events managed to be both exciting and scientifically ludicrous. For instance, mighty hurricanes formed over land, whereas in fact they can only ever be born over water. And a supposedly climate-driven tsunami swamped the streets of New York, although such tidal waves cannot be caused by rising temperatures.

As global warming awareness has taken hold, disaster scenarios like these have become increasingly popular. There have been many books, articles and films about impending climate disasters, some of which are just as lurid as *The Day After Tomorrow*. The question is, are they true?

There are certainly some wild cards in the climate and every chance that, if we don't curb emissions, the result will be even worse than a mere multiplying of the effects that we described in Chapter 3. In this chapter we will separate the myths from reality, starting with the least likely and working our way upwards.

## Shutdown of the oceans' circulation

This is perhaps the scenario most beloved of disaster-mongers, and is also the one at the heart of *The Day After Tomorrow*.

Despite their appearances, the world's oceans are not just chaotic individual masses of water. Beneath their surfaces lies a supremely organised conveyor belt of currents that transports unimaginable quantities of water around the world. There is at least one region where this conveyor belt can be switched on and off: a few relatively small patches of water located between Greenland, Iceland and the north coast of Norway.

In that part of the world, sea water moving north at the surface experiences two important changes. First it becomes very cold. Second, it becomes much saltier, because the top part of the ocean begins to freeze into 'fresh' sea ice, leaving much of its salt in the water beneath.

Cold, salty water is much heavier than normal sea water, and so begins to sink. As it sinks, it pulls surface water in to replace it, in the same way that when you take out the plug in a bath surface water races towards the end of the bath to replace what's disappeared down the plughole. In this case, the descending arm of the conveyor belt drags balmy tropical waters – the famous Gulf Stream – up north, where they lap the shores of several northern European countries and help to explain why these are much warmer than parts of North America at the same latitude.[1]

In the scenario described in *The Day After Tomorrow*, a shutdown of the conveyor belt stopped the Gulf Stream from heading north, and hence brought a spectacular ice age to northern Europe and North America. However, although there were early fears that this might indeed take place, scientists now believe that switching off the conveyor belt would only lower European temperatures by a few degrees, and would probably just barely cancel out the global warming there.

This sounds as if it would be a good thing. But the sinking, and dragging northwards of surface water, sets in motion an entire network of ocean-wide currents which stretch down the Atlantic, around the southern coast of Africa, through the Indian and southern oceans and around the Pacific. This gigantic conveyor belt carries not just water, but salt and warmth right around the globe. Switch it off, and you have the potential to change climate worldwide.

For instance, similar changes in ocean circulation in the past seem to have significantly changed the pattern of tropical rainfall, including the monsoons that ultimately provide much of Asia with its food.[2] Europe and North America would also not escape scot-free. Changing the ocean currents in this way would also redistribute sea water, making the North Atlantic rise by up to a metre, in addition to the rise that had already come from melting ice.[3] It's also possible that the shifting currents would change the location of the food supply for schools of fish, so that lucrative Atlantic fisheries could collapse.

The best way to switch off the conveyor belt would be to melt large amounts of ice right on top of the main sinking point. That would leave a freshwater 'lens' that could act like a plug, stopping the water from getting dense enough to sink in the first place. That's exactly what's already happening in the Arctic. Both the floating sea ice and the land-based Greenland Ice Sheet are already delivering freshwater exactly where it could hurt.

The good news is that, as yet, they're not delivering nearly enough. Ocean modellers have compared the output from eleven different models and have concluded that the amount of freshwater needed to shut down the North Atlantic conveyor belt would be about the same as that now coming from the Amazon.[4] At the moment, the Arctic has hardly reached a quarter of the model's lowermost threshold. And of course the sea ice won't be around for much longer to keep contributing.

The IPCC report states that it is extremely unlikely that the conveyor belt will shut down in the twenty-first century, whatever we choose to do about climate change. However, if Greenland starts to melt more quickly (see below), there is still a chance that the conveyor belt could be vulnerable in the longer term. In the meantime, there are already signs that the system may be weakening, and models predict that, if we do nothing to halt carbon dioxide emissions, the conveyor belt could be 50 per cent weaker by the end of the century. The danger is that this might bring a similar pattern of effects as for a total shutdown, albeit of a lesser magnitude.[5]

Likelihood: the collapse of the ocean conveyor belt is very unlikely over the next century, and improbable even in the following hundred years. There is also virtually no chance that shutdown would cause a European ice age. However, if we don't constrain climate change, weakening of the circulation by the end of this century could still reduce tropical rainfall, including the Asian monsoons, as well as raising sea level in the North Atlantic.

## Massive, abrupt sea-level rise

The sea is already rising, as melting glaciers add their load to oceans that are expanding as they warm. But what if the world's ice sheets tipped over a threshold and suddenly, irreversibly, slid into the sea? There are three major ice sheets to worry about, two in Antarctica and one in Greenland. So far, these three together contribute only about a tenth of the current global sea level rise of three millimetres per year. But the signs are that the melt could be accelerating, and there is a frighteningly large amount of ice at stake.[6]

## Antarctica

Antarctica's two great ice sheets are linked at the centre like slightly misshapen butterfly's wings. The larger of these, the East Antarctic Ice Sheet, contains enough fresh water to raise sea levels by more than forty metres. However nobody thinks it will melt in the near future. The eastern sheet is old, cold and set in its ways and recent satellite data have even shown that it is putting on weight rather than losing it.[7] (That's not a contradiction to the global warming story, by the way. The models predict that, in one of the many counter-intuitive consequences of warming, as the seas warm and sea ice melts around Antarctica, more water will be sucked up into the air, and this will then fall as extra snow in the frozen interior. Unfortunately, the amount of extra snow captured is still only enough to slow sea level rise by about a tenth of a millimetre per year.)

However, the smaller, western sheet is more vulnerable, because most of its glaciers sit on a thin film of water – rather than being frozen to the rock like the eastern half. If the West Antarctic Ice Sheet did slide into the sea, it would still raise global sea levels by a horrifying five metres.

Clues as to how this might take place come from the doomed Larsen B ice shelf. The collapse of Larsen B isn't necessarily a sign that global warming has already come for the rest of Antarctica. Its home was the Antarctic Peninsula, a finger of land that sticks out towards South America, and that is so northerly and relatively balmy that old Antarctic hands refer to it as the 'banana belt'.

Though the peninsula has certainly been getting even warmer lately, with temperatures rising by around 0.5°C a decade since the 1950s, the rest of the continent has remained much more stable. And though recent evidence suggests that

Larsen B had previously remained intact for at least 10,000 years,[8] it is still just about possible (though increasingly unlikely) that the warming there is merely part of a natural fluctuation. Also, the collapse of Larsen B made not one iota of difference to sea level. Floating ice doesn't raise or lower the water level as it melts. You can see this for yourself by putting an ice cube in a glass of water. As the cube melts, the water stays at exactly the same level in the glass.

But, disturbingly, behind Larsen B were a set of flowing glaciers that the ice shelf had previously held back. With the shelf gone, these glaciers have now started to accelerate.[9] When glacier ice flows from land into the sea it adds water that wasn't there before. It other words, it raises sea level.

Those glaciers are relatively small by Antarctic standards. But there are much, much larger ones draining ice from the mighty West Antarctic Ice Sheet into the sea. And all of these are held back by two vast floating ice shelves that dwarf Larsen B. If these shelves were to shatter, it's possible that most of the West Antarctic Ice Sheet could then slide into the sea.

Fortunately, these gigantic ice shelves are much less vulnerable than Larsen B was, since they are at least five times thicker. Few researchers think they will break up soon, even if climate change is allowed to go unchecked. But they are still being very closely monitored, just in case.

The glaciers/ice shelves systems make up roughly two-thirds of the West Antarctic Ice Sheet. Until recently, the remaining third was relatively unstudied, largely because the weather there is awful even by Antarctic standards. However this region, called Pine Island/Thwaites, contains three of the continent's largest glaciers, which drain ice from the high interior out into the sea. Because the front ends of these glaciers are exposed directly to the sea, without the benefit of shelves of ice to buffer them, they have been called the 'soft underbelly' of Antarctica. And there are worrying signs that these glaciers are speeding up and draining more ice.[10]

Likelihood: the massive East Antarctic Ice Sheet is virtually certain to stay intact, and might continue to soak up some sea level rise through extra snowfall. Most of the West Antarctic Ice Sheet is unlikely to collapse sufficiently to provide an abrupt dramatic rise in sea level this century, though this conclusion depends on aspects of its internal dynamics which are as yet unclear. The Pine Island/ Thwaites glaciers could be more vulnerable. How likely they are to collapse remains uncertain – and is now a subject of urgent study. If they collapsed, taking with them the ice they drain from the interior, that could still raise global sea level by about 1.5 metres, drowning much of the world's coastline.

## Greenland

Melting the entire Greenland Ice Sheet would increase sea levels worldwide by a full seven metres. Because the Arctic is warming much faster it is – probably – more vulnerable than its Antarctic cousins.

But is it melting? In the past few decades the picture has been anything but clear, with different measures giving different answers. In some places a glacier was receding, while in others one was surging forwards. But of late all the signs have begun to point in the same direction. Greenland is indeed beginning to melt.

Though satellite measurements of Greenland's interior sug- gest that snow has recently been building up there, the edges of the ice sheet are also getting thinner.[11] Greenland's mighty outlet glaciers seem to have been speeding up, too, more than doubling its annual loss of ice over the past decade.[12]

The good news is that this process has still not yet doomed the Greenland Ice Sheet to extinction. In 2007, modellers calculated that it would take a global average warming of a full 3°C to push Greenland over the edge,[13] a threshold that we probably still have time to avoid.

But there is another important factor that the models didn't include. In 2002 several researchers noticed that something alarming seemed to be happening in one region during the summertime. Just when the summer sun began melting parts of the surface of west-central Greenland, the glacier there began to slip more quickly.[14] That's surprising because Greenland's glaciers are hundreds of metres thick. And because they slip on their bellies, something that happens on the surface shouldn't make any difference. It turned out, though, that the melting was producing giant lakes on the surface, whose water then poured down through cracks and crevasses creating inner waterfalls that flow to the land below and lubricate the ice's sliding edge. That's worrying because in principle it means that the entire Greenland Ice Sheet could be more vulnerable than we think to the steadily warming air.

The models don't incorporate this mechanism because they can't. Nobody yet knows how widespread the effect might be, or even where the cracks are. What's more, even before it reaches the point of no return Greenland can still raise sea level by amounts that we humans would find catastrophic. The ice sheet didn't disappear during the last warm period, around 130,000 years ago, when temperatures in the north were a few degrees higher than they are today.

And yet the latest analyses suggest melting Greenland ice increased the sea level then by between two and three metres. That would be more than enough to cause serious trouble in today's world.

Likelihood: the Greenland Ice Sheet is already melting. Unconstrained climate change with a global average temperature rise of 3°C could doom the ice sheet to eventual disappearance within the next few centuries – which would condemn future generations to a sea level rise of seven metres (though even if it tipped over this threshold, the entire ice sheet would still take many more centuries to melt entirely). However, as with the West Antarctic Ice Sheet, this assessment of the vulnerability of Greenland depends on aspects of its internal dynamics – for instance, whether the glaciers will begin to slide more quickly as surface meltwater falls through cracks – which are as yet uncertain. If these mechanisms cause Greenland to melt more quickly than we expect, sea level could rise by a matter of metres over the next century, which would cause grave danger for our civilisation. Greenland is one of the most convincing reasons we have for the urgent need to curb climate change.

## Melting permafrost

In the frozen wastes of the Arctic lies a climate wild card that makes even the soberest scientists afraid. From Alaska and northern Canada across northernmost parts of Europe and Siberia lie millions of square kilometres of frozen Earth. In some places, the land is forested with black spruce; in others there are sedges, mosses, frozen lakes and marshes. But around the fringes, and sometimes in the heart of this freezing land, the thaw has already begun.

Spruces in northern Canada have begun to lurch drunkenly as the ground falls beneath their feet. Giant holes have opened up in Alaska as the ice that once held the soil together turns to water and trickles away. Siberia's lakes have begun to awaken from their frozen sleep. And they are all, inexorably, putting out carbon.

This is the Arctic permafrost, so-called because it contains a layer of soil that stays frozen through summer and winter. This soil acts like a freezer, trapping carbon in the form of leaves, roots, dead mosses, anything that was once alive. But the power to the freezer has been turned off, and the carbon inside is beginning to rot.[15]

The danger is that the warming caused by our own, human, emissions of carbon dioxide is triggering a thaw of the north, and that that in turn will emit yet more carbon of its own in a vicious cycle that accelerates the warming. This is another example of a positive feedback, positive not because it's good but because it exacerbates the original effect.

In this case, what's frightening is the sheer scale of the potential problem. Some researchers have estimated that there could be a full 900 gigatonnes of carbon waiting to be released from the rotting Arctic soils, which is more than we have currently in the entire atmosphere. If even a small percentage of that escaped, it could double or triple the effect of our human emissions. And then, all climate bets would be off.

Also frightening is that when it comes to thawing permafrost we have very few facts to go on. Until recently research efforts have been too patchy and sporadic to put the whole picture together. Now Arctic scientists are scrambling to understand exactly what will happen.

We do know that the Arctic is already warming up. Temperature measurements show that not a single part of the region is cooling down and most are seriously heating up, in some places at more than double the global average rate.[16] We also know that the permafrost is already thawing in the fringe regions where it is at its thinnest and patchiest. However, there are also worrying signs that parts of the much colder interior may have begun to release their carbon, as bubbles of methane emerge from lakes in Arctic Russia.[17]

What's more, the form in which the carbon comes out can make a big difference. In the muddy marshland of northern Sweden, the thaw has actually decreased the overall amount of carbon emerging, because the water has blocked off the soil from the air, which in turn slows down the rotting process. But much of the carbon that does come out is now in the form of methane – marsh gas – which packs a much greater punch in the global warming stakes than carbon dioxide. The upshot: though the overall amount of carbon released has dropped by 13 per cent, the warming effect has gone up nearly 50 per cent.[18]

Likelihood: uncertain but very worrying. Nobody yet knows what will happen to permafrost in the future. The first tentative attempt to model the effect suggested that if emissions continue unabated, by the end of the century 90 per cent of the permafrost will be gone. This figure is probably an over-estimation, and better models will be available in the next five years or so. But if even a few per cent of the available carbon comes back out of the ground that would effectively double our current human emissions at a stroke. And the resulting climate disaster doesn't bear thinking about. Though it has more or less escaped the attention of the writers of disaster scenarios, permafrost is the most frightening wild card in the deck.

## Something we don't know about yet

It might sound facetious, but the biggest dangers could come from a disaster scenario that nobody has yet noticed. The climate records written in ice and rocks suggest that our atmosphere is supremely temperamental, capable of tipping over a dramatic edge into a new state in a very short amount of time. For instance, at the end of the last ice age the sudden melting of vast amounts of ice shut off the ocean circulation, which caused an abrupt refreezing. Though it's still not clear exactly how global the event was, Greenland's temperature dropped by 15°C, and northern Europe's by 5°C. The freeze happened over several centuries, and at first scientists studying ice cores thought the thaw had taken equally long. But as new, more detailed ice cores were drilled, researchers discovered to their astonishment that the shift back to warm temperatures at the end of this deep freeze probably happened within a decade. (As one researcher put it, dryly, the climate shift took place within a 'congressional lifetime'.)

What's more, similar abrupt lurches from cold to warm and back to cold again seem to have happened throughout the ice age itself, and in spite of intense research nobody is yet sure exactly why.

And then there's the time, around fifty-five million years ago, when some unknown event apparently triggered the release of massive amounts of carbon, which in turn raised global temperatures abruptly by some 8°C.

In this context, it's alarming to think that, thanks to our human burning of fossil fuels, carbon dioxide levels are higher today than they have been for at least 650,000 years and probably much longer. Renowned climate scientist Wally Broecker from Lamont Doherty Earth Observatory has likened the climate to an angry beast that we are now poking with a stick. If we keep on poking, we don't know what will happen next. But we do know that it could happen swiftly enough to take us completely by surprise.

Even without these disaster scenarios, the IPCC report shows that we have ample reasons to fear unabated carbon dioxide emissions. The changes that we described in Chapter 4, and which are now inevitable, are just a hint of what we would have in store if climate change were allowed to continue unabated for the next century or more.

This alone should provide us with a serious incentive to stop our greenhouse emissions before things get even worse. But the wild cards that we have described in this chapter put into even starker perspective the arguments for kicking our carbon habit. Take sea level, for instance. The IPCC report suggests that, if carbon dioxide emissions continue as foreseen, by the end of the century sea level will have risen by between a quarter and half a metre. Especially at the higher end of the range, that would bring the danger of flooding to millions more people.

However, it's also worth remembering that the IPCC is inherently a conservative body. Some researchers have since suggested that, if anything, this prediction is likely to be an underestimate. In particular, it doesn't include any of the mechanisms by which the ice sheets could crumble. If all the possible ice mechanisms add together to conspire against us

– if, for instance, meltwater at the surface does indeed flood down to the base; if that sends the ice sliding ever faster on Greenland and West Antarctica; if the buttressing ice shelves do start to crack; and if warm sea begins to lap at the vulnerable mouths of the Pine Island glaciers – then there is a serious chance that by the end of the century the sea will have risen by a matter not of centimetres but of metres.[19] That's not a chance we should want to take.

Another potential danger lies in the capacity of the environment to soak up the carbon dioxide that we emit. To date, the oceans and the ecosystems on land have soaked up around half of the emissions that we humans have put out. That's just as well. If it weren't for this particular ecosystem service we would now be experiencing much more severe effects from climate change.

But the trouble is that at some point in the future the natural world might become saturated and lose its capacity to soak up emissions. When and whether that will happen in the oceans is a complicated question. The ability of the oceans to take up carbon dioxide depends on their chemistry (how warm and acidic they become), their physics (whether ocean circulation patterns change) and their biology (what happens to the organisms that trap carbon in their bodies and are then buried in the sea floor). No model has yet managed to give a convincing answer to how these different effects will combine.

On land, the picture is a little clearer, but also bleaker. Even without considering the effect of thawing permafrost, the IPCC report suggests that the capacity of land-based ecosystems to soak up carbon dioxide will saturate around 2030. If we don't restrict emissions, by 2070 plants and soils may even become a net source of carbon dioxide – which would add to our human contribution of greenhouse gases and accelerate the warming.[20]

If we continue to burn fossil fuels with abandon, the more distant future will be much worse than anything we've described so far. There's enough fossil carbon in oil, gas and – especially – coal to keep the world going for centuries. Long before it's exhausted, we will have passed the threshold for all the eventualities described in this chapter, and more. In the end the atmosphere could contain thousands of ppm of carbon dioxide, a level not seen since the time hundreds of millions of years ago when hyper-hurricanes lashed the Earth's surface with acid rain.

There are plenty of excellent, well-researched books that have looked into this disturbing crystal ball.[21] Here, we prefer to assume that mankind will not be foolish enough to let that happen. Our generation is the last to have the chance of averting the worst of these scenarios. All we need is the right combination of new technologies, and economic, political and social will. The next two sections of the book will look at each of these in turn.

# Part II: TECHNOLOGICAL SOLUTIONS

Now that we know the scale of the problem, the next question is what to do about it. Applying existing technologies and developing new ones will be a large part of the answer – though that's not all it will take. In this section of the book we explain what low-carbon technologies and strategies are already available and what else is on the horizon. The tools we describe will need to be used on every scale, from the personal, to that of cities, to that of countries. They will involve many different sectors of the economy, different greenhouse gases and different ways to produce and use energy. We'll explain how these technologies are likely to affect your life, and then later, at the end of the book, we'll outline specific ways in which your individual choices about employing these approaches will make a difference. First, though, we need to establish a target for the ultimate levels of greenhouse gas at which we should be aiming.

# 6

# WHAT SHOULD WE AIM FOR?

To tackle climate change we will have to reduce our emissions of greenhouse gases. There is no other way. But what figure should we aim for? This is the first and most important question to answer. Until we have a specific target, we will have no idea what technological or political solutions will enable us to achieve it.

Many previous attempts to decide how far we should allow our climate to go began with the idea that we should stop climate change before it becomes 'dangerous'. However, it's too late for that. As we explained in Chapter 3, climate change set the stage for the 2003 European heatwave that killed more than 35,000 people. At a scientific conference convened by the British government in 2005 whose theme was 'Avoiding Dangerous Climate Change', one delegate commented dryly: 'Relatives of the heatwave victims will think we are past the dangerous level already.'

A better question is how much climate change we can afford before things become truly catastrophic. Though the answer is full of scientific uncertainties, a broad consensus is beginning to emerge.

# How hot is too hot?

The global average temperature has already risen by some 0.75°C since the nineteenth century. If we switched off every fossil-fuel power station, grounded every plane, car and train and went to huddle around wood fires, there would still be another 0.6°C of warming to come, as the atmosphere catches up with the greenhouse gases we have already put into the air. Thus the minimum possible temperature rise for the world, compared to pre-industrial times, is around 1.4°C. There is nothing we can do to stop at least that much. Below we outline some of the changes predicted by the IPCC report for warming of 2°C and upwards.[1]

## Vulnerabilities at warming of up to 2°C

- Global crop yield will be higher than today but this masks an inequality. In some middle and high-latitude countries crop yields go up, but in the tropics they are already falling. 10–30 million more people at risk of hunger.
- Increase in human health problems from heatwaves, malnutrition, floods, droughts and spread of infectious diseases.
- Less water availability and more drought in the middle latitudes and semi-arid tropics. 0.4–1.7 billion people suffering increased water scarcity.
- Environmentally driven migration with the potential to exacerbate conflicts over scarce resources and cultural invasions.
- More intense individual rainfall events, causing potential for flooding even in regions that are otherwise suffering from more severe droughts.

- Increase in intensity of hurricanes.
- Increased heatwaves in continental areas, as well as more droughts and fires in mid-latitude continental areas as the storm tracks move polewards.

## Additional vulnerabilities at warming of 2–3°C

All of the above plus:
- 0–3 million more people at risk of flooding.
- Up to a further 10 million at risk of hunger.
- Most of the world's coral reefs bleached.
- Commitment to widespread de-glaciation of the Greenland and perhaps the West Antarctic Ice Sheet with potential sea level rise of several metres.
- Considerable weakening of the ocean conveyor belt, with potential for significantly reducing monsoon rains.
- Further increase in intensity of hurricanes, enough to exceed infrastructure design criteria, cause significant economic loss and threaten large numbers of lives.
- More flooding in North America and Europe as winter rainfall increases and less water is stored as snow.
- Rapid increase in frequency of serious heatwaves causing many deaths and crop failures, loss of forest and fires.
- Extreme drought in increasingly larger areas.
- Serious threat of inundation in low-lying coastal areas and small islands.
- Accelerated shrinking and eventual loss of tropical mountain glaciers.
- Considerably more environmentally driven migration.
- 20–30 per cent of all species on Earth at increasingly high risk of extinction.

## Additional vulnerabilities at warming of 3–4°C

All of the above plus:
- Increasing likelihood of near-total melting of Greenland and West Antarctic Ice Sheets leading to eventual sea level rise of twelve metres over the coming centuries.
- Rather than soaking up carbon as they do today, terrestrial ecosystems switch to being a net source of carbon, accelerating the warming rate.
- Major species extinctions around the world.
- Widespread death of coral reefs.
- Falls in food yields in some parts of the higher latitudes. Global food production begins to fall.

## Additional vulnerabilities at warming of 4–5°C

All of the above plus:
- Food yields fall even at the most favourable locations in higher latitudes. Global production plummets.
- Increasing risk of serious, abrupt changes to the climate system including shutdown of the ocean circulation and major release of carbon from thawing permafrost.
- Up to a fifth of the world's population affected by flooding.
- Up to 120 million more people at risk of hunger.
- 1.1–3.2 billion people suffer from increased water scarcity.
- Loss of almost all high-latitude forest and very large tracts of the Amazon rainforest.
- Ecosystems covering 40 per cent of the world's land area subject to major changes.
- Very substantial increases in human deaths from malnutrition, diseases, heatwaves, floods and droughts.

## Additional vulnerabilities at warming of 5–6°C

- The IPCC didn't want to go there, and nor do we.

## Two degrees of freedom

Looking at the above lists, none of the outcomes are desirable, and they become increasingly less so as the temperature scale rises. All things being equal, to keep the 'danger' as low as possible we would pick the lowest possible rise, in other words set a temperature limit of 2°C. (In addition to the 1.4°C that's already inevitable, that would allow us just 0.6°C of leeway in which to kick our carbon habit.)

Even before the advanced model predictions in the IPCC report were available, researchers had been trying to put a figure on how much warming humans can bear. Perhaps surprisingly, and through quite different reasoning, many of them have hit on exactly the same figure of 2°C.

One early strategy was to avoid 'dangerous' climate change by keeping our warming to within the upper limits of natural variability during the relatively stable 10,000 years since the end of the last ice age. Pioneering economist of climate change William Nordhaus from Yale University suggested back in 1979 that this limit might be of the order of 2°C, though he admitted the great level of uncertainty in the data.[2]

In 1995, the German Advisory Council on Global Change (WBGU), an independent science council set up by the German government in the run-up to the Rio Earth Summit, published a report suggesting that the highest global mean temperature in the past several hundred thousand years had been about 1.5°C above pre-industrial levels. They added an extra 0.5°C on the principle that the Industrial Revolution has at least brought us more capacity to adapt to a changing world, and proposed the same maximum temperature limit of 2°C.

This isn't necessarily the best way of deciding on a 'safe' temperature rise. For one thing, during the last warm gap between ice ages, which occurred about 130,000 years ago, the global mean temperature was only a whisker higher than it is today. But thanks to slight wobbles in the Earth's orbit, the heat was distributed differently, the Arctic grew much warmer, ice melted and sea levels were several metres higher than they are now. Looking at the past can be a useful guide to the future, but it's still not a mirror image.

Moreover, temperature rises that occurred before humans existed — and long before there were more than six billion of us living in our fixed cities and depending on our industrial lifestyles — have little to say about what we might find 'dangerous' today.

However, the more we discover about the dangers of our interference with the climate system, the better that almost accidental figure of 2°C looks. The above lists show that the most serious effects begin to kick in somewhere between 2 and 3°C and become increasingly dangerous as the numbers go up.

In 2003 the WBGU produced another report[3] which set out the specific dangers likely to be faced for different temperature windows. They concluded that, based on dangers such as floods, famine, heatwaves, droughts and extinctions, temperatures should not be allowed to rise beyond 2°C. The report added: 'This climate window should be agreed as a global objective . . . The European Union should seek to adopt a leading role on this matter.'

This conclusion was not limited to green Germany. In 2005,

the International Climate Change Taskforce, a grouping of scientists and politicians from around the world, published a report.[4] The taskforce was co-chaired by British MP Stephen Byers and American Republican Senator Olympia Snowe, and, as well as the usual concerned faces from the industrialised world, also included members from China, India, Malaysia and Australia. Their conclusion? To avoid the worst effects of agricultural losses, water shortages, costs to health, damage to coral reefs and terrestrial ecosystems, and the increasing risk of passing a dangerous climate tipping point: 'We propose a long-term objective of preventing average global surface temperature from rising by more than 2°C above its pre-industrial level.'

That same year, the European Union confirmed the adoption of this figure as its official policy. The entire continent is now committed to attempting to keep global temperatures from rising more than 2°C above pre-industrial values, and to persuade the rest of the world to follow suit.[5]

## Now for the really bad news

The very serious problem, which few people appear yet to have noticed, is that it's now almost certainly impossible to restrict warming to 2°C. If we had started two decades ago we would have had a good chance. But in the present climate, that target looks increasingly out of range.

To guarantee staying below a given temperature we need to know exactly how sensitive the climate is to rises in greenhouse gases – how much temperature 'bang' you get for every greenhouse 'buck'. Our estimates for this sensitivity are getting better all the time, but they're still uncertain. If the sensitivity is at the lowest end of the range, we still have a slight chance of staying below 2°C. But if it's at the higher end, even 3°C may already be beyond us.

Whether the climate is thick skinned or highly strung depends on the various feedbacks that act with carbon dioxide to boost its effect. For instance, as we described in Chapter 1, warmer air soaks up more water vapour – which is a potent greenhouse gas in its own right – and thus causes even more warming. Also, melting shiny white sea ice and replacing it with dark sea water enables the world to soak up more sunlight, causing more warming. The strength of all of these feedbacks added to the power of $CO_2$ and the rest of the greenhouse family together determine the climate's sensitivity.

Because they all treat the feedbacks in slightly different ways, climate models come up with a variety of numbers for the sensitivity. Putting these together gives a range of probable temperatures for any given amount of greenhouse gas in the air. Forgive us for presenting yet another blizzard of figures, but they are vitally important to the story:[6]

- For 450 ppm $CO_2$eq, the temperature rise will probably be between 2 and 3.5°C with a likeliest value around 2.5°C.
- For 550 ppm $CO_2$eq, the rise will be between 3 and 5°C, with a likeliest value of about 3.5°C.
- For 650 ppm $CO_2$eq, the rise will be between 3.5 and 6°C, with a likeliest value of around 4°C.

These numbers should ring very loud alarm bells. The concentration of greenhouse gases in today's atmosphere is currently around 430 ppm $CO_2$eq. This means that 450 ppm is the lowest we can possibly hope to achieve. And yet look at the range. The *likeliest* value for the temperature rise even if we

The likely changes in global temperature (°C) for greenhouse gas stabilisation levels of 450, 550 and 650 parts per million. Note that the curves are not symmetric – in each case the tail at the higher end stretches out further than the one on the lower end. Thus the most probable value for the temperature rise does not coincide with the peak of the curve, but sits slightly to the right. The likeliest temperature increase for 450 ppm is around 2.5 °C, for 550 ppm is 3.5 °C and for 650 ppm is 4 °C. The asymmetry of the curves also means there is a greater risk of temperatures considerably above these 'likeliest' values than there is of temperatures that fall below. All in all, these curves show how big a risk we are already taking with our greenhouse future. (Source: The Hadley Centre, based on work published in G. R. Harris et al., 'Frequency distributions of transient regional climate change from perturbed physics ensembles of general circulation model simulations', *Climate Dynamics*, vol. 27, no.4, pp. 357–75, 2006)

manage to stick at this value is already 2.5°C. If we're very lucky, and the sensitivity is at the lowest part of its range, we might stay below that. But if we're unlucky, even at the lowest greenhouse gas level we can conceivably achieve, we could still find ourselves heading for a highly dangerous 3.5°C. If we allow the greenhouse gases to rise above 450 ppm, the situation is even worse. 550 ppm, which has long been the target that was supposed to keep us below 2°C, has no chance at all of doing this, and might even take us up to 5°C. That doesn't even bear thinking about.

For all of these reasons, we believe the only choice we have is to keep greenhouse gases at the lowest level we can possibly stay below. In other words, we have to go for 450 ppm $CO_2$eq. This is the number to look for in every policy statement, and every climate agreement.

Note that this number is lower than many climate policies that were set in motion in the past decade – including that of the UK. The reason for this is that the latest science tells us that our earlier estimates were too optimistic. For instance, the UK policy was based on a report produced in 2003 by the Royal Commission on Environmental Pollution, which suggested that keeping $CO_2$ levels below 550 ppm would be enough to prevent temperatures from rising more than 2°C above pre-industrial levels. But the science has moved on and we now know that's not enough. We'll talk about the political implications of this in Part III.

For now, the message to hold on to is this: although dangerous climate change is already with us, we still have a good chance of being able to cope with it if we stay below 450 ppm $CO_2$eq. This is the number we have to aim for. Any higher, and the risk of catastrophic climate change becomes just too great.

# How can we get there?

Much of what we've said so far sounds like unremitting bad news. But there is still hope. Though it's now almost impossible for us to stay below 2°C, it's not a dramatic threshold above which something bad would suddenly happen. Rather, it's like a speed limit in that the higher you go above 2°C the greater the risk of a serious disaster. Everything we've said so far in this chapter should be an extra spur to action, rather than a cause for dismay. Because the good news is that we do still have a chance of keeping greenhouse gases to that 450 ppm limit.

We will, however, have to act fast. Global greenhouse emissions will need to peak within fifteen years, and by 2050 they will have to have fallen to half their current levels. That sounds like a lot to ask, especially when you consider that much of this

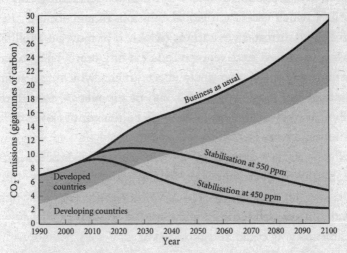

Predicted future greenhouse emissions according to several different scenarios. To convert from gigatonnes of carbon to gigatonnes of carbon dioxide (used throughout this book) multiply by 3.67. (Source: UK Department of Environment, Food and Rural Affairs)

change will have to come from developing countries that are currently much more focused on improving the wretched lives of their citizens than worrying about the global climate.

The pace of emissions is also picking up alarmingly. If we don't do anything to change our ways, in 2035 the air will already contain 550 ppm $CO_2$eq.[7] By the end of the century, emissions could be 250 per cent of today's level, with greenhouse gases heading hotly towards the 1,000 ppm mark. The IPCC report describes the challenge of turning this around as 'daunting'.[8]

However, the good news is that many of the technologies that we will need to curb greenhouse gases are already available or in the pipeline. In the next few chapters we will describe these in more detail. But first, just to show you how, together, these technologies can solve the problem, we'd like to mention an ingeniously simple approach put forward in 2004 by two Princeton researchers, Steve Pacala and Robert Socolow.[9] The researchers broke the problem down into a series of 'wedges', each of which would cut global emissions of greenhouse gases by 25 billion tonnes of carbon (which is just over 90 billion tonnes of carbon dioxide) over the next fifty years. They called them 'wedges' because their effects gradually increase from nothing right now, at the thin end of the wedge, to a thick billion tonnes of carbon (about 3.7 billion tonnes of carbon dioxide) per year in fifty years' time.

Pacala and Socolow originally added seven wedges together to show how you could turn a rising graph of emissions into one that stayed level. In fact, as we've shown above, staying level isn't enough – the graph has to fall. By the same analogy, to do this you could add more wedges.

The wedges include the following for fifty years' time (in each case we would need to scale up our efforts in a straight line, starting from zero today):

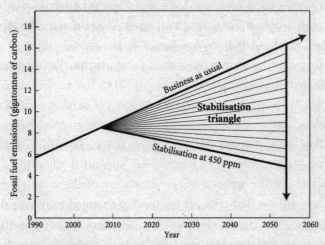

The 'wedges' strategy for reducing future greenhouse emissions from the 'business as usual' path to stabilisation at 450 ppm of carbon dioxide. To convert from gigatonnes of carbon to gigatonnes of carbon dioxide (used throughout this book) multiply by 3.67. (Source: adapted from S. Pacala and R. Socolow, 'Stabilisation wedges: solving the climate problem for the next 50 years with current technologies', *Science*, vol. 205, pp. 968–72, 13 August 2004)

- Double the fuel economy of two billion cars.
- Halve the annual average distance travelled by two billion cars.
- Cut carbon emissions from buildings and appliances by a quarter.
- Capture and store carbon dioxide from 800 gigawatts of coal power plants.
- Capture and store carbon dioxide from 1600 gigawatts of natural gas power plants.
- Build two million 1 megawatt wind turbines (about fifty times what we have today).
- Stop all felling of tropical forests and plant 300 million hectares of new trees in the tropics.
- Double the current amount of nuclear power.

- Quadruple the amount of natural gas used to generate electricity by converting coal-fired power stations (since gas produces fewer greenhouse emissions than coal).
- Increase the use of biofuels in vehicles by fifty times today's level.
- Use low-tillage farming methods on all the world's cropland.
- Increase the global area of solar panels by a factor of seven hundred.

You could imagine other wedges put together from the technological solutions that we've described here. Note that none of these require any major technological breakthrough.[10] If you added in a few new approaches along the way, the task would become even more possible.

In February 2007, Richard Branson, the entrepreneurial head of the Virgin Group, announced a prize of $25 million for anyone who can devise an effective way of removing 1 billion tonnes of carbon dioxide or more from the atmosphere per year for at least a decade. (Branson was inspired, he says, by the prize of £20,000 offered in the eighteenth century for measuring longitude, which was won by clockmaker John Harrison, and also by the $10 million Ansari X Prize for private human spaceflight, which was won in 2004.) The closing date for the Virgin prize is 8 February 2010.

If you want to have a go, be warned that the problem is harder than it sounds because carbon dioxide is so widely dispersed. There are only four molecules of $CO_2$ for every 10,000 molecules of air, so any attempt to capture it will also have to find a way to make it much more concentrated.

One promising approach was announced in April 2007 by Klaus Lackner from Columbia University, working with research and development company Global Research Technologies. The idea is to do the opposite of what chimneys normally do. Instead of pumping $CO_2$-laden air out into the atmosphere, gigantic chimneys would draw polluted air in from their surroundings, before a mineral soaked up the carbon dioxide and then released it as a pure stream of gas ready for storage underground. An advantage of this approach is that the chimneys wouldn't need to be near the places where the $CO_2$ was emitted. Instead of being bolted on to power stations or trailed behind cars, chimneys such as these could strip the $CO_2$ out of the air half a world away – for example, right next to a potential site of carbon dioxide storage.

The company estimates that a million such devices, each with an admittedly huge opening of a hundred square metres, would be able to soak up a billion tonnes of $CO_2$ a year. If we started very soon with pilot projects, gradually increased our efforts and ended up in fifty years' time with about four times that capacity, this could make up one of Socolow and Pacala's wedges.[11]

Another way to take carbon dioxide directly back out of the atmosphere would be to let biology do the concentrating for you. Plants build their bodies from carbon dioxide in the air. Normally, this returns to the air when the plant's body is broken down, by being digested in the gut of an animal, say, or burnt in a fire. But what if you protected the body so that its carbon stayed safely stored?

For instance, planting new trees in the tropics and then protecting them from being logged or burnt would be an excellent way to soak up carbon dioxide from the air – which is why it shows up in one of Socolow and Pacala's wedges.

Another intriguing approach that has recently emerged is the technology of 'biochar'. The idea is that you take some kind of agricultural leftover – perhaps the stalks and cobs from maize – and burn it at a very high temperature in the absence of oxygen. Some of the carbon forms into an oil that you can then use to burn and make energy. The rest forms a hard, black form of charcoal in which, its proponents believe, it will stay locked up for hundreds of years. The economic benefits of the oil can then help pay for the costs of sequestering the rest of the carbon. One neat side benefit of this approach is that in principle the charcoal could then be spread on fields. It wouldn't break down, but it could help the soils to hold on to nutrients and water, which would reduce the need for both artificial fertilisers and irrigation. The idea is still in its infancy, but it could well be one to watch.[12]

One approach we don't recommend is to try to engineer our way directly out of trouble by somehow balancing the warming we have caused with an equal amount of cooling. This idea has a troubled history, partly because many of the schemes proposed over the years have been wildly impractical. Suggestions have ranged from the wacky (paint as much of the world as possible white so that it will reflect more sunlight) to the ultra-expensive (put gigantic mirrors in space that would block sunlight – and would also cost trillions of dollars to make and deploy).

Moreover, this approach, which involves letting the carbon dioxide do its stuff and then wiping out the warming effect, does nothing for the other consequence of high carbon dioxide. One upside could be that the extra carbon dioxide might help to fertilise plant growth without the usual associated droughts that send crop yields tumbling in a warmer world. But a much more serious downside is that, as we explained in Chapter 3, more carbon dioxide in the air means a more acidic ocean – and putting a mirror in the sky would do nothing to stop that.

But the main reason that most climate scientists have given the idea of geo-engineering short shrift is that they are suspicious of any quick fix that leaves us with our old bad habits intact. As Meinrat Andreae from the Max Planck Institute for Chemistry in Mainz, Germany, put it: 'It's like a junkie figuring out new ways of stealing from his children.'[13]

In 2006, atmospheric scientist and Nobel laureate Paul Crutzen made the bold suggestion that we should inject clouds of sulphur dioxide into the air to make an artificial haze – a cloudy mirror in the sky – that would reflect sunlight back out to space and help to balance the greenhouse warming.[14] However, deliberately messing with something as complex as the atmosphere in this way could be even more dangerous than the problem it's trying to solve.

The history of our dealings with the atmosphere is littered with unintended (and often unfortunate) consequences. For instance, the chemicals that nearly destroyed the ozone layer – which protects us from cancer-causing ultra-violet rays – were invented by a well-meaning chemist who was trying to improve the environment. Trying to fix the problem by putting yet more pollution in the sky seems perilously like the children's song 'I know an old lady who swallowed a fly . . .'

# 7

# MORE FROM LESS

The first and perhaps most important thing we need to do to tackle climate change is to get smarter about how we use energy. Fossil fuels have provided us with such a cheap source of power that we've become foolishly profligate with our energy usage. It's amazing how much we waste, without even

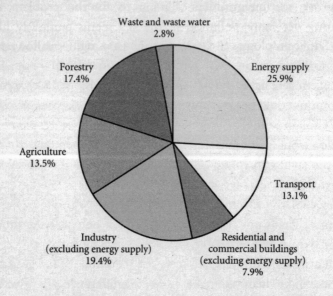

Total greenhouse gas emissions from different sectors. (Source: IPCC)

noticing how much it costs us. In fact, far from being expensive, many of the strategies we could use to reduce carbon dioxide emissions by improving efficiency will actually save money. This is the low-hanging fruit of the emissions game, the gaps that should already have been plugged if the energy market had been truly doing its job.

## Buildings

Globally, buildings are responsible for greenhouse emissions of around 9 billion tonnes of $CO_2$eq per year,[1] which is about 18 per cent of the total. Most of this comes from energy use, or abuse. Although insulation has become better and appliances more efficient over the past few decades, the way we use energy in our buildings is still incredibly wasteful, a combination of pouring greenhouse gases into the atmosphere and money down the drain.

The technologies already exist to put this right. For example, by upgrading to the best available insulation levels and using the most efficient lights and appliances a typical UK building's annual footprint could be cut at a stroke by nearly three-quarters.[2]

Though some of this would cost money to implement, much would come absolutely free, or even save money, thanks to the savings in energy costs. Even in the short term, over the next fifteen years we could cut at least 30 per cent from the projected rise in emissions from buildings without paying a penny. That's not counting changing our behaviour in buildings, which would enable us to cut even more.

This is one of the many areas of the climate change game where individuals can make a dramatic difference. Many of the following strategies can apply to your own home, place of work, school or place of worship. If we all start to put some or all of them into place, that will have a huge effect on global emissions.

## Insulate and isolate

In cold, overcast climates, we need to stop cold air from entering buildings in winter and from escaping in summer. All this takes is good insulation in walls and lofts and making sure that windows and doors seal properly in the winter to minimise draughts. It really is as simple as that.

In warmer regions, the building itself can act as a filter, selectively letting in daylight, warmth and cool air, depending on the needs of the moment. If this sounds high tech, it's probably worth mentioning that early architects were doing this before anyone had even heard of oil or electricity. The designers of Moorish palaces in Andalucía, for example, knew all about how to set the slope of a roof so that it blocked the searing overhead summer sun, but let in the gentler, more sloping sunbeams of winter. Modern buildings can also be designed to do this expertly, but in the meantime any of us can work with what we already have. When the sun is full on the windows, shut the shutters or draw the blinds. When you need to cool down and there's plenty of wind outside, open a window.

## New lamps for old

Lighting is one of the easiest ways to cut the emissions from buildings, which could drop by up to 90 per cent using technologies that are already available. For instance, swapping old incandescent lights for the lowest energy ones available can cut the energy used in half. Designing buildings to make proper use of incoming daylight around the edges can cut the remainder in half again, while a very simple strategy called task/ambient lighting can reduce it still further. This involves having a relatively low background lighting level, with more light at individual workstations. Not only does this take less energy, it's also often more restful on the eyes.

Finally, about one-third of the world's population has no access to any form of modern energy, and depends on lighting that burns fossil fuels directly – such as kerosene or paraffin lamps. These provide only 1 per cent of the world's lighting but 20 per cent of its lighting-related emissions. Switching to off-grid solar lighting would avoid almost all these emissions, while also creating fewer hazards to health from fumes. India's The Energy Research Institute (TERI) is trying to encourage just that with an immensely ambitious camapign called 'Lighting a Billion Lives', which aims to bring solar lighting to a billion homes in developing countries[3]. This is one example of how, if developing countries can get the funds and knowledge to 'leapfrog' to modern technologies, the whole world will be better off.[4]

## Appliance of science

Increase the efficiency of the appliances inside the building and reduce their number. Take frequent inventories to make sure that you don't have appliances that are too numerous, or too big. When you're replacing household appliances, always go for the most efficient new ones. In 1978, the US government introduced simple federal standards for appliance efficiency. By 2020, this will have cut residential greenhouse emissions there by about 10 per cent.

## Pull the plug on standby

Amazing though it sounds, those little lights on TVs and videos and all the other accoutrements of appliance standby modes really do make a big contribution to greenhouse emissions. It's a testament to our profligacy with energy that even mobile phone chargers that are not in use continue to draw electricity as long as they're plugged in. The International Energy Agency (IEA) estimates that standby mode could be causing a full 1 per cent of the world's greenhouse emissions, which is nearly as much as the entire aviation industry.[5] In 1999, the IEA launched the so-called 'one watt initiative' to encourage manufacturers to limit standby mode to one watt or less.[6] In the meantime, though it sounds absurd it really does make a big difference if you switch everything off at the wall as soon as you're no longer using it.

## Change behaviour

Even when houses are otherwise identical, one classic study showed that a single family can easily use twice as much electricity as its next-door neighbour.[7] In another study among nine identical children's homes in London there was a 50 per cent difference in electricity use. Tellingly, when the people in charge of the homes knew their electricity use was being monitored, it fell dramatically.[8] More recently, a survey of fifty projects worldwide looked at whether or not a household would change its consumption if its members knew how much electricity they were using compared to the same month the previous year, or compared to a neighbour. The upshot was an energy saving of 5 per cent.[9] This all shows how, if we're properly informed about how much electricity we're using and we pay attention, we're much more likely to use less. It's amazing how a 'smart meter' ticking away next to the fridge can encourage you to switch off the lights when you leave a room.

## Do-it-yourself

Otherwise known as micro-generation, this approach involves using the resources of your building to make your own energy.

We'll describe low-carbon methods for generating energy in more detail in Chapter 9, but it's important to note that many of these can apply quite well on the small scale. For instance, you can use the Sun directly for warming water or generating electricity through solar panels; heat pumps can also carry warm or cool air in or out of the building; and individual wind turbines can also play their part. Small-scale 'combined heat and power' (CHP) units will also be available soon to make use of both the heat and the electricity generated by burning natural gas.

Many of these technologies are currently expensive compared to their fossil-fuel equivalents, but they will become less so as economies of scale begin to kick in. More flexible national grid networks could even mean that individual households could export electricity that they don't use back to the grid itself. If it's satisfying to watch a smart meter tell you that you're saving electricity, how much more so would it be if the meter told you that you were selling electricity back to the power companies?

## Industry

Overall, industry is responsible for some 12 billion tonnes of greenhouse gases, almost a quarter of global emissions. Most of these come from the use of fossil fuels to make energy; direct use of fossil fuels for chemical processing and smelting; or direct production of carbon dioxide as part of the processing (for instance, in making cement from limestone).

Almost all the energy use is in a handful of energy intensive industries: iron and steel, chemicals and fertilisers, cement, glass and ceramics, pulp and paper. There are already plenty of ways to cut down on the energy needed. For instance, in so-called 'heat cascading' the waste heat from the highest energy processes is used to feed a series of successively cooler steps until the final output is used for heating the factory itself.[10] It would need no new technological advances, no legislation, and many factories could do it tomorrow.

Another technology that is already available to improve efficiency is variable speed motors.[11] It sounds prosaic, but more than half of all electricity generated is used to drive motors, and if they were more efficient that could make a huge difference. A motor that operates continuously and flexibly at relatively low speeds uses much less power than one that comes on and off at a fixed high speed. Similarly flexible motors on fans could save up to a third of their energy, and lifts could regenerate energy when going down.

Industries could also use the heat generated by electricity power plants, which is usually just wasted. If the factory were sited close enough to a power plant, the heat that normally disappears into the air via the cooling towers could instead be piped in to feed the heat-hungry processes. (This approach could also deliver heat to individual towns through district pipe networks.)

For the industries that generate carbon dioxide directly – such as the cement industry, which is currently responsible for some 3 per cent of global greenhouse emissions – the most promising approach would be to capture the carbon and store it before it can reach the atmosphere.

## Agriculture

Agriculture accounts for around 13 per cent of global greenhouse gas emissions, about the same as transport. Almost none of this comes from carbon dioxide. Though huge amounts of $CO_2$ do pass between the atmosphere and agricultural crops every year, the balance is more or less zero. It's the sister greenhouse gases – methane ('natural gas') and nitrous oxide ('laughing gas') – that matter most here.

Agricultural methane comes from a variety of places, and almost always involves microbes feasting on organic matter in places where there is little or no oxygen. Thus the biggest sources are the guts of cows, sheep and water buffalo. A smaller amount of methane comes from rice paddy fields, and from the burning of biomass. (Biomass burning, especially of forests, also contributes significant amounts of carbon dioxide, but we'll deal with this separately.)

Nitrous oxide comes directly from soils, especially when they have a surfeit of nitrogen-containing compounds because they have been doused with nitrate fertilisers or with animal manure.

Nobody has yet come up with a detailed study of exactly how these emissions will increase in the future if nothing is done to try to stop them. However, the IPCC report estimates[12] that by 2030 the agricultural contribution to these two greenhouse gases will have risen by 31–37 per cent.

There are various ways to control agricultural emissions. They almost all involve increasing the efficiency of how we use our land, and the technologies by and large already exist. For instance, better diets for livestock makes them – to put it frankly – belch less. In New Zealand, scientists are studying how to change the microbes that cows use to digest their food to encourage them to make sugars instead of methane. Even independently of climate change this makes good agricultural sense, since any loss of carbon by methane means less carbon to add to the bulk of the animal's body. It's also possible to control the nutrients in the soil by more natural means than adding nitrate fertilisers. For instance, the practice of agroforestry involves planting crops that contribute to each other's nutritional needs side by side. Agricultural lands could even be encouraged to become net sinks of carbon, by reducing the amount of ploughing – which disturbs the soil and encourages microbes to mobilise the carbon that it contains.

None of these practices would necessarily come cheap, or be immediately practical for the farmers in developing countries who will contribute the bulk of the growth in 'business as usual' greenhouse emissions. But if we come up with a way to make emissions cost money, by putting a decent price on the heads of all the greenhouse gases, this could help to pay for the agricultural changes we need. The IPCC report says that with a price up to $50 per tonne of $CO_2$eq, total agricultural emissions in 2030 could be reduced by about a third, and with a price up to $100 per tonne they could be cut in half – which would more than wipe out all the projected increases.[13]

## Forests

Chopping down and burning trees contributes some 8 billion tonnes of carbon dioxide to the atmosphere each year.[14] That's a huge amount, more than 16 per cent of the total human greenhouse gas emissions – more than comes from either agriculture or transport. And yet it's very largely unnecessary. Destroying forests is one of the maddest forms of messing with the climate that we humans have yet come up with.

Most of the carbon dioxide from deforestation comes from the burning of tropical forests, especially the Amazon rainforest. Reasons for cutting it down range from logging of individual hardwood trees, or slash and burn for subsistence agriculture, to large-scale agricultural plantations of palm oil. Even logging of individual trees often creates mass destruction. Bulldozers blast through the remaining trees to get to their prize; felling of individual trees often brings down their neighbours as they are bound together with woody lianas; the holes thus created in the leaf canopy let in the hot tropical sunlight which dries out the forest and allows for the outbreak of accidental fire; and loggers usually make themselves roads, which encourage the influx of subsistence slash and burn farmers.[15]

Models suggest that by 2030 a combination of preventing current deforestation, better management of forest and reforesting appropriate areas[16] could easily and cheaply reduce annual emissions by up to 14 billion tonnes per year.[17] Few studies have made predictions as to what the baseline 'business as usual' scenario would be for this time period, though there is some suggestion that deforestation emissions would be more or less the same per year in 2030 as they are today – in other words, 8 billion tonnes per year. In that case, applying all these tactics would mean that we wouldn't just reduce forest emissions to zero; forests would actually be soaking up considerable amounts of the emissions that came from other sources, helping us to meet the overall global reductions that we need.[18]

There would also be very little loss of food production. The soil that supports tropical forest is relatively poor in nutrients, most of which are bound up in trees, leaf litter and endless biological recycling. Thus, they are inadequate for growing crops for more than a few years, which is one reason why slash and burn farmers need to keep moving. In central Brazil, advances in soil science have allowed farmers to grow crops such as soybean in the previously infertile Cerrado region, which has taken pressure off the Amazon while the overall agricultural production has actually gone up.[19]

What's more, any reduction in emissions from forests would be relatively cheap, especially when compared to other ways of cutting carbon. Economic research suggests that the direct yield from forest land that's been converted to farming – including the proceeds from the sale of timber – is the equivalent of less than \$1 per tonne of $CO_2$ in many areas, and usually well below \$5 per tonne.[20] Any economic system that makes it expensive to emit carbon dioxide by putting a price on the head of every tonne of $CO_2$ would wipe out these profits many times over. Analyses suggest that almost half of the reduction would cost less than \$20 per tonne of $CO_2$, and more than two-thirds would cost less than \$50 per tonne.[21] As we'll show in Chapter 10, these numbers look eminently sensible when compared to the likely prices that will be set in future carbon markets.

How to ensure that the countries where deforestation rates are highest have both the funds and the incentive to put a stop to it is a political rather than a technological question; Chapters 10 and 11 discuss some of the strategies that are already in place, as well as ideas for how to strengthen them. What's clear is that we need to make it happen. It's true that many developed nations, especially in Europe and North America, converted their forests to agricultural land centuries ago, and that this laid the foundations for their subsequent development. That's one reason why the developed world should help pay to reduce tropical deforestation. To those who exploit them, tropical forests might seem like a cheap and almost infinite resource. But the emissions they are putting out as they burn are costing all of us the Earth.

## Waste

Waste is a relatively small contributor, at around 1.2 billion tonnes $CO_2$eq per year, which is just a few per cent of the global total. Still, it's also easily reduced. Most of the emissions come in the form of methane from landfill sites which is relatively straightforward to capture and can often be used to generate electricity. For instance, in the past decade, the UK has reduced its methane from landfill sites by 55 per cent.

Even more important, though, are the indirect emissions from waste – which are much harder to quantify but likely to be very substantial. From a climate point of view it's foolish to use things once and then throw them away. The archaeologist E. W. Haury wrote: 'Whichever way one views the mounds [of waste], as garbage piles to avoid, or as symbols of a way of life, they . . . are the features more productive of information than any others.'[22] If alien archaeologists began to uncover our own particular piles of plastic bags that have been used only once and then thrown away, wrappings, cartons, tins and papers that have served us very little but cost us dear in carbon emissions to make, it's not hard to imagine what conclusions they might draw.

## Population

One important issue very commonly raised in the context of climate change is the world's burgeoning population. There are currently some 6.7 billion people on Earth, compared to just one billion in the mid-nineteenth century, and the United Nations predicts that global population will rise to a staggering 9 billion by the middle of the century. Generally speaking, the more people we have on Earth, the more overall carbon dioxide emissions there will be. So it seems obvious that if we are to tackle climate change we need to curb this dramatic rise in population.

However, the devil is in the details. The first problem is that it's not clear exactly how to go about this worthy goal. Many of the strategies that different countries have adopted to try to curb their populations have now been discredited, or have come with disturbing side effects. Some population dynamicists now advocate strategies to reduce unintended pregnancies by a combination of more effective sex education and greater availability of birth control methods. However, though this might be effective in wealthier industrialised nations, the birth rate there is often already falling. In developing countries, on the other hand, large families are often highly desired. This is an inevitable consequence of poverty - arising from a combination of high infant mortality rates, limited options for economic advancement and the need for family support in sickness or old age[23].

To deal with rising population effectively you need to understand the underlying causes. Although many of the wealthy industrialised nations currently have low birth rates, that has not always been the case. For example in the UK, from the Middle Ages through to the eighteenth century, birth rates were typically 7 or 8 per woman, but most of these children did not survive to adulthood so the population was relatively stable. As conditions improved through the introduction of clean water, sanitation and health care, more of the children lived into maturity to have their own children and the British population spiked. However, since these developments also came with an increase in the level of education and empowerment of girls and women, the number of births per woman began to fall and the population stabilised again. This same dynamic has applied in the past to most currently industrialised nations and is also beginning to apply to parts of the developing world.

Thus, by far the most effective way to curb population growth in the long term is to educate and empower girls and women. Many different studies have shown a direct correlation between the level of education of a country's female population and the rate of population growth[24] – the more educated girls are, the more economic opportunities they have and the fewer children they bear. This is a desirable goal and should be a target for developmental policies the world over even regardless of climate change.

It is also worth noting that not all populations are equal when it comes to greenhouse emissions. As we describe in Chapters 12 and 13, there is already a very marked disparity between the amount of emissions produced per person in industrialised nations and in poorer developing countries. Coupled with this is the question of how the consumption behaviour of the population is likely to change in the future. Increasing urbanisation in rapidly developing countries is likely to cause a large rise in the emissions per person, whereas in the ageing populations of industrialised nations the emissions per head might start to decline even without deliberate policies to curb emissions. The upshot is that it's very hard to calculate exactly what contribution rising populations will make to the overall greenhouse gas budget[25].

Finally, there is the question of timing. Thanks to our previous tendency to ignore the problem, tackling climate change has now become urgent and immediate. As we explained in Chapter 6, we will need to make radical changes to our greenhouse gas emissions in the next two decades, a timescale over which population policies have little effect. Yes, in the long term we will need to curb population growth, both to rein in emissions of carbon dioxide and to ensure that we can sustainably feed, house and clothe everybody on Earth. But in the immediate future the only way to tackle climate change is to change the way energy is used by those of us that have already been born.

# 8

# PLANES, TRAINS
# AND AUTOMOBILES

Transport has received so much attention in the climate change story that we have given it a chapter of its own. This sector currently makes up 13 per cent of global greenhouse emissions, and after power generation it is by far the fastest growing.[1] It's also by far the most talked about, probably because it's the one area in which individuals can make the most dramatic difference. Almost all the energy for transport comes from petroleum, and unless there is a dramatic change from our current path, greenhouse emissions from transport will be 80 per cent higher in 2030 than they are today.[2]

Part of the problem is that wealth and carbon-hungry transport have long tended to go hand in hand. The richer the world gets, the further it wants to travel and the less carbon efficient the means it chooses. As the wealth of a nation rises, its citizens change from walking and cycling, through buses and local trains, to cars, high-speed trains and air travel.[3]

Most of the projected rise over the next few decades will come from developing countries, but it's hard to argue that the citizens of those countries should not enjoy the advantages of travel already afforded to those in the industrialised world.

Curbing these emissions will take a combination of new low-carbon technologies, increased efficiencies and the provision of attractive enough alternatives to encourage us all to turn readily away from the most polluting methods of moving around.

## Biofuels

First, a few words about one of the highest profile and most notorious new technologies for transport – low-carbon fuels, known collectively as biofuels. Though most of the strategies for low-carbon energy produce electricity, transport almost always needs a liquid fuel that can easily be delivered to individual cars, buses, trains and planes. (Electric cars are one promising exception to this, as we discuss below.) One way to provide a liquid fuel without damaging the atmosphere would be to make new green fuels that use carbon-neutral biomass as a feedstuff. That way, we could keep doing more or less what we do now, but with fewer carbon consequences.

This is such an attractive notion that two of these so-called 'biofuels' are already in use – bioethanol, which is a direct substitute for petrol, and biodiesel, which is just what it sounds like. Bioethanol can be made from more or less any crop containing sugar or starch. The starchy crops, for instance wheat or potatoes, would then need an additional chemical process to convert their starch into sugar. Yeast is then added to the sugar and the mixture fermented, as for making alcohol to drink. Similarly, biodiesel comes from crops that make oil, for instance rapeseed, sunflowers or oil palms.

In principle, biofuels like these should be carbon neutral because the emissions given out by burning the fuel balance the carbon dioxide taken up by the crops from the air in the first place. But as with so many other attempts to replace fossil fuels, the environmental devil is in the details.

First, there is the danger that agricultural land can be diverted from food production, or that grains that would have been used for food are diverted instead to make fuel. That in turn would drive prices for existing foodstuffs higher, which hurts those least able to afford to feed themselves.

This is, famously, already happening. In June 2007 the United Nations Food and Agriculture Organization published a report warning that the demand for grains and vegetable oils to convert into biofuels was already driving prices very high. The report estimated that food import prices for developing countries had risen by a shocking 90 per cent since 2000.[4] Considering that many of those same developing countries are already suffering the effects of climate change brought on them by the West's use of fossil fuels, this attempt to right the wrong looks more like heaping injury on injury. But the rise in prices has also had an inflationary effect on first-world countries too, at a time when many economies are struggling with the threat of recession.

In June 2008 world leaders converged on Italy for a high-level conference to consider the role that bioenergy has played in soaring food prices, though they emerged with little more than a declaration calling on developed nations to provide increased assistance to the developing world.

Growing the necessary crops also means using nitrogen fertilisers, which in turn cause the soil to put out nitrous oxide – a potent greenhouse gas in its own right. Then ploughing, harvesting and processing the crops requires energy, which is usually supplied by burning fossil fuels. Each extra step – converting starch to sugar, converting sugar to alcohol – takes more energy still. There's even a possibility that certain biofuels could produce more greenhouse gas emissions than the old fossil fuels they seek to replace.

Former US President George Bush has sought to boost his climate change credentials, and the prospect of improved fuel security, by spearheading a rush to make bioethanol from corn. And yet, the evidence suggests that this could hurt as much as it helps. Many researchers have tried to do a so-called 'lifecycle analysis' of bioethanol from different crops, but it's still hard to know exactly what numbers to put in the calculations. For instance, a group of scientists from Berkeley, California, reviewed a whole set of studies and concluded that bioethanol made from corn produced some 18 per cent fewer greenhouse emissions than normal petrol. Though it's nowhere near 100 per cent, that might still sound promising. Until, that is, you notice the uncertainty. Though 18 per cent is the researchers' best guess, they still acknowledge that the real number could be anywhere from 36 per cent less than petrol (which would be better still) to 29 per cent *more* than petrol (which would obviously be much worse).[5]

A report from the International Energy Agency published in 2007 concluded that the typical $CO_2$ reduction for biofuels based on corn was 15–25 per cent compared with petrol. Using sugar cane as a feedstock, on the other hand, produced up to 90 per cent $CO_2$ reduction and should be considered a much more viable alternative.[6]

It's also important to calculate exactly how much carbon dioxide biodiesel costs to produce. And as well as the processing costs, there's the question of exactly where in the world the vegetable oil to make it comes from. In 2003, the EU committed its member states to blending fuels with 5.75 per cent biofuels by 2010, which sparked a new oil rush. Since the Continent doesn't have enough land to supply the necessary vegetable oils, it would have to import on a huge scale to meet this target. That would be good news for countries like Malaysia and Indonesia, which produce most of the world's palm oil. But environmental groups warn that these countries intend to cut down large tracts of virgin rainforest to convert to palm oil plantations.

Replacing a vivid, varied ecosystem with regimented rows of a single species of palm isn't just an aesthetic loss (though it could be the final blow for that charismatic primate the orang-utan), it's also dangerous. The sheer variety of species in a rainforest protects it from incoming diseases, whereas a disease that specifically targets oil palms could wipe out an entire plantation almost overnight.

Then, of course, there's the issue of carbon dioxide. Burning vast amounts of virgin rainforest, together with the potential of such fires to spread to the region's carbon-rich peat lands, could put enough emissions into the atmosphere to outweigh the carbon benefits of biodiesel for decades. Such so-called green fuel would therefore be anything but.[7] A United Nations report published in 2007 was careful to state that, though most biofuels provide fewer carbon emissions than their fossil-fuel rivals, this is only 'provided that there is no clearing of forest-land or . . . draining of peat lands that store centuries of carbon'.[8]

All this is not to say that biofuels are bad. In fact, they can work very well. For the past thirty years they have been a superb resource for Brazil – which responded to the 1970s oil crisis by converting sugar cane to bioethanol and now produces over half the world's supply. The scheme has worked well there at least in part because the country has large tracts of well-watered agricultural land which is perfect for sugar cane production. Brazil is now sharing its expertise with countries in southern Africa, to enable them to resuscitate their moribund sugar cane industry and put it to biofuels use.

But the important point to make is that not all biofuels are equal in the fight against climate change. The UN report suggested a way round the problem of rogue emissions during the planting and processing, in the form of an international certification scheme to state exactly how much greenhouse gas the bioenergy has saved, or indeed cost, throughout its lifetime.[9] 'While developing and implementing a widely accepted certification scheme will be a challenge,' it adds sternly, 'this should not deter governments, industry and other actors from making the effort.' The UK is now looking into such a scheme for imported biofuels, and Belgium has already begun to use one.

The best way round the problem of competition with food would be to find a way to use cellulose, the material that lines the cell walls of plants and makes them stand tall. Unlike horses and cows, humans can't digest cellulose, but it is nonetheless packed with sugars. If these sugars could be converted into ethanol, this would open up the possibility of using stalks, woodchips and tough wild grasses that would never compete with food crops. Termites have the technology. They secrete an enzyme that helps them digest cellulose for food and we would do well to learn from their example. A few small factories are being built in the US to convert crop leftovers into ethanol in Iowa, New York, Tennessee, Michigan, Georgia, Kansas, Colorado, and Florida. (An intriguing alternative to this biological route would be the development of an industrial-scale catalyst that could convert plant waste matter into ethanol, something that David King is currently working on[10]). Moreover, the tide in the US is turning. While President Obama has advocated subsidies for bioethanol, he emphasies the need for non-food sources and has promised considerable funding for research into second-generation biofuels as part of a $150 billion investment into clean energy over the next 10 years. Meanwhile, in September 2008, the EU voted to revise its biofuels targets. The new rules require that member states achieve 5% renewable energy in transport by 2015, and 10% by 2020. However, a fifth of the 2015 target and two fifths of the 2020 target will have to come either from second-generation sources such as cellulose, or from other low-carbon forms of transport such as electric/hydrogen powered cars (see below).

While in many ways this seems sensible, there is a danger that changing regulatory regimes on such a short timescale might shake the confidence of industries taking their first tentative steps into the low-carbon world. With its revision, the EU effectively reduced its target from 5.75% biofuel in petrol by 2010, to a mere 4% by 2015. This has angered some members of the biofuel industry, who have already made considerable investments based on the earlier target.

## Planes

Aeroplanes have become the new villains of climate. In terms of overall numbers that's not strictly fair. Aviation is directly responsible for about 700 million tonnes of carbon dioxide each year, which is just 1.6 per cent of global greenhouse emissions.[11] However, molecule for molecule the emissions count for much more than they would on the ground because planes are very efficient at causing greenhouse warming. High-altitude deliveries of nitrogen oxides (which form ozone, another greenhouse gas), as well as the water in contrails that can go on to form cirrus clouds, together enhance the direct effect of carbon dioxide by up to a factor of three.[12]

There's also the inequality argument. One reason why planes contribute so little to the overall greenhouse gas burden is that relatively few of the human population can afford to use them. A return flight from London to New York, for example, generates a hefty 1.5 tonnes of carbon dioxide per passenger. Without even counting the extra greenhouse effects involved in flying, that's as much as an average Indian citizen emits in an entire year. (To be fair to aviation, this argument also applies to power generation. As we've already mentioned, fully a third of the world's population has no access to modern energy sources.)

The third reason why aircraft receive so much attention is that, unlike other carbon-hungry forms of transport, there are no likely alternatives to fossil fuels on the horizon. Hydrogen could work, and would be especially low-carbon if it was made from renewable energy sources rather than fossil fuels. However, it would probably have to be carried on the plane in liquid form, which would be much heavier than the kerosene that aeroplanes use now and would also need to be refrigerated. Worse still, the output from burning hydrogen is . . . water. That's fine on the ground, but up in the air it would contribute to making further cirrus clouds, which would in turn help to warm the Earth.

Another possibility would be to make kerosene artificially. This process is already well established starting from coal, or in some cases natural gas. In principle it could also be done using biomass, such as the waste left over from food crops, for a low-carbon alternative. The technology just needs to be adapted, but it's not clear whether it would become competitive, given the relative cheapness of pulling the feedstuff for kerosene out of holes in the ground.

Biofuels are perhaps more promising. However, ethanol yields less energy, pound for pound, so tanks would have to be much larger to accommodate fuel for the same distance travelled. And biodiesel freezes at the low temperatures encountered aloft, so the fuel tanks and engines would have to be heated.

One alternative might be butanol, which is like ethanol but with twice as many carbon atoms in its chemical backbone. Because of this, butanol packs more energy punch for its weight, and also freezes at much lower temperatures. (Furthermore, it's less corrosive than ethanol, so would be much easier to transport in pipelines.) In 2007 Virgin Atlantic and Boeing announced a joint initiative to work with engine manufacturer GE Aviation on developing a plane that could fly on biofuels. The plan is to test fly one of Virgin's Boeing 747s some time in 2008, with a mix of biofuel in one of the four engines.

The head of Virgin, Richard Branson, suspects that butanol might be the answer, though he's not ruling out finding something else that will work even better. In 2006 Virgin announced that profits from its flights and trains over the next ten years (more than $1 billion) will be ploughed into a new venture, Virgin Fuels, which is dedicated to finding new low-carbon fuels for transport. This seems to be sound business sense rather than well-meaning philanthropy. Whoever invents an effective low-carbon fuel system for aeroplanes will be able to look Bill Gates in the bank balance.

Oil giant BP is also betting on butanol, though not necessarily for planes. In 2006, it announced that it was investing $1 billion to develop new biofuels, and other large energy companies – as well as the US Department of Energy – are also starting to commit funds.

Even if the biofuels experiments pay off, they're unlikely to replace standard jet fuel for several decades.[13] So for now most of the efforts to reduce the environmental effects of aircraft depend on improving their fuel efficiency. Partly because jet fuel already makes up a high proportion of the cost of flying, aircraft manufacturers have a good record for improving efficiency. Modern planes are some 70 per cent more fuel efficient than those of forty years ago.[14] The new Boeing 787 'Dreamliner' uses lightweight composites for its body and is 20 per cent more efficient again.

Research into other fuel-saving technologies, which was abandoned in the 1990s when oil prices plummeted, are re-entering the arena. For instance, suction systems to reduce turbulence, new body and wing designs and rear-mounted, open turbo-prop engines could all improve fuel efficiency by up to a further 60 per cent.[15]

Changing the way planes fly would also help. Plenty of fuel is wasted by taxiing, and by endless waiting in holding patterns. Several airlines are looking into the possibility of towing planes to the runway, and not switching on the engines until just before take-off. Better air traffic control could also ensure that planes fly the minimum possible distance and land immediately on arrival.

However, even if all these strategies for increased efficiency come into play, they are still likely to be swamped by yet bigger increases in passenger numbers. According to the IPCC report, a 'business as usual' scenario, which incorporates projected improvements in efficiency, would produce 2.5 times the current aviation emissions by 2030. Even with more drastic improved efficiency, the emissions would still almost double.[16]

Thus, until a new fully green jet fuel can come into play, the most immediate strategy will have to be to persuade people out of planes, especially in cases where other, less carbon-hungry forms of travel are readily available. In particular, short-haul flights produce disproportionate emissions because so much of the flight is taken up by taxiing, waiting, climbing and approaching. The message here is that if you can take a train, do so.[17]

Meanwhile, it's worth making a point here about international shipping which has so far escaped the accusing fingers that are being pointed at aviation. Most international freight travels by sea, and ships are responsible for around 800 million tonnes of carbon dioxide per year,[18] which is slightly more than from aviation. Like air travel, shipping is also growing at an extraordinary rate. Also like air travel, questions about which country is ultimately responsible for the emissions are so contentious that it is not even included in national emissions tallies. There's more about how to resolve this issue in Chapter 11.

## Trains

Trains are already a relatively carbon-friendly way of getting around even using standard fossil fuels. Emissions can be as little as 10 per cent of that of the equivalent journey by car, depending on how many passengers are in the car, and exactly what fuel the train is using.[19] Trains are also much more pleasant than the combination of endless security queues and limited room that constitutes modern air travel – so there's large potential for convincing us all to switch. Even for shorter journeys trains could be made attractive given the right pricing incentives and timetables. In the UK, for instance, 60 per cent of the population live within a ten-minute drive (or a fifteen-minute cycle ride) of a railway station.

There are ways to improve trains still further. Using a low-carbon fuel such as biodiesel would cut carbon emissions almost to nothing, as would electrifying trains and taking advantage of new low-carbon technologies as they come on to the grid. Fuelled by France's electricity, which is 80 per cent nuclear, the famous TGV train is one of the lowest-carbon ways to travel in the world, short of cycling or walking. If you live in Europe and want to travel to almost anywhere in France, this is your best carbon bet.

Coordinating the ticketing and use of trains over long distances and between countries and extending the coverage of high-speed networks will all be important if trains are to compete effectively with short-haul planes. In July 2007, a new Europe-wide network called Railteam was launched which will soon allow people to book a single ticket for travel across several different countries, and coordinate connections.[20] Though elsewhere in the world trans-national train networks are not so advanced, the drive to reduce emissions, especially from freight, might even breathe new life into the long-awaited Trans-Asia Railway, with the aim of coordinating gauges and prices and connecting European countries directly with a broad swathe of Asia.

## Automobiles

Three-quarters of all transport emissions come from road vehicles, and if no one acts to intervene there will be more than a billion vehicles on the roads by 2030, and a billion more again by 2050.

To solve this impending transport emissions crisis we will need to find some alternative way to drive that does not also produce carbon dioxide. An approach already on the market is hybrid vehicles. Present hybrids, of which the Toyota Prius is the market leader, combine a normal petroleum-fuelled internal combustion engine with an electric motor and battery. The idea is that the battery is recharged when the engine is running, and especially during braking. Such hybrids use the electric motor/battery to boost power during acceleration, to run power steering and other accessories, and to drive the engine at low loads when normal internal combustion engines are at their least efficient.

Under standard US driving conditions, this improves fuel efficiency by up to 50 per cent, with an equivalent drop in greenhouse gas emissions. They might do even better than this in heavily congested urban settings, when the battery can gain proportionally more from braking, and when the electric motor can be used proportionally more for slow, otherwise inefficient driving. They also have the general advantage that they can be used with the current petrol distribution systems and produce cars that are barely distinguishable in range, power and size from their fossil-fuel counterparts. In 2005 worldwide sales of hybrid vehicles totalled more than half a million. (While that's impressive, it's still only a tiny fraction of the sixty-three million motor vehicles sold that year.[21])

Better still, from a greenhouse perspective, would be all-electric vehicles that could be powered directly from the electricity grid. That way, as more renewable and low-carbon energy made it on to the grid, transportation could gain the low-emission benefits. In fact, electricity powered some of the first motorised vehicles, until they were outcompeted by the cheap, easily available fossil fuels that powered the internal combustion engine. A few modern electric cars exist but they suffer from short driving range and very limited battery life.

'Plug-in' hybrids might be a good intermediate step. In 2007 General Motors and Ford announced that they were starting development of hybrid vehicles that could travel short distances without using petrol at all, and be easily recharged at a regular electricity socket. This would be particularly useful if the electricity came from a low-carbon source.

Another important strategy is to improve the fuel efficiency of the cars themselves. More aerodynamic designs, using lighter materials and increasing the efficiency of engines, will all help to reduce emissions – though there is always the danger that such innovations will simply provide an excuse to make bigger, more powerful cars. This is another area in which consumer choice is likely to have a considerable effect on the future of cars. If we as consumers insist on cars that are lightweight and economical rather than pointlessly large and power-hungry, manufacturers will have to respond to our demands. If, on the other hand, we stick with the tired old notion that big is beautiful, manufacturers will inevitably do the same.

Something else to look out for is exactly how much emissions your car has produced while being created. There are now moves to design cars whose 'cradle to grave' emissions are as low as possible. For instance, they could be built from lightweight, strong, biodegradable materials prepared at low temperatures, unlike stainless steel.

We will also need to change the way we use our cars. One promising approach is so-called eco-driving, which encourages drivers to use their cars to the maximum possible efficiency. Techniques include smoother deceleration and acceleration, keeping engine revolutions low, turning off the engine when idling, reducing maximum speeds and ensuring that tyres are properly inflated. Studies in Europe and the US suggested that such measures could improve fuel economy by an extraordinary 20 per cent and in the Netherlands eco-driving is part of the standard driving school curriculum. Some cars are also already fitted with on-board technology aids to get the most out of every litre of fuel.

Still better would be making it attractive to people to be less reliant on cars and to use less carbon-intense forms of transport, especially for short journeys. Cars consume more energy and emit more greenhouse gases per passenger kilometre than any other surface form of transport. Almost anything would be better. Cutting down on the number of cars on the roads would also bring us all many side benefits: imagine living in a world where the roads were safer, where there were fewer boring traffic queues, less air pollution and less vulnerability to erratic oil prices.

However, history shows that most of us are unlikely to change our ways unless the alternatives are both readily available and more attractive. This could be especially important for short trips. In Europe fully half of journeys made by car are for less than five kilometres. That's understandable in rural areas, but in large cities where public transport is weak the situation can be even worse. In Bogotá in 1998, for example, 70 per cent of private car trips were for less than three kilometres. The city now has a project, funded by the Clean Development Mechanism, using buses that travel frequently along dedicated bus lanes, which makes them both quick and easy to use. This is projected to save the city more than 7 million tonnes of carbon dioxide over the next thirty years, at a cost of less than $20 per tonne.[22]

Another possibility in cities where public transport is already advanced is to use internet and even wireless technology to make it more reliable. Seattle's 'BusMonster' website has already begun to offer locals a mix of maps and real-time information on the whereabouts of their buses. Before you leave home you can check the internet to find out exactly when your bus will arrive at the nearest stop, and how long – given current traffic conditions – it will take to get to your destination. In the future, this sort of information could be sent directly to your mobile phone, and be readily available at every bus stop.

In rural areas, 'on-command' buses could soon rival the attraction of the car. In 1999 in the United Kingdom the so-called 'Wigglybus' began operating in Wiltshire. It has a core circular route but if you phone in a booking it will also make a detour to pick you up. The bus is satellite-tracked and the call centre sends a list of pick-ups to the driver. There are now three separate routes in operation, where rural passengers can make a call and be picked up shortly afterwards, often outside their front doors.

Integrating transit with efficient city design will be especially important in the most rapidly developing areas of the world. The populations can be so great that even a relatively small percentage shift from cars to public transport can make a big difference. One study suggested that strategies like these could almost halve the projected transport emissions in a rapidly developing city like Shanghai by 2020.

In the longer term, low-carbon fuel might be the answer. One approach that has received plenty of attention is hydrogen. The idea here is that some low-emissions energy source is used to split water and make hydrogen gas. Hydrogen could also be made from natural gas. Although this generates carbon dioxide emissions, it is still more carbon-efficient than burning regular petrol. And if the carbon could be captured and stored the emissions could drop almost to zero.

In most versions of this vision, the hydrogen is stored, transported and delivered to a device known as a fuel cell which generates power when called on to do so.[23] Fuel cells are highly efficient and are silent when operating. In fact cars running on fuel cells would be so quiet that it might even be necessary to manufacture noise artificially, to warn pedestrians of the presence of a car. But the beauty of this approach is that all that comes out of the car's exhaust is water.

The technology is reasonably advanced, and a handful of test vehicles are now on the roads. Iceland opened the world's first hydrogen fuelling station in April 2003 and is hoping to become a fully hydrogen economy by 2030, with the hydrogen created using the country's carbon-free geothermal energy. Norway's first hydrogen station opened in August 2006, and the government there has plans for a 580-kilometre hydrogen corridor between Oslo and Stavanger. The European Union is testing hydrogen buses and China plans to use some at the Beijing Olympics in 2008. California has plans to introduce hydrogen in twenty-one interstate highway filling stations.[24]

At present, though, the technology is still some way from being fully commercial. The main problems are finding the right way to store and distribute the hydrogen, as well as improving the efficiency of the fuel cells and bringing their costs down. However, many large car manufacturers, including General Motors, Chrysler, Mercedes, BMW and Toyota, are now working very hard to resolve these issues, and Toyota has provided prototype fuel cell cars to all Japanese government ministers. When the technology develops to the point of mass production, which could be before 2020, the necessary changes to the existing petrol-based infrastructure should become commercially viable.

Another way to reduce emissions from the road might be to use biofuels. Most petrol cars can run with up to 10 per cent ethanol in their fuel mix without any modification, and some new cars can burn the pure stuff. The technology was introduced in Brazil in the 1970s, and the flexi-fuel adaptation allows cars to be run on petrol, alcohol or any mixture of the two. Biodiesel can also be used with relatively little modification in both cars and trains. Many countries now have targets for the proportion of biofuels to be used in road transport, though, as we describe above, it's vitally important to know exactly where the biofuels have come from, and how many emissions have been produced during the unseen parts of their life.

# 9

# POWER TO CHANGE

Our enthusiasm for burning fossil fuels has scarcely dimmed since we first came up with the idea during the Industrial Revolution. The last three decades of the twentieth century in particular saw a dramatic growth spurt of 70 per cent in human emissions of greenhouse gases, so that by 2004 we were putting out a grand total of 49 billion tonnes of $CO_2$eq per year.[1]

Those emissions are projected to continue their rise for the foreseeable future. Between them, coal, oil and gas make up almost all our current energy use. There's enough oil and natural gas in the world to last us for decades, and enough coal for centuries.[2]

By far the largest rise since 1970 came from power generation, which increased by nearly 150 per cent and now accounts for around a quarter of our global greenhouse emissions.[3] One way to reduce these emissions will be to make existing fossil-fuel plants more efficient. For instance, switching from the worst fossil fuel in terms of emissions (coal) to the best (natural gas) typically reduces emissions by 50 per cent.[4] However, if we are to have any chance of staving off the most dangerous effects of climate change, this won't be enough. We will have to find new ways of making power that don't also involve making greenhouse gases.

Unfortunately, although the technological cupboard is not exactly bare, it's not replete with alternatives either. In spite of the increasing interest in climate change over the past few years very little serious industrial attention has been paid to alternative energy sources. Comparing the amount of research and development spent by an industry to its total turnover tells a woeful story. In the US, the figure for research into power is just 0.5 per cent of turnover, compared to 3.3 per cent for the car industry, 8 per cent for electronics and 15 per cent for pharmaceuticals.[5] Worldwide, investment in energy research and development has remained roughly constant over the past couple of decades and in some countries – including the UK – it has even gone down, as oil prices have fallen and deregulation of energy companies has led them to focus more on short-term gains than on long-term research.

But the world is finally starting to wake up to the technological challenge and efforts are now beginning within the energy industries and in collaboration between them. In the UK, for instance, one of us (David King) devised and set up the Energy Technologies Institute, which will soon be opening its doors for business. A partnership between the government and a consortium of industries, it will receive £1 billion over ten years to focus on developing new, low-carbon forms of energy.

The International Energy Agency (IEA) predicts that more than $20 trillion will need to be invested between now and 2030 to meet the world's growing hunger for power.[6] Governments and businesses around the world will soon be making decisions about exactly where their investment should go. Here are the low-carbon technologies that will need to be on the world's shopping list to meet this demand.[7] (It's worth mentioning that many of these technologies come with their own side benefits, especially reducing local and regional air pollution.)

## Hydroenergy

Hydroelectric power is currently the biggest of all the renewable energy supplies.[8] In 2004 it provided 5 per cent of all global energy and a full 90 per cent of electricity from renewable sources. However, flooding land to make new reservoirs for hydropower often comes with its own environmental cost. For instance, there is often a loss of ecosystem services. Many of the nutrients that once fertilised the land following the annual flooding of the River Nile now end up instead on the floor of Egypt's giant Aswan Dam, and for the first time in the country's very long history Egyptian farmers are having to put artificial fertiliser on their fields. And flooding any region to create a dam also usually means the social cost of forced resettlement.

Moreover, there are still some question marks about exactly how much carbon emissions a hydro plant can save. Though the electricity generation itself doesn't cause any greenhouse emissions, shallow reservoirs can give off methane, which is a much more potent greenhouse gas than carbon dioxide. On balance, however, most hydro plants do much better for greenhouse emissions than their fossil-fuel equivalents.

Because of this uncertainty over the environmental benefits of large hydroelectric plants, the UN has excluded them from its Clean Development Mechanism through which industrialised countries can fund low-carbon technologies in the developed world. (Chapter 10 has much more about the Clean Development Mechanism, and how it works.) This blanket ban doesn't seem the best position to take. We believe it would be considerably better to judge potential projects individually, by doing a full environmental and greenhouse gas analysis, and only then deciding if it is worth sponsoring from both an environmental and climate point of view.

## Geothermal

Using naturally hot rocks to heat up steam and make electricity is clearly a good idea. The only problem with geothermal energy is that you need to be lucky enough to have the hot rocks in the first place. Iceland, which stands over a series of volcanoes, needs merely to drill into the ground to find the heat it needs. But for most other places, there isn't enough heat below ground to generate a significant amount of electricity.

Geothermal heat can still be used to warm buildings directly, using heat pumps. The electricity it takes to pump the heat up from below ground is more than balanced by the savings from more conventional, fossil-fuel-powered heating sources. Many areas are suitable for this, and such heat pumps should become a standard feature of homes throughout the world. New urban developments are best, since it's easier to drill the required bore holes before you build the houses.

Still, geothermal energy presently makes up just 0.4 per cent of the overall power generation mix, and it's unlikely to grow significantly in the future.[9]


## Bioenergy

This involves generating heat and/or electricity by burning more or less any biological material (also called biomass). That could include logs of wood, wood chippings, straw, agricultural leavings (such as stalks and leaves), fast-growing trees, dedicated crops grown especially for their energy properties and even the solid waste from sewage or the methane from landfill sites. Globally bioenergy makes up an impressive 10 per cent of the energy supply, though most of this is in simple (and inefficient) wood fires in the developing world, the smoke from which leads to significant health problems. The IPCC report estimates that every year in India alone, indoor air pollution kills half a million women and children.[10]

To make a big dent in the greenhouse problem, biomass would need to be used to replace fossil fuels for large-scale electricity and heating. One problem with this is that biomass is not a particularly concentrated form of energy, especially compared to fossil fuels, whose energy was compressed over hundreds of millions of years. Still, it's already being used as an additive to coal in more than 150 coal-fired power plants around the world.

In the longer term, biotechnological research might produce crops that can be grown specifically for their high-energy characteristics, though as yet there are no such varieties on the horizon.

As we explained in Chapter 8, crops could also be a useful source of low-carbon transport fuel.

## Nuclear power (fission)

Nuclear fission power comes from the energy that spills out when you split heavy atoms. Long the *bête noire* of environmental groups, it has begun to enjoy a green renaissance thanks to its relatively low greenhouse emissions. In principle, nuclear power should generate no carbon emissions because it doesn't involve burning any fossil fuels. However, the processing of uranium ore to make the feedstock takes energy, as does the building and eventual decommissioning of the plant itself, and at least for now this is usually supplied by fossil sources.

All detailed studies agree, however, that nuclear power is a very low-carbon energy source and hence a good candidate for the new energy mix. In particular it is one of the very few technologies that are currently ready to go. It's not renewable, in that the uranium ore has to be mined and will eventually run out. But the current stocks should be enough to last for several centuries even if the industry expands significantly – and technological developments in fuel recycling could extend this to several thousand years.[11]

More problematic are the issues of waste, safety and nuclear proliferation, all of which have made the nuclear option a highly contentious one in many countries. Partly, the hostility to nuclear power is a leftover from early designs which were both less safety conscious and generated more waste than the models now available.

Between 1980 and 2005 the efficiency of output from US nuclear power plants (the percentage of energy achieved compared to the theoretical maximum) went up from 60 to 90 per cent, and the next generation of power stations will generate even less waste for each unit of energy they produce.

Because of this, the waste from this new generation of power plants will add only a small fraction on to the amount that already exists in countries that have relied on nuclear power in the past. In the UK, for instance, replacing every current (and soon-to-be-decommissioned) nuclear power station with a new one, and running these new stations for forty years, would increase the country's existing waste levels by a mere 10 per cent.

There is still the issue of how to dispose of the high-level waste, which will remain radioactive for thousands of years. But Finland, Sweden, France, the UK and the US are all investigating geological options for burying the waste in apparently stable rock formations.

Safety is, of course, a paramount consideration for nuclear

power, though we should also point out that, historically, many other forms of power generation have come with their own hazards. Even in the developed world, coal miners are still dying in underground accidents, and from silicosis – the bitter legacy of breathing so much coal dust for so long.

However, the dangers of a wider nuclear accident have led designers of nuclear power plants to make significant advances with regard to safety. Perhaps the most interesting is the recent drive towards 'walk-away safety' in which the machine is designed to shut itself down immediately should anything go wrong.

In the new Westinghouse AP1000 (which is currently available, though hasn't yet been used on a commercial scale) large tanks of water sit inside the reactor containment. If there is a drop in pressure in the main cooling circuit, a valve opens in the tank and the water falls down to cool the reactor. The valve is fail-safe in that it needs power to keep it closed. So if the power cuts off it also opens automatically. The upshot is that in case of trouble, the operators could walk away and the reactor would shut itself down.

Another design that uses the principle of 'walk-away safety' is the South African Pebble Bed Nuclear Reactor, so-called because its fuel is made up of 'pebbles' of graphite containing thousands of tiny fuel particles. Over a period of several months, the pebbles slowly make their way to the bottom of the reactor, where they are extracted, inspected for damage and then blown pneumatically back to the top. This effectively makes it impossible to melt the core. The first demonstration plant is due to come on-stream in South Africa in 2011.

Another objection often raised is that peaceful nuclear power might encourage the dangerous proliferation of nuclear weapons. Although the materials for a nuclear bomb don't arise automatically in a nuclear power station, they can be separated out given the technology and the time. Designers are working hard to address this for future generations of nuclear power stations, but it's unlikely they will be able to eliminate the threat completely.

However, the Treaty on Non-Proliferation of Nuclear Weapons has been signed by nearly 190 countries, and the thorough inspection routines by its watchdog committee, the International Atomic Energy Authority (IAEA), have to date picked up suspicious activities extremely quickly. For instance, they successfully blew the whistle on countries such as North Korea and Iran – which were using their nuclear power plants to mask their attempts to make weapons – thus focusing the world's attention on the problem. Moreover, the motivation for any country to try to develop nuclear weapons has very different origins from the need for energy from nuclear power plants. North Korea did not seek to develop weapons because France had nuclear energy.

Nuclear power currently accounts for about 5 per cent of global energy, and in some quarters it is predicted that this could double by 2030. Because of the advances that have been made in addressing the apparent disadvantages of nuclear power, and because it is one of the very few low-carbon technologies that is ready to go, we believe that a further generation of nuclear power stations will be at least a very necessary stop-gap in countries that already possess the technology, and perhaps for others, too, while we wait for other low-carbon energy sources to become available.

If your gut instinct is to react against nuclear power, do consider the arguments here very carefully. Individual and community support will be vital for new nuclear power stations to go ahead, and the problem of climate change will require us all to make some very hard choices. As we've already said, nuclear power is one of the very few low-carbon technologies that are already on hand, and though it is not necessarily an ideal way to make energy, the dangers of climate change are certainly far worse.

## Wind energy

Wind sounds like the perfect solution to the energy crisis. The air moves around anyway, so why not harness its energy for free, with no carbon emissions to boot? Partly because of this, wind turbines are springing up around the world. Installations have been growing by 28 per cent a year since 2000, with a record 40 per cent leap in 2005. However, this all started from a very low base, and wind still makes up a mere 0.2 per cent of the global energy mix.

One reason is that wind energy comes with its own public perception problems. There are claims that turbines are noisy, and that they cause problems for radar and airline flight paths, as well as for unwary birds and bats that stray into their blades. But most of all, many of the best places to put them on land are big, windy, open expanses, which are often also very beautiful. Even supporters of renewable energy rarely want to see giant turbines marching across their precious wildernesses. In the UK, for instance, while just over 2 gigawatts (GW) of potential wind energy have made it on to the National Grid, another 9 GW are currently mired in contested planning permissions. (An average power plant generates 0.5 GW and the UK's peak demand is around 60 GW.)

As with nuclear power, this is another area where your individual attitude can make a big collective difference. If a wind farm is proposed for land near where you live, it's worth thinking about your reaction very carefully. It's not necessarily a good idea to put turbines up in places that are outstandingly beautiful and wild. But those aren't the only sites where wind power could be productive. Ultimately, wind will have to be a large part of the overall mix for tackling climate change and none of us can afford to dismiss it out of hand from our own backyards.

The more successful onshore wind farm schemes have involved starting with small-scale installations and working up. It turns out that turbines are neither noisy nor particularly ugly (especially compared to electricity pylons), and when one or two are in place it's easier to be enthusiastic about scaling up. Some small, windy towns have discovered that a large wind turbine can provide electricity to the whole town at very little cost. In these cases, far from being an eyesore the turbine can become a testimony to the smart – and responsible – action of the townspeople. If you live in such a town, it's well worth talking to your local council about this.

Another possibility is to place wind farms offshore, where there would be fewer worries about blighting the view. However, the windiest places also tend to be the ones with the harshest conditions. New materials will need to be developed to stand up to the buffeting they would receive, and transportation of the generated electricity could also be a problem. Recently, planning permission has been given for a large-scale wind farm to be built in the Thames estuary. But this approach is in its infancy even in countries like the UK that have very windy coasts.

One final potential problem with wind is that, like many other renewable sources, it is inherently fickle. Denmark, which has 5 GW of installed wind power, has managed this by exporting electricity to its near neighbours – Norway,

Sweden and Germany – when the wind blows, and importing – for instance from Norway's hydro plants – during lulls. Still, for those countries that do not have alternative providers so near at hand, the sporadic nature of wind will remain a problem, at least until we can come up with ways of storing wind electricity along with better methods of forecasting when the wind is on its way.

However, none of these problems is insurmountable, and wind will certainly have to be a vital component in the future low-carbon energy mix, with the most promising sites in northern Europe, on the southern tip of South America, Tasmania, and in North America in the Great Lakes and along the north-eastern and western coasts. Germany already has a significant wind capacity, as does the United States, and other countries are following suit. One study predicted that, in principle at least, wind could generate 126,000 terrawatt-hours of electricity per year by 2030. That, by the way, would be five times the global electricity requirements.

## Solar heating

Enough sunlight falls on the Earth to meet our energy needs 10,000 times over. However, it's very highly dispersed. Various technologies already exist to concentrate the sunlight using parabolic mirrors and focus it on to tanks of liquid – usually water or oil. If you're lucky enough to live in a sunny country, solar heating panels like these are excellent ways to heat water for individual homes. They sit on the roof rather like a satellite dish and provide baths and showers that are satisfyingly hot and guilt-free.

Solar heating can also be used on a much larger scale, by

making the hot liquid drive an engine to generate electricity. Clouds can get in the way, so electricity from solar heating would have to be supplemented from time to time from another source (probably coal, natural gas or bioenergy). The best places to site solar heating power stations would be in low-latitude deserts, which receive intense sunlight and suffer relatively few cloudy days.

Solar heating plants have been installed in California since the late 1980s. New projects are now either being built or planned in eleven other countries including Australia, Spain, Israel and Morocco. Analysts estimate that by 2040 solar heating could be contributing 5 per cent of the world's electricity needs. However, the potential is very much greater. If just 1 per cent of the world's desert areas could be linked to the rest of the world by high-voltage cables that would be enough to meet the world's entire global electricity needs, as forecast for 2030. By this means North Africa, for instance, could exploit its sunshine to export large amounts of energy to parts of neighbouring Europe.

## Solar photovoltaic (solar panels)

Unlike solar heating, this technology uses individual rays of sunlight to dislodge electrons inside an electronic panel. It thus generates an electric current directly instead of having to go through the intermediate step of using hot liquid and an engine.

Estimates vary, but there are enough solar panels like this around the world to generate at least 5 GW (which is just 0.004 per cent of total world power). Solar panels have the major advantage that they can be placed directly where the energy is required, which avoids the need for power lines. Thus, they are especially popular in rural areas of developing countries, where normal grid electricity is either unavailable or unreliable. However, the panels remain too inefficient at converting sunlight to electricity, and too expensive to manufacture, to make them fully competitive with other forms of electricity in the developed world.

One reason they are expensive is that solar panels tend to be based on silicon, because industry already has plenty of experience of making silicon chips for computers. A cheaper alternative would be to use plastics, ceramics or some other material, perhaps devised through the emerging science of nanotechnology. This will require technological break-throughs and probably won't be available for several decades. But it does have fantastic potential to yield an energy source that is cheap, free of emissions and waste, and has an unlimited fuel supply (the Sun). Solar panels could also be used in conjunction with direct solar heating, so that you could even exploit the heat generated by the electronic chips themselves.

## Carbon capture and storage (CCS)

This could be the most important bridging technology be-tween using fossil fuels and new, low-carbon alternatives. It's so important, in fact, that many people are now talking about CCS as if it were already established, though as yet it is only at the pilot stage.

The idea is to burn fossil fuels in the normal way to generate power, but then to grab the carbon dioxide and bury it before it can escape into the atmosphere. This has the great advantage that it can remove emissions from traditional fossil-fuel plants, thus buying the world some time to develop new low-carbon alternatives. CCS is likely to be especially important for countries like India and China, which are currently exploiting their vast coal reserves at an increasing rate to fuel extremely rapid economic growth.

Critics of CCS say that it would allow us to keep our old, bad, polluting habits and discourage fossil-fuel companies from switching to alternative forms of energy. But it's now too late to raise this sort of objection. The typical lifetime of a coal-fired power station is forty years. And developing countries with large coal reserves are bound to make use of them. Even with strong action to encourage the use of renewable and low-carbon energies, the International Energy Agency predicts that fossil fuels could still make up half the energy supply in 2050.[12] If we are to have any chance of reining in climate change some form of CCS will be a vital part of the mix.

The technology is likely to work best when applied to a single large source of carbon dioxide, for instance a power plant, or the chimneys from a major energy-intensive industry. Studies suggest that CCS could reduce emissions from fossil-fuel power plants by 80–90 per cent, though this will come at a price. The present technologies for capturing carbon are still expensive; and electricity generated from a fossil-fuel plant using carbon capture will always cost more than from one that vents its carbon dioxide into the atmosphere. For CCS to be economically viable there will have to be some kind of pricing system that rewards reductions in carbon emissions.

In principle CCS can be applied to any design of power plant, though in practice it is much cheaper and more efficient when used in modern 'cleaner' designs that already produce relatively concentrated streams of $CO_2$ in their outflow. (These designs also produce much less local pollution, although they tend to be more expensive and are rarely used in the new power plants springing up in the developing world.) Also, and most importantly, scenario studies suggest that, regardless of the design of power plant, CCS will always be both more efficient and cheaper to implement if it is built into the design of the plant rather than retrofitted at a later date. Given the rate at which new power plants are now being built, especially in India and China, it is imperative that CCS systems are installed in pilot schemes in a range of different power plant designs as soon as possible. Studies suggest that, technologically at least, CCS pilots could be up and running within five to ten years, but that will require a combination of political will and economic incentive.

Once captured, the carbon dioxide can be compressed into liquid form to be transported via pipeline or ship, or 'fixed' into some inert solid chemical compound. As for storage, the likeliest option would be to inject the gas into some deep geological network of tunnels and cracks, such as an empty oil or gas field or a salty aquifer. (Freshwater aquifers tend already to be in use to provide water for drinking and irrigation.) Empty oil and gas fields would probably be the easier option, since they exist in large numbers and we already know that they have been capable of holding on to their contents for hundreds of millions of years. However, coal–rich countries such as China and India have no access to empty oil fields of their own. Thus, the challenge will be to find a secure way of exploiting aquifers. There should, however, be plenty of space available. The IPCC estimates that known gas and oil fields could store between 675 and 900 gigatonnes of $CO_2$, and that saline formations could take at least another 1,000 gigatonnes,[13] while other reports suggest that this is a very conservative estimate.

In 2007, the UK government announced a competition for funds to develop a CCS demonstration plant. The European Union is also funding a similar demonstration plant to be sited in China, under the so-called 'Near-Zero-Emissions Coal Initiative'.[14] The UK and China signed an agreement in 2005 to detail specifically UK-funded action on the project, and a similar agreement was signed between the EU and China the following year, with the aim of having a demonstration project up and running by 2014. Projects like these should help to identify and overcome technical difficulties associated with the capture and storage.

There have, however, been some disappointing backward steps in the pursuit of this vital technology. In January 2008, the US Department of Energy withdrew from the public-private partnership FutureGen, which was to have created pilot energy plants for CCS. BP pulled the plug on a similar scheme at Peterhead, citing regulatory uncertainty, though they are now proceeding with projects in California and Abu Dhabi.

Opinions differ over the likely spread and scope of CCS in the future. Some scenarios suggest that CCS will only ever be a bridging technology that will be deployed rapidly but then superseded in the middle of the century by other low-carbon technologies. Others assume that it will be widespread until at least the end of the century.[15] An IPCC special report on CCS, published in 2005, calculates that between 30 and 60 per cent of global emissions of $CO_2$ from power generation could be suitable for capture and storage by 2050, and that a further 30–40 per cent of emissions from industries such as cement making could also be amenable to capture by then.[16]

An enticing prospect is that CCS could be used to capture and store the carbon dioxide from burning biomass. In that case, the result would be a net loss of carbon dioxide from the air, which could help with achieving that low stabilisation target of 450 ppm $CO_2$eq.

## Nuclear fusion

As we mentioned above, 'normal' nuclear power works by splitting an atom. By contrast, fusion works by 'fusing' the nuclei of two atoms together. This is the process that fuels the Sun, and it has several distinct advantages. For one thing it produces virtually no radioactive waste.[17] For another, the feedstock is very plentiful. Nuclear fusion uses a naturally occurring, heavy form of hydrogen, which is abundantly present in sea water, along with lithium metal, which is very abundant on Earth. In principle, using nuclear fusion, one bathful of water and the lithium from a single laptop battery could provide all the energy needs of a UK citizen for a full seven years. The waste product, non-radioactive helium gas, floats away.

The problem, though, lies in persuading those two nuclei to overcome their natural distaste for each other long enough to merge, and release copious amounts of energy. Copying the Sun's strategy means heating the gas to extraordinarily high temperatures. That takes a lot of energy in the first place, and also requires materials that can survive the heat.

The Joint European Torus, JET, in the UK has produced 16 megawatts of fusion power, by confining gas in a magnetic bottle and heating it to more than 100 million °C, and the Japanese torus at Naka, which is modelled on JET, has achieved similar results. These two projects are the largest fusion devices in the world. However, a fusion power station will need to be some ten times the size of these projects, and operate around the clock.

Acting on behalf of the EU, David King helped to broker an international consortium to address this problem. Comprising the EU, Russia, Japan, China, South Korea, India and the US, this is the biggest ever international technological enterprise. Uniquely, it spans countries from the developed and developing worlds, from both East and West. Each country is contributing a hefty €500 million, and the EU and France even more.

Together, the consortium members are about to begin constructing an experimental device, called the International Thermonuclear Experimental Reactor, in France. The device will cost some $10 billion, will be on the scale of an eventual power station and will operate for twenty years in an effort to resolve the scientific and engineering challenges of fusion. If all goes well, the first commercial fusion power could be available within the next forty years – or sooner if the governments involved increase their investment in the project.

## Final note

Most of the technologies and approaches that we have described here are ready to go, or will be soon. The rest are ripe for investment. The International Energy Agency estimates that $20 trillion will be invested in energy over the next twenty-five years. If a significant part of this goes into fossil fuels, rather than the low-carbon alternatives, it will be very difficult to go back. Even technologies such as carbon capture and storage, which work alongside traditional fossil-fuel power plants, would be much more expensive to retrofit than to design into new power stations from the start. In other words the techno-logical picture tells the same story as the science: the need to change our carbon habits is urgent, and the time to start is now.

# Part III: POLITICAL SOLUTIONS

By now it should be clear that the world needs to reduce its greenhouse emissions and has both the technical wherewithal and ingenuity to do it. But the science and the technology are the easy part. They provide the way. What we need next is the will. This section of the book covers the economic and political aspects of climate change. Much of this is necessarily the concern of big business and nations, but individuals are still important as a source of pressure from below. These chapters will explain what to look out for in political agreements. They are a handbook, if you like, to show you whether your politicians are doing what they should. At the end of the section, we put all of these solutions – both technological and political – together to show how your personal choices can make a difference.

# 10

# IT'S THE ECONOMY, STUPID

## Pay now or pay later

For a while now, economics has been at odds with science on the issue of climate change. Almost from the beginning, science has been saying: act now before it's too late. But until recently some economists have been saying: wait until we're all richer, or until new technologies come along.

That's because many economic theorists have consistently argued that kicking the carbon habit will damage the world economy, producing serious economic pain for relatively little climate gain. Even some of those who accepted that climate change was more than a soppy green theory have tended to argue that it would be better to wait until economies had grown and the world was richer. That way we could use our future wealth to tackle what was largely perceived as a future problem.

This argument was apparently confounded in 2007 when UK economist Sir Nicholas Stern led a team that published the world's most extensive review, *The Economics of Climate Change*, commissioned by the British government. The *Stern Review*'s 600-plus pages contained many detailed analyses of the economic blessings and curses of climate change. But the one that made headlines around the world was this: according to Stern, tackling climate change immediately to the tune of a maximum value of 500–550 ppm $CO_2$eq would cost just 1 per cent of global per capita consumption per year; leaving the problem till later would raise the bill inexorably; and letting climate change continue unabated could eventually cost the world a full 20 per cent of global consumption per year.[1]

Paying 1 per cent now to save 20 per cent later sounds like a good deal in anyone's books. But other economists immediately leapt on Stern's assumptions, claiming that he had built this answer into his models. More conventional models, they said, would give a much lower future benefit, and probably a higher present cost. Stern vigorously defended his choices and the battle rumbles on.

Why exactly can't these economists agree? The reason illustrates how economic models differ fundamentally from scientific ones and also – we would argue – why in the end they can't tell us with any degree of certainty how much it will cost us in the future if we ignore climate change today.

The argument is a bit technical, but it is worth persevering. Because once you understand the origin of the Stern spat, you will also understand just how little faith you should have in any bold, specific economic assertions about the future costs of climate change.

Generally speaking, economic models that are looking at the effect of any change try to work out whether it will make people in the future better or worse off. To put it at its very simplest, suppose something happens that makes me £5 richer but costs four other people £5 each. On balance the five of us are worse off.

Models looking at the consequences of climate change do something similar. Though the models are more complex and include many more factors, it's still more or less a case of adding up the consequences for everyone in the world to get a figure for global wellbeing which might be positive (on the whole the world will be better off) or negative (on balance, things will get worse).

There is, however, an extra twist, which economists call 'discounting'. Discounting the future is economist-speak for the 'bird in the hand' principle. The idea is that a loaf of bread is worth more to you today than it would be next week because the future is uncertain. Looking on the bright side, by next week you might have won the lottery and be rich enough not to care about the price of bread. Looking on the dark side, you might no longer need it because you've been run over by a bus. Either way, it counts for more now than it would then, and the difference is the 'discount rate'.

The discount rate that Stern chose for his climate calculations was unusually low. In other words a loaf of bread would be worth almost as much to you in a week's time as it would in your hand right now. This makes problems in Stern's future cost very much more than many economists are comfortable with. By choosing a low value for the discount rate, claimed his critics, Stern was skewing the costs of future climate change so they counted for more than they should.

On top of that, Stern used an unusually low figure for the discounting level between rich and poor.[2] Other economists were indignant that Stern was not more egalitarian in his choice, saying that this too builds in an excessive weight for future generations. Since economies tend to grow, people in the future are likely to be richer than we are today. Giving less weight to the poor (i.e. us) and more weight to the rich (i.e. our grandchildren) also makes damage to the future seem more expensive.[3]

Stern stands by his choices. He says that discounting heavily for the future is all very well when something happens in your lifetime. But since the time frame for the global warming problem runs into centuries, a large discount is equivalent to saying that people born in the future matter less than we do today. In the above example, it would be like saying a loaf of bread is worth more to you than it would be to your unborn grandson. Making this kind of assumption about future generations who aren't here to stand up for themselves is something that Stern finds unethical.

He also makes the undeniable point that if we can say 'let's leave the problem for the next generation' the same argument could hold for them, too. By taking this route, humans would consistently hand on the challenge of dealing with climate change to successively more remote descendants, while the world crashed and burned around them.

As for the rich/poor discounting figure, Stern points out that the critic advocating a much higher value should logically support massive redistribution of wealth between the rich and poor of today's world.[4] (The IPCC report also noted dryly: 'In most other policy areas, the rich do not reveal as much concern for the poor as is implied by the equity weights used in many models.'[5])

Nonetheless, by choosing unusual values for these two figures, Stern does seem to have encouraged the future to cost as much as possible. Cambridge economist Sir Partha Dasgupta (who has no problem with Stern's low figure for future discounting, but finds his relative inequality between rich and poor harder to swallow[6]) points out that we don't actually know how big a difference these choices made to Stern's findings.

The trouble, he says, is that the future cost of excessive carbon is extraordinarily sensitive to the discounting figures you choose. The IPCC report agrees. It says that discounting the future at 3 per cent means that one tonne of carbon bears an ultimate 'social cost' of around $62. Dropping the rate to 2 per cent increases the cost to $165 per tonne. Set the discount rate at 0 per cent and the number goes up to a massive $1610 per tonne.[7] That's a big difference in cost for something – how importantly we rate our grandchildren – that is an ethical rather than a financial call.

The bottom line is that the hard numbers of the future economic costs of climate change depend very sensitively on what are essentially touchy-feely choices. Put that way, any attempt to put a firm price on future damage seems hopeless.

This problem is exacerbated when you add in the risk that the Earth's climate could tip over one of the thresholds that we described in Chapter 5. The level of uncertainty that this brings to economic models makes concrete predictions all but impossible. As Dasgupta puts it: 'Climate change and biodiversity losses are two phenomena that are probably not amenable to formal, quantitative economic analysis. We economists should not have pressed for what I believe is misplaced concreteness. Certainly, we should not do so now.'[8]

However, even if we can't put exact economic costs on to the future, we still know a changing climate will bring direct misery – flood, drought and famine – to very large numbers of human beings, along with all the indirect dangers associated with mass migration and resource wars. In fact, it's already doing so. You could argue that there's little need to worry about how much climate damage might cost us in the future, when its effects are already being felt today. And many of the future variables are in any case incalculable. What value would we put on leaving Venice intact for future generations? Or London? Or Cairo?

Bearing in mind all these problems, how exactly do we decide whether it's a good idea to act now, or leave the problem till later? One way is to listen to the science. As we explained in Chapter 6, if we want to avoid leaving future generations with very serious – even dangerous – changes in climate, we need to stabilise greenhouse gas levels at 450 ppm $CO_2$eq. And to do that we have to act now. To get greenhouse gases down to this level, we need global emissions to peak within the next fifteen years. If we waited to act, 450 ppm would very soon be beyond us. (In fact, even higher stabilisation levels would require us to act in the next twenty years.) The coming decade is the only window of opportunity we, or any other generation, will ever have.

Put this way, the economic question becomes not so much 'How much will it cost us if we don't pay to stop it now?', but 'Can we afford to pay if we do?' And the answer is that the cost of reducing emissions could be surprisingly low.

## How much will it cost?

The Stern report considered a wide range of potential costs that could be incurred in the tackling of climate change, as well as savings from improving efficiency. Overall, it concluded that the annual cost of putting ourselves on a path to stabilising the atmospheric levels at 550 ppm equivalent or below by 2050 would be between -1.0 and +3.5 per cent of GDP with an average of around 1 per cent.

The IPCC report roughly agrees with these figures, though the range is shifted slightly higher. It suggests that the cost for 550 ppm by 2050 would be between 1 and 5 per cent of GDP;

that for 650 ppm it would be 'less than 2 per cent of GDP' and that for 450 ppm there are too few studies to give a reliable estimate.[9]

A report in the business journal the *McKinsey Quarterly* has an intriguing way of considering the problem.[10] The authors made a list of all possible ways of reducing greenhouse gas emissions up to a 'marginal cost' of €40 per tonne. (That's to say that many of their methods actually save money; many cost a little but still much less than €40 per tonne; but none costs more.) Then they line these different ways up on a graph.

The graph bears all the usual suspects. It starts on the far left with the methods that will bring the biggest savings: building insulation (very big savings of more than €150 per tonne); improving efficiency in lighting (savings of €100 per tonne); heating (savings of €50 per tonne) and so on. At around zero net cost lies reducing industrial emissions of greenhouse gases other than carbon dioxide. Then the price begins to go positive for nuclear energy (around €1 per tonne) up to carbon capture and storage on coal power plants (net cost of €30 per tonne) on up to the most expensive methods such as waste emissions recovery and biodiesel (just short of €40 per tonne).

Going that far, say the authors, would produce enough overall savings between now and 2030 to set the world on a stabilisation path for greenhouse emissions at 450 ppm equivalent. Encouragingly, their approach uses only methods that either exist now or are in the immediate pipeline (for instance carbon capture and storage). It doesn't require any immediate technological breakthrough.

The authors also add up all their savings and costs to arrive at an overall price for following this path. They say that using every method they describe to its fullest potential would mean

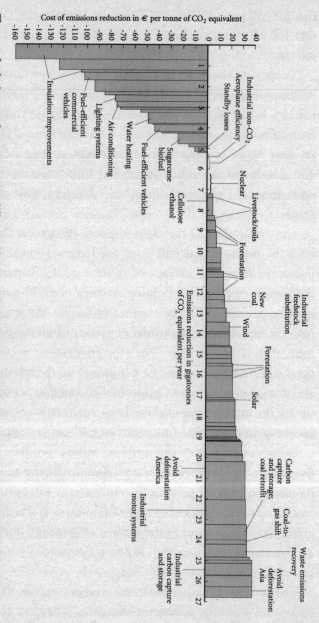

The cost of reducing greenhouse gases using different technological approaches up until 2013. Anything below the axis saves money, while anything above the axis costs. All the strategies shown here, taken together, would be enough to keep greenhouse gases below 450 parts per million. The balance of costs and savings also shows that the overall cost of this would be relatively low. (Source, 'A cost curve for greenhouse gas reduction', P. Enkvist et al., *The McKinsey Quarterly*, no. 1, p 35–45, 2007)

that by 2030 we would only be paying out some 0.6 per cent GDP. Even if some of the methods fell short, it would still cost just 1.4 per cent GDP by 2030.

Could we afford to pay these sorts of sums? That's more a political than an economic question. Dasgupta points out that 1 per cent GDP globally would mean a cost of around 1.8 per cent GDP for the rich countries who would need to bear the brunt of the costs, a sum that adds up to more than seven times the annual global aid budget. Put that way the task of persuading our governments to pay out sounds hard. It becomes tempting to think of the money needed to pay for climate change as a sort of opportunity cost. Why don't we just spend the money directly on aid instead, and save lives right now instead of waiting till later?

However, that's a false argument. We don't have a single pot of money that the world has contributed to, and which we now need to decide how to spend. If the money doesn't go on dealing with climate change, it's very unlikely to go instead to aid. Moreover, in many cases the money to deal with climate change is already there in a different pot, marked 'energy'. As we mentioned in Chapter 9, the International Energy Agency predicts that more than $20 trillion will need to be invested between now and 2030 to meet the world's growing hunger for power. The question we face regarding this pot is: should it be invested in fossil fuels or in low-carbon sources?

Also, we believe that the model of thinking about the cost of climate change as an alternative form of aid is misguided. This isn't about handing over money to poor people to make their lives a little better. It's about changing the culture of the entire planet, so that we leave behind a climate that all our grandchildren will be able to weather. As we've already said, the next two decades are our only possible window of opportunity to rein in greenhouse gases to a level that will achieve this goal. After that, however rich some parts of the world then become, it will be too late.

Because of this, we believe it's better to think of the costs of climate change not so much as a handout as an insurance policy against a dangerous future. The authors of the *McKinsey Quarterly* article point out that even excluding life insurance, in 2005 the global insurance industry's turnover was 3.3 per cent of GDP, which makes the cost of dealing with climate change seem much more reasonable. In fact, investing in new forms of energy and claiming all the savings from improving our efficiency could even boost our economic growth.

## How do we pay?

Normally, we rely on market signals – for instance, prices – to make decisions about how to spend our money. But the price we currently pay for energy takes no account of the effect it has on the climate; it gives no encouragement to do things the low-carbon way, nor does it provide economic penalties for taking a high-carbon path. Because of this, the Stern report describes climate change as 'the greatest market failure the world has ever seen'.[11]

To rectify this, many economists advocate that we adjust the market. The simplest way would be to put a tax on every tonne of greenhouse gas emitted. That way, the price of any activity that created greenhouse gases would reflect the true cost to the environment and the market would clamp down on the biggest offenders, making it cost-effective for them to turn to low-carbon solutions.

There is some evidence that this can work, at least on a national level. In the early 1990s, Norway introduced a carbon tax on emissions from energy and it did seem to encourage technological innovation.[12] However, the problem comes when you try to apply this approach globally. Agreeing on international taxes is notoriously difficult – witness the problems the European Union has experienced trying to regularise the complex and myriad differences in its members' sales taxes. And although Sweden, Finland and Denmark also introduced carbon taxes during the 1990s they have not harmonised their approaches with Norway or with each other. If such similar countries can't come to agreement, there is little hope for doing so with the vastly more disparate countries in the rest of the world. Moreover, it's hard to imagine any country welcoming, or even tolerating, an annual tax bill from the World Bank.

An approach more likely to work politically is the so-called 'cap and trade scheme'. This is modelled on the successful approach used by the US in the mid-1990s to reduce sulphur dioxide emissions and thereby cut down on acid rain. The 'cap' part is that every participant in the scheme has a cap on how much they can emit in a given year. They are then awarded a set of permits equal to that cap. The 'trade' part is that anyone going over their limit can buy permits from anyone who has emissions to spare. Every year the cap gets a little lower, and emissions fall inexorably – aided by the invisible hand of capitalism.

One clever thing about cap and trade is that it ensures that the fall in emissions occurs as economically as possible, since if it's cheaper for me to pay you to cut emissions than to cut them myself, I can buy your permits. This worked beautifully in America for reducing sulphur, as emissions dropped faster than most people had imagined, and at a fraction of the cost that doomsayers had been predicting. In 1999 BP set up an internal market for emissions trading of carbon dioxide among their various subsidiaries. It cost $20 million to set up, and by encouraging energy efficiency over the following three years saved the company an impressive $650 million.

The United Kingdom was the first country in the world to set up a national carbon emissions trading scheme, in 2004. A Europe-wide scheme swiftly followed the next January, which the UK scheme merged into. This was the world's first international trading scheme for carbon.[13] It's open only to members of the European Union, but – especially with the addition of ten countries from Eastern Europe in 2004, and a further two in 2007 – the EU countries are now so varied, and differ so greatly from each other in economic development, that they make an effective microcosm showing how a world-wide trading scheme might look.

Participation in the European scheme is mandatory for a number of industries in every member state. Energy generators, metal manufacturers and producers of cement, bricks, pulp and paper are all obliged to adhere to an emissions quota. (Together these industries account for almost 40 per cent of the EU's overall emissions.) Individual governments decide how to distribute permits among these industries, and the bulk of the cuts usually fall on the electricity generators since they are less likely to suffer from international competition.

The process sets a natural price on carbon emissions per tonne that arises out of the standard economic model of supply and demand. In the European scheme, the price per tonne was holding up well at between €10 and €20 per tonne for the first year of trading, a value that would certainly make emissions savings worthwhile. However, in April 2006, disaster struck. Actual emissions figures from the industries involved over 2005 were much lower than had been predicted. Cap and trade only works if the permits are relatively scarce – and therefore desirable. The caps have to be considerably lower than the actual emissions, or there's no point in having them. But it turned out that in many of the countries involved, predictions for emissions had been wildly overestimated. The price of carbon plummeted, and permits for the first phase became almost worthless.[14]

This was a painful lesson in the hazards of setting up a brand-new market. It's now clearer than ever that for a market like this to work, it must create real scarcity in permits, making the right to emit greenhouse gases a rare and valued commodity. The EU has already taken this on board. The second phase of the project, which runs from 2008 to 2012, has set very much more stringent caps, and permits for that phase are holding their prices up well at more than €25 per tonne.[15] So, in spite of these teething troubles, the market is now well established and will surely be a powerful tool for reducing emissions in a region that adds up to the world's largest combined economy.[16]

Similar schemes have been springing up all over the world. In New South Wales in Australia, emissions trading has been mandatory for electricity companies since 2003. California now has its own carbon trading scheme, as does a consortium of north-eastern American states. The Chicago Climate Exchange has been operating successfully (dealing with voluntary emissions caps) since 2003, and when the international climate treaty, the Kyoto Protocol, came into effect in February 2005 it too involved an emissions trading scheme for those countries that had ratified the treaty.

In May 2008, the World Bank reported that the global carbon market had grown more than sixfold in the previous two years, from $10 billion in 2005 to $64 billion in 2007, most of which came from the sale and resale of European Union

Allowances,[17] which is certainly encouraging. Meanwhile, as well as tightening up its emissions, the EU is investigating ways to bring new sectors under the trading umbrella, especially transport and international shipping. In July 2008, the European Parliament voted overwhelmingly to include aviation emissions from all flights starting and landing in the EU in the ETS from 2012, the first time that products from countries outside the EU have been included in the scheme.

In another important development, unlike the first phase of the European Trading Scheme where permits were issued free of charge, a small proportion of permits in the second phase are being auctioned. However, the EU has restricted this proportion to a mere ten per cent. This is a missed opportunity. When the cap and trade market becomes fully global it will involve a trillion dollars or more, and if all these permits were initially auctioned, that would generate several hundred billion dollars per year. This isn't as simple as it sounds, because it will be important to establish who should run the auctions and manage the funds. However this money could then be used to pay for adaptation in the developing world, and for the technology transfer that developing countries will need to make the transition to a low-carbon economy[18].

Carbon markets won't, in themselves, be enough. The 2007 World Bank report on the state of the carbon market noted that 'the enormity of the climate challenge . . . will require a profound transformation, including in those sectors that cap and trade cannot easily reach'.

For instance, agriculture, private transport and homes would require far too many of us individuals to be amenable to the sort of monitoring and auditing that a cap and trade scheme would require. In cases like these, governments will also need to oblige energy companies to use more renewable energy, to introduce standards for efficiency and, above all, to point us all in the right direction by providing reliable information about exactly how much greenhouse gas an individual product is responsible for throughout its lifetime.

The World Bank report also singled out the need for individual governments and international consortia to encourage investment in developing new, low-carbon technologies. One important way to do this will be to set up public–private partnerships to encourage investment in research and development, such as the UK's Energy Technologies Institute.[19]

## The Robin Hood effect

Most analysts agree that the burden of payment should fall most heavily on the world's richest countries, which are not only in the best position to pay but have also been, historically, the main cause of the greenhouse problem. But the costs will not fall evenly. In another of the nasty ironies associated with the greenhouse problem, solutions that actually save money (such as insulating homes) tend to fall in the rich nations' patches whereas the solutions that cost the most (such as capturing carbon from Indian power plants or preventing deforestation in Brazil) fall on the poorer nations, who have done least to create the problem in the first place. Any arrangement for who pays, and how, will have to ensure that money from the richer nations passes effectively to the poorer ones, specifically targeted towards cutting emissions in the most economically efficient way possible.

In principle, cap and trade allows funds to be transferred between nations. But in practice, we need to go further to ensure that money flows from rich countries to poorer ones. This isn't

just some twenty-first-century Robin Hood principle of generosity to the poor. In fact, it is the only way to encourage
developing countries to 'leapfrog' the old, bad polluting habits of
the industrial world and invest directly in low-carbon habits
instead – which is something the entire world needs them to do.

The Kyoto Protocol brought in two other mechanisms to
channel money from the most industrialised countries to ones that
are less developed, and the EU trading scheme is linked to both. In
the jargon of treaties, these are known as 'Joint Implementation'
(JI) and the 'Clean Development Mechanism' (CDM).

Joint Implementation means that one developed country
can gain carbon credit by setting up a programme to reduce
emissions in another relatively well-developed country. For
instance, France could pay to set up efficiency improvements in
Romania. (Joint Implementation mainly works for countries
from Eastern Europe and the former Soviet Union, which are
relatively developed, but where a small amount of investment
can make a big difference to energy efficiency.)

The Clean Development Mechanism is similar, but applies
between developed and much poorer developing countries.
Thus, France could gain credit by setting up a programme to
reduce emissions in India. The idea is that this brings two
benefits. Emissions reductions become relatively cheap for the
developed country, while developing countries receive funds
that enable them to adopt new, low-carbon technologies.

There are several potential problems with both these approaches. For one thing, critics have claimed that they let
developed countries off the hook. In principle these mechanisms could allow you to meet your targets, while ignoring all
the new technologies and approaches that we have already
described. You could buy your way out of short-term trouble
without doing any long-term investment to enable you to kick

your own carbon habit. That would also have the disadvantage that the rich nations are less inclined to develop new technologies which can then be passed on to developing nations.

Another problem is ensuring that the projects included really do reduce overall emissions, and that they wouldn't have happened anyway. What if a forest that was planted specifically to soak up carbon dioxide emissions is then harvested for firewood? Or a company providing solar panels folds before the panels are supplied? What if the project would otherwise have found funding from other sources? Questions like these have especially bedevilled the Clean Development Mechanism.

In June 2007, the Worldwide Fund for Nature (WWF) published a report called 'Emission Impossible' in which they highlighted what they saw as a host of problems with the operation of the CDM as applied to the European Emissions Trading Scheme.[20] First, the WWF worried that the current scheme apparently allows countries in the EU to offload their entire emissions cuts on to developing countries without needing to change anything at home. The rules do set a limit on what percentage of the proposed emissions cap can be allocated overseas. For instance, France is restricted to 13.5 per cent of its cap, and the UK to 8 per cent. The problem is that this percentage is applied to the *entire emissions allowance*, not just to the difference between the capped emissions and the 'business as usual' scenario. By almost any predictions, the difference between cap and 'business as usual' for France, say, is less than 13.5 per cent of the total emissions. In other words, the WWF showed that these percentages amounted to most, if not all, of the actual amount by which each country would have to cut.

As long as the officials take note of this, it can easily be fixed by just reducing the allowed percentages. More troubling, perhaps, is a series of investigations into the quality of the projects chosen for the CDM. Developing countries that have ratified the Kyoto Protocol can put forward proposals for projects that, they say, will reduce carbon emissions. These are then assessed by a CDM Executive Board based in Switzerland. The idea is to check especially whether the projects will deliver the proposed emissions savings, and whether the savings are 'additional' in that they wouldn't have happened without the extra funding provided through the CDM. Moreover, the board is supposed to check that the projects fit with the general aims of sustainable development in the countries involved.

The WWF has come up with a list of approved projects that, they say, don't meet one or more of these criteria. For instance, they say that a hydropower project in China was accepted in 2006 even though the CDM board received a submission saying that 'revenue from CDM credits was irrelevant to the decision to go ahead with the project', and adding that 'construction began in October 2003'. An article in *Nature* also criticised the CDM,[21] and in Britain the *Guardian* newspaper claimed that up to 20 per cent of all the carbon credits issued so far under the CDM could be doubtful.[22]

Again, the solution to this is simple, as long as it's effectively implemented. The European trading scheme is currently under review and the WWF recommends that the next phase is linked only to those CDM projects that are certified by the so-called Gold Standard.[23] This is an independent benchmark set up to accredit schemes to cut emissions in developing countries both for international and individual investors. The Gold Standard, for instance, admits only renewable energy and efficiency projects and is highly conservative in its estimate about whether a project is truly 'additional'.

Another problem has arisen with projects involving so-called "trace" greenhouse gases, which exist in only tiny quantities in the air but punch far above their weight when it comes to warming. One of the most potent of these is HFC-23, which is a by-product of the manufacture of another chemical called HCF-22. Weight for weight, HFC-23 causes nearly 12000 times as much warming as carbon dioxide, which is why it is mostly banned in the developed world. But that also means that tonne for tonne, it is vastly cheaper to eliminate than $CO_2$. An article in *Nature* in 2007 calculated that some 30% of CDM credits to date involved the elimination of this gas, largely from factories in China and India, at a total value of almost €5 billion[24]. This represents a massive windfall for the factories involved – eliminating the unwanted by-product can even end up being more profitable than making the refrigerant in the first place. To stop companies setting up new factories simply to gain huge profits from eliminating HCF-23, the UN even had to modify its rules. Any factories claiming CDM credits for HCF-23 now have to have been in operation in 2003. What's more, this is a tremendously expensive way of eliminating the gas. The *Nature* article also calculated that it would cost only 100 million to install scrubbers to remove HFC-23 directly from the factories involved, and suggests that it would be better to take non-$CO_2$ gases out of the CDM system completely. This approach does provide a much more reliable guarantee that the required emissions will be achieved. On the other hand, by excluding projects such as reforestation, the Gold Standard is also somewhat limiting. Better still would be a new standard, agreed by governments, that would take into account the full range of possible ways to reduce emissions in the developing world, and provide a reliable method of emissions accounting even for the projects that are harder to quantify.

All these problems notwithstanding, the CDM is clearly working in its endeavour to draw foreign investment into developing countries to enable them to cut emissions. The World Bank report on 2007's Carbon Market says that the Kyoto Protocol mechanisms have generated $8 billion in new resources for developing countries, which have in themselves attracted a further $16 billion in associated investments for generating clean energy. When these initial problems with the CDM have been resolved, it will be a vital component of the climate toolkit.

A final note on this topic concerns the question of deforestation. The *Stern Review* identified halting the rate of deforestation as one of the most cost-effective means of rapidly cutting carbon dioxide emissions. In principle, it's obvious that slowing the rate at which forests are cut and burned will also reduce carbon dioxide emissions. However, the Kyoto Protocol, and thus the CDM, found this too hard to turn into a formula, and therefore stuck to reforestation and afforestation projects.

The *Stern Review* notes that a hectare of forest generates an income of just $2 per year if converted to pasture, $1,000 per year for soybean or oil palm production, or between $240 and $1,035 as a one-off return for selling timber. It then calculates that, even assuming a modest carbon price of $30 per tonne, the same hectare of forest could be worth $17,500 if kept intact.[25]

At present, though, there is no provision for earning credit by protecting forests. This leads to some obvious absurdities. For instance, environmental groups claim that forests in Malaysia and Indonesia are being cut down and burned to clear land that is then used to grow sugar cane for 'low-carbon' biofuel.

After pressure from scientists, in 2007 the United Nations Framework Convention on Climate Change launched a two-year consultation for a mechanism to encourage the reduction of deforestation levels, provisionally called 'Reducing Emissions from Deforestation' (RED).[26] One approach, proposed by Papua New Guinea and Costa Rica on behalf of the Coalition of Rainforest Nations, was to mimic the cap and trade schemes with a separate scheme built around deforestation credits. The idea is that each nation establishes a baseline rate of deforestation, converted into tonnes of carbon dioxide. Any reductions below this baseline could then be sold in a carbon market. Emissions above the baseline would automatically disqualify a country from trading.[27] This would also require some solution to the problems that Kyoto Protocol negotiators encountered: how to estimate a reliable baseline for the rate of deforestation before intervention; how to ensure that the forest remains intact permanently rather than just for a few years until attention passes elsewhere; and how to avoid 'leakage' whereby people displaced from cutting down one part of the forest simply move to another part.

## Adaptation

As we explained in Chapter 4, every country will need to adapt to the climate change that is already occurring, and which is inevitable. The countries that will be hardest hit will be those that can least afford to pay (and that have contributed least historically to the climate problem).

There are already three global funds aimed at aiding the least developed countries to adapt. The Least Developed Country Fund takes contributions from developed nations and uses them to help the poorest countries draw up adaptation plans. By April 2006 it had received a total of $89 million in pledges and actual funds. The Special Climate Change Fund supports direct adaptation activities and has received some $45 million to date. Finally, the Adaptation Fund arises directly from the Clean Development Mechanism. Each CDM transaction pays a 2 per cent levy into this fund, which is also used to support adaptation projects in the poorest countries. The World Bank estimates that by 2012 this will have raised up to $500 million.[28]

However, the first two funds are dependent on aid, which some developing countries consider to be an inappropriate model. Indeed a levy is a more appropriate tool than relying on a country's generosity – and potentially diverting resources from other aid projects. The third fund is based on a levy, but carries the economic problem that, since it is effectively a tax on the money invested, it provides a perverse financial disincentive to invest in the CDM. (One way round this would be to apply the same levy on all carbon trades, so as to remove the distinction.)

Various alternative proposals have been put forward.[29] One attractive possibility is that a levy could be applied to some voluntary and polluting enterprise such as air travel. (This would help compensate for the long-time exemptions that air travel has had from tax on fuel duty, as well as helping control the projected massive growth in air travel.) Another approach would be to come up with a separate fund levied on industrialised nations as a function of their GDP, or, more appropriately still, as a function of their historical greenhouse emissions. Finally, as we pointed out earlier in this chapter, most of the tradable permits to emit carbon dioxide are currently allocated free of charge. However if instead they were auctioned off in a global market, this could generate a massive fund to the tune of several hundred billion dollars a year – which could enable developing countries both to adapt to climate change and to begin to decarbonise their economies.

## The colour of money

All in all, the problem of climate change is beginning to shift from a scientific and technological issue to an economic one. Around the world, brokers and businesses have noticed the amount of money changing hands over climate change and are eager to join in. The business world, too, has spotted that climate change comes with opportunities, as well as risks.

In some cases, companies seek to attract consumer support by taking a climate-friendly stand. For instance, companies as widely diverse as liberal-leaning Google and the right-wing and normally anti-environmental Fox News network have recently pledged to go carbon neutral. Others seek to be ahead of the game by improving their own efficiencies, while yet others are looking to develop environmental products to sell. BP (which has dropped its original name 'British Petroleum' and switched to the so-called tagline 'Beyond Petroleum') has said that it will spend $8 billion on developing alternative energy over the next decade. (Unfortunately it has pulled out of a carbon capture and storage scheme at Peterhead in Scotland, although it is proceeding with projects in California and Abu Dhabi. Disappointingly Shell has also recently blotted its green copybook. In May 2008 the company withdrew from its 1000-MegaWatt offshore wind project in Kent, although the two remaining partners, E.ON and the Danish utility Dong Energy, later agreed to buy Shell out by upping their own stakes to 50:50, effectively keeping the project on track.)

Wal-Mart, the world's biggest retailer, is heavily pushing its low-energy light bulbs, as well as pledging to implement emissions-savings efforts across the company[30]. The UK's biggest retailer, supermarket chain Tesco, has also put climate change at the top of its agenda. The company is committed to reduce its stores' energy use 50% by 2008 and to halve its overall greenhouse gas emissions by 2020.

Eurostar, which runs trains from London to continental Europe, has given a green edge to its competition with the carbon-hungry airlines. Not content with simply pointing out that train journeys necessarily produce fewer emissions than the equivalent flight, Eurostar has used a combination of electricity from British Energy – whose nuclear-fueled energy is extremely low carbon – and offsetting the remaining emissions, to make all its journeys carbon-neutral. Unlike other schemes this requires no extra payment from the passenger. The company says that the extra custom its carbon-neutrality has generated more than compensates for the extra cost.

Others want to be in on the act when it comes to setting the inevitable constraints on greenhouse emissions. For a report entitled 'Getting Ahead of the Curve' the Michigan-based Pew Center on Climate Change surveyed thirty-one major American corporations.[31] Almost all of them believed that government regulation of greenhouse gases was imminent, and 84 per cent believed it would happen before 2015. General Motors, Ford and Chrysler are the latest additions to the US Climate Action Partnership, which is lobbying the US government to set obligatory limits on emissions.

The Pew Center report quotes Linda Fisher, Vice-President of DuPont, thus: 'We need to understand, measure and assess market opportunities. How do you know and communicate which products will be successful in a greenhouse gas constrained world? How should we target our research? Can we find creative ways to use renewables? Can we change societal behaviour through products and technologies? The company that answers these questions successfully will be the winner.'

The colour of money is now officially green.

Though this was encouraging, the fallout from the credit crunch led some to suggest that we could no longer 'afford' to deal with climate change. President Obama has inherited the worst financial situation in living memory and the argument goes that he and other world leaders could be too bogged down by this to pay proper attention to kicking the carbon habit. However, the financial crisis could just as easily be a springboard for investing in low-carbon energy. Many of the world's biggest financial institutions have been placed into temporary public ownership. Regulation is the new watch word – especially with a new political will to deal with climate change emanating from Washington – and governments could see this as the perfect opportunity to incorporate the cost of carbon into a new, improved international financial system.

Moreover, as the world tries to spend its way out of trouble, governments will be seeking vital, future-proof projects for their public financing. The latest buzz-phrase is a 'Green New Deal' whereby the investments needed to wean the world off carbon could also be the ones that pull us out of the financial doldrums and reinvigorate the global economy. Conversely, any companies, or indeed governments, that ignore the climate imperative in these endeavours are likely to leave themselves with 'stranded assets'; money-hungry projects such as coal-fired power stations, airport runways or drilling projects that become worthless because they were designed for the old world and have no place in the new.

The financial crisis also provides a graphic example of what happens when governments take their eyes off the regulatory ball and allow institutions to smash and grab resources now without heed for the future. The current financial crisis was bad enough for business. An unchecked climate meltdown would be very, very much worse.

# 11

# THE ROAD FROM KYOTO

The famous Kyoto Protocol was born out of the 1992 Rio
Earth Summit, the midwife being the United Nations Framework Convention on Climate Change (UNFCCC). This was
the world's first climate treaty. It came into force in 1994 and
has since been signed by 189 countries – including the USA
and Australia – which is as near to global unanimity as any
international treaty that has ever existed.[1] Its stated objective is
to achieve '. . . stabilisation of greenhouse gas concentrations
in the atmosphere at a level that would prevent dangerous
[human-induced] interference with the climate system'.

Technically the Kyoto Protocol was an amendment to the
UNFCCC treaty, assigning specific obligatory emissions cuts
to each of the signatories. Any signatory who then went on to
ratify the Protocol agreed to be bound by its terms. In total, the
Protocol was designed to cut global emissions by 5 per cent of
their 1990 levels by 2012. Though this was far too low to make a
significant difference to the problem, it was always intended to be
a first step, after which the levels would be ratcheted upwards.

   Though any party to the UNFCCC could sign and ratify the
Protocol, only the so-called Annex 1 countries – the most

industrialised nations – had any obligation to cut their emissions. A developing country that ratified would then be allowed to put forward projects for the Clean Development Mechanism, which we described in Chapter 10, and through which the richer nations could satisfy some of their obligation by investing in clean technologies in the poorer ones.

Kyoto may have had its flaws, but it was still an important first step in the tortuous process of reaching international agreement to tackle climate change. As witness to that, nearly everybody signed up. A full 176 of the available 178 parties have now ratified the Protocol. Of the remaining two, Kazakhstan intends to ratify but has not yet done so for technical reasons relating to its change in status from developing to developed country.

The only country that has not ratified, and that has declared that it will never ratify, is the United States.[2] The US has been increasingly isolated in its opinion of Kyoto in particular and agreements to cap greenhouse emissions in general. The US government is, however, starting to change its tune on climate change and we will talk much more about this below and in Chapter 13. The US is particularly important. As one of the world's highest greenhouse emitters and the world's richest economy, its participation in a future agreement will be essential.

The first phase of the Kyoto Protocol will end in 2012 and the world urgently needs to settle on a new agreement that is much more ambitious in its targets. While the science tells us that we must reduce emissions drastically, we are presently on the wrong track. Global emissions are accelerating. In the decade during which Kyoto was devised and signed, the 1990s, greenhouse emissions from fossil fuels and industry grew at a rate of 1.1 per cent per year. By the early 2000s, this had risen to more than 3 per cent per year and counting.[3]

The lack of emissions targets for developing countries was

claimed to be a major sticking point for the US. It's true that most of recent growth in emissions has come from countries outside Annex 1. But that's not the whole story. In 2004, the combined emissions of developing and least developed economies (which comprise some 80 per cent of the world's population) accounted for 73 per cent of emissions *growth* but still only 41 per cent of total global emissions, and just 23 per cent of cumulative emissions since the mid-eighteenth century.[4] Moreover, almost all developing countries have much lower emissions per head of population than their richer, more profligate, industrialised counterparts. The new agreement will have to include developing countries but will also have to take into account their relative contribution and means.

## Where do I sign?

The new international agreement will need to cover four main points:

### Global target

Everybody involved in the agreement (which is to say every nation on Earth) will have to agree on the overall global objective. Just how much are we prepared to let temperatures rise before we can stop climate change in its tracks?

Whatever target is agreed on by the international community, it will have to be flexible enough to respond to the latest developments in climate science. This, together with the gravity of the potential climate catastrophes, would suggest that we should aim for the lowest achievable target – on the principle that it's simpler to ease restrictions, as new information comes to light, than to tighten them. However, the lower the target, the more immediate the action required, and the more difficult it will be to achieve technically, economically and politically.

Of all the decisions in the new international agreement this will be at once the most difficult and the most important. It will make the biggest overall difference to each country's actions, regardless of how the reductions are ultimately divided among them. It will also make the biggest difference to our chances of averting global catastrophe.

The science of targets, though unfortunately full of uncertainties, is progressing rapidly and will need to continue to do so. But it's already too late to wait and see. Dangerous climate change is now with us. The new agreement will have to come up with the best available figure that will try to avoid even worse consequences, especially the catastrophic outcomes described in Chapter 5.

The atmosphere already contains around 430 ppm of greenhouse gases. As we explained in Chapter 6, to avoid the worst consequences of climate change we will need to end up at 450 ppm equivalent.

Roughly speaking, to reach this figure industrialised countries will need to cut their emissions from 1990 levels by 80 per cent by the middle of the century.[5] We will also need to set interim targets for, say, 2025 or 2030, so that we can be sure we're on the right track. For developing countries the numbers vary much more widely, depending on the way that the burden of cuts is distributed.

## National targets
Once the overall target is set, the next task will be to decide exactly how the reductions should be divided among the nations of the world. This will be fiendishly difficult, given the need to reconcile the economic needs and political ex-

pectations of countries with such wildly different backgrounds. The criteria for handing out responsibility might include a country's greenhouse emissions per head of population; its overall emissions; its historical responsibility for the current atmospheric load of greenhouse gases; its wealth and economic capacity to change; and its vulnerability to near and long-term threats from climate change.

One of the hardest questions will be exactly where to start. That is: what should the baseline emissions level be when deciding how much each country needs to cut? The Kyoto Protocol used 1990 as the baseline, which is one reason why the US refused to ratify it. By 1997, when President Clinton signed the Protocol, emissions in the US had already sky-rocketed from their 1990 level. Many American politicians felt the resulting targets would be too draconian for the good of America, and both Democrats and Republicans subsequently voted it down. Meanwhile, thanks to the economic slow-down that followed *perestroika*, emissions from the former Soviet bloc had plummeted relative to 1990. They could more than meet their Kyoto requirements without doing anything at all, and any subsequent agreement based around 1990 would leave them with billions of dollars' worth of emissions permits to burn. Thus, though 1990 remains a point of reference for most of the world, the former Soviet bloc would benefit too much from it and the US too little. (When the G8 summit in Japan in June 2008 issued a joint statement promising to 'consider and adopt' a target of reducing global emissions by 50% by 2050, it said nothing at all about what the starting point for this should be – because the issue of 1990 was too controversial.)

One way round this that many analysts are now adopting for a post-Kyoto agreement is to set the 2010 Kyoto targets, which are a percentage of 1990 emissions, as a starting point for most of the signatories, but to make actual 2010 emissions the starting point for the US and the Russian Federation. The disadvantage of this is that it might seem to reward American profligacy; the advantage is that it makes the US very much more likely to sign. This solution would cost Russia its chance to sell those billions of dollars' worth of emissions permits that arose from its economic freefall in the 1990s. But until now Russia has made no effort to sell – probably because nobody other than the US could afford to buy on that scale and the US is emphatically not a member of the Kyoto trading scheme. Since the US is also most unlikely to agree to any future scheme that would keep 1990 as the baseline date, it is doubtful that these permits are of much worth to Russia in any case.

Once the target date is set, the next question is how to spread the load. First will be the important – and contentious – issue of how to incorporate aviation and shipping into the mix. Both of these sectors are projected to increase dramatically over the next few decades, albeit from a relatively low base. But it's difficult to decide exactly how to allocate emissions from international flights and shipping: do they belong to the initiating country, the receiving country or the country that has most passengers or freight on board? There's also the danger that if not all countries have signed up, operators would be able to dodge regulations by fuelling up in a country that's not compliant. For reasons like these, both aviation and shipping remained out of the Kyoto agreement and are not formally counted in any individual nation's greenhouse tally. Yet, as Friends of the Earth memorably put it, 'a carbon management system that simply leaves these emissions out is rather like a calorie-controlled diet that opts to exclude calories from chocolate'.[6]

Next, and even more importantly, the new agreement will need to find a way to distribute the load between industrialised and developing countries. During his administration, President Bush repeatedly said that the US would not sign up to any agreement that did not involve developing countries. His argument was strengthened by the fact that the rate of emissions growth is highest in the developing world, and that, at least according to one source, China has just overtaken the US as the world's largest individual emitter.[7] On the other hand China can very reasonably respond that its emissions are high because of its vast population. If you recalculate emissions per head of population, America remains far above most of the rest of the industrialised world, and head and shoulders above China. (US emissions per capita in 2004 were 24 tonnes of $CO_2eq$ compared to China's meagre 5.)[8] And all the countries of the developing world can also argue that they want for their citizens the standard of living that Americans already have.

Also important will be to acknowledge that the world's rich countries got where they are today by exploiting cheap energy and thereby filling the atmosphere with most of its current greenhouse load. Carbon dioxide in particular lasts so long in the atmosphere that a significant proportion of the molecules generated by the steam engines and coal fires of the early Industrial Revolution are still around in the air today.

During the 1997 Kyoto negotiations, Brazil made a suggestion which has since become known as the Brazilian Proposal. Their idea was that countries should now share the burden of emissions cuts according to how historically responsible they were for the problem. In other words, we should calculate what concentration of greenhouse gases each country has put into the atmosphere over time, and use those figures to allocate emissions cuts. That would mean, for instance, that countries such as Germany and the UK, which have been emitting for longer, would bear a larger share than their current emissions implied. It would also mean that big emitters that had developed their industries more recently, Australia for instance, would bear less of a share.

It sounds brilliantly simple and fair – the 'polluter pays' principle with historical accounting thrown in. However, there are some problems with calculating how much each country has contributed to the current greenhouse effect. Methane, for instance, has a much shorter atmospheric lifetime than carbon dioxide, so early emissions matter less today. Also countries that developed early (and historically have high emissions) benefited economically, but have since passed on many of those benefits to other more recent developers.

To date, the Brazilian Proposal has not been adopted, but it does show how imaginative thinking will be needed to come up with a way of distributing the burden of emissions cuts that is clearly fair, will achieve the required target, and – most importantly – that everyone will be prepared to sign up to. The eventual agreement will have to find some way of accounting for the different state of development, and historical responsibility, of the signatories. It will have to be flexible, cost effective and do the climate job. Here are some of the ideas already on the various negotiating tables, along with the buzzwords to look out for. Note that these are all ways to distribute national targets, and they say nothing about how the individual countries will go about achieving them, or what will happen if they don't:

*Contraction and convergence[9] (or, 'We'll meet you in 2050')*
This is the buzz phrase on many negotiators' lips. The 'convergence' part of the phrase refers to a certain low target of greenhouse emissions per head of population, which every country agrees to converge on by, say, 2050. This target would depend on how low overall we were trying to go, as set out in

the first part of the agreement. For instance, a global target of 450 ppm of greenhouse gases would mean convergence in 2050 at around 2 tonnes of $CO_2$eq per head, where 550 ppm would be closer to 3 tonnes per head.[10] This figure would necessarily be much lower than the current emissions per head of the richest countries, and probably higher than the current figure for most developing countries.

Thus, the industrialised world would need to 'contract' its emissions to meet the target, whereas developing countries would be allowed to increase their emissions and develop their economies before everyone eventually converges on to the same spot. According to this approach, the emissions paths for some developing countries might rise above the eventual target, before falling as their economies became stronger.

There is even a provision for the lowest emitting (and least developed) countries to receive more emissions allowances than they would need. They could then sell the excess 'hot air' to get international funding for their development efforts.

Contraction and convergence has the benefits that every nation is involved from the beginning, that it's a transparent, straightforward concept and that it produces a definite final concentration of greenhouse gases. However, its very simplicity is also a flaw, since it doesn't easily take into account the very different circumstances of different nations, nor their historical responsibility for the mess we are now in.

*Differentiated convergence (or, 'You start, we'll follow')*
A slightly more complicated version of contraction and convergence was devised in 2006. The richest countries, those covered by the Kyoto agreement, would similarly agree to converge their emissions per head to a certain low figure within an agreed time frame. Individual developing countries would

also agree to converge to the same figure, but they wouldn't have to start until their emissions per head reached a certain percentage of the (steadily declining) global average.

If they never pass the threshold, they never have to make cuts. In that case, if they wish they can choose to take on an emissions target. If they stay below the target, they can sell their excess emissions permits, but if they go above they aren't penalised. (Unless, of course, they reach the threshold, and have to join in the contraction to convergence.)

This has many of the benefits of the first scheme, with the additional attraction that it puts a little more of the onus on the countries that have been historically responsible for the problem, while giving more breathing room to the developing countries trying to catch up.

*Multi-stage targets (or, 'Climb up when you're ready')*
This approach is just what it sounds like – it involves a set of different stages with different levels of commitment, and countries graduate from one to another when they pass certain thresholds (for instance, emissions per head, or GDP per head). Stage 1, for the least developed countries, would be no commitments at all. Stage 2, then, might be that countries commit to sustainable development, with greenhouse objectives built in – for instance, the phasing out of inefficient equipment. Stage 3 could involve a moderate target for cutting emissions, and Stage 4 could require a more stringent and immediate target. Industrialised nations would start at Stage 4, while the rest would move up the ladder as their state of development changed.

A lot would hinge, of course, on the choice of thresholds, as well as the nature of the commitments in the later stages. One of the hazards of this approach is that the emissions accounting is inherently very complex. It would be difficult to be sure of reaching a set global target, given the uncertainties in the different development paths, and there would also have to be inbuilt incentives, which would be guaranteed to hold over time, to encourage countries to act when they passed the different thresholds.

Using this approach it would just about be possible to make the 550 ppm greenhouse limit. 450 ppm would require most developing countries to enter Stages 2 or 3 immediately, and Stage 4 would require drastic (and probably impossible) reductions of up to 9 per cent per year.[11]

### Global triptych (or, 'Do what you can')

The triptych approach was invented as a way to divide the overall EU emissions allowances from the Kyoto Protocol between individual European states. It's called 'triptych', which means 'threefold', because it originally looked at the three sectors responsible for most of a country's emissions: power generation, energy-intensive industry and 'domestic' (homes and transport). Thus, it could take into account developments in low-carbon power sources, the potential for improved efficiency in industry and the relevance of living standards in the carbon budget.

The idea is to give allowances for each individual sector, then add them up to a fixed national allowance for each country. Only the overall national target is obligatory – the country can find whatever way it likes to get there – but the process is supposed to make sure that the target is reasonably achievable.

Though the global version of this approach is more complex, and involves more sectors (for instance, agriculture and waste), the basic principle still holds. The great advantage of this approach is that it specifically takes national circumstances into account. The main disadvantage is its inherent complexity.

It would require huge amounts of reliable data for each nation, would be highly complicated to negotiate and the burden of specificity and detail wouldn't exactly lead to a result that was transparently fair. Applying it globally would thus be a tremendous challenge, but it might still be useful to divide allowances among nearby, and similar, countries – as it was for Kyoto in the EU.

*Sector by sector (or, 'I will if you will')*
The idea here is to alleviate concerns about the effect of emissions reductions on global competitiveness by applying the same rules to an individual sector regardless of the country involved. So, for example, the entire world car industry could agree to a standard level of emissions per passenger kilometre, regardless of where the car was built or driven. Or the steel industry could agree to emit no more than a certain amount of carbon dioxide per tonne of steel produced.

One way this could work is if the industrialised countries adopted absolute emissions targets, as for Kyoto but more stringent, whereas the most rapidly developing countries would work on their energy and heavy industry sectors across the board. Involving the top ten highest emitters in each sector would cover 80–90 per cent of the emissions from developing countries.

This would certainly help deal with the worry that any company that cut emissions from its own power plants would then lose customers to ones that continued to pollute, but produced cheaper electricity. But it would not guarantee that we stay below that magic threshold of maximum greenhouse gases in the air.

*Intensity (or, 'Never mind the total, feel the efficiency')*
This approach abandons the idea of overall emissions targets in

favour of calculating the emissions per unit of economic growth (GDP). The obvious benefit of this is that it would ensure that future economic growth is as carbon efficient as possible, and that if future growth patterns change the target doesn't move.

The major, and perhaps overwhelming, disadvantage of this approach is that it says nothing about how much greenhouse gas ends up in the air. Even if every country in the world drastically improved its carbon efficiency, as economies continued to grow, greenhouse gases would continue to rise, and the climate would be left free to do its wicked worst. As one assessment puts it of this approach, 'environmental effectiveness not guaranteed'.[12] It was, however, much favoured by President Bush.

No single approach will be acceptable to everybody, and the final answer may well end up being a compromise. However, and perhaps surprisingly, the choice of approach makes relatively little difference to the requirements for most countries, adding or subtracting only a few percentage points to the overall target. It will probably matter most to those developing countries that might participate earlier or later depending on the strategy adopted. For the rest, the most significant factors will be the overall target chosen, and the baseline date.

## Carrot and stick

The third pillar of the new agreement will be an ultra-reliable mechanism to encourage nations to meet their targets, and provide sanctions if they don't. Both the carrot and the stick are likely to be financial.

For encouragement, emissions trading is the best game in town. The more emissions you save, the more money you can earn by selling your excess. Pricing commodities is a formula that markets, and governments, understand very well, and setting a price on carbon is the best way to repair the great market failure that is global warming.

For sanctions, the likeliest instrument is the World Trade Organization. All countries know that it's good for their economies to be part of the global trading club. In the intense horse-trading that preceded the activation of the Kyoto agreement, Russia finally agreed to sign up as a straight swap for EU support of its application for WTO membership. Since the WTO sets global trading rules, it will also need to ensure that every country accepts that economic benefits go hand in hand with meeting climate obligations, and that the world won't tolerate, and can't afford, climate freeloaders. Public opinion could also play an important role in the individual countries. The *Stern Review* puts this nicely: 'As the science of climate change is widely accepted, public attitudes will make it increasingly difficult for political leaders around the world to downplay the importance of serious action.'[13]

## Flow of resources

Finally, the agreement will need a mechanism to transfer both technology and funds from the richest countries to the developing world.

### *Technology transfer*

Developing countries will need to be able to continue their economic growth without pouring out carbon dioxide, by leapfrogging over the dirty polluting technologies that got the first world where it is today. It's in nobody's interest if countries don't meet their targets because they can't afford to. Nor can the world afford to have developing countries make the same mistakes as the West. And no developing countries will come on board and agree to curb their emissions unless some kind of technology transfer is in place. It is likely to be based on some form of Clean Development Mechanism, driven by a carbon emissions trading market. It will also be important to encourage bilateral and multilateral technological collaborations. Finally, this part of the agreement will need to include some way to pay for preserving forests through cutting deforestation rates, which is something that Kyoto didn't do.

*Adaptation funding*

As we've repeatedly stated, the science of climate change makes it very clear that the countries least responsible for causing the problem will be the ones to suffer most. They are also the countries least able to pay for the sorts of adaptations that are already necessary. At a pinch, and with the right political will, the US could protect its coastline from another Katrina-type flooding disaster, and the UK is already protecting its own coast. But the same doesn't apply to Bangladesh which, as well as having the potential to be harder hit, has a much weaker economy. The international agreement will have to deal with this issue by ensuring the flow of adaptation funding from rich to poorer nations.

Both technology transfer and adaptation funding will probably go hand in hand. For instance, it could be part of the agreement that if a rich nation exceeds its agreed emissions it can either buy unused permits from elsewhere, or provide technological or adaptation costs.

## Last-chance saloon

It's unlikely that all the details of such an agreement can be thrashed out among the 189 countries that have signed the

Kyoto Protocol. For such delicate negotiations, this group is just too unwieldy. However, there is more hope to be found in a new grouping of the topmost polluting nations. This group, now enshrined as the Gleneagles Dialogue, comprises the G8 richest nations, the EU, and – in particular – the top five most rapidly developing economies: the so-called G8 + 5. If these very disparate countries, the world's major emitters, can be brought to agreement, the rest of the world might well follow. The next two chapters will look at these key countries in more detail.

Above all, the new agreement needs to come soon. It's not just that the Kyoto Protocol runs out in 2012. More importantly, we are running out of time to get to grips with climate change. If we had acted three decades ago we might have been able to prevent the dangerous effects that we are witnessing today and will continue to witness, come what may, over the next few decades. Now it's too late for that.

But we do still have time to stop the worst of the possible future consequences. As we've already said repeatedly, that will probably require emissions levels to peak within the next fifteen years, before starting to fall – which in turn means we need to act fast. Given how long it takes to set the wheels of government turning, even with the best will in the world we have to have an international agreement in place as early as possible in 2009.

The key international meeting to look out for is the UN Climate Summit in Copenhagen in December 2009. All the signatories of Kyoto will be present and this is when the essential elements of the new treaty will finally have to be settled on.

When it comes to climate change there's no more time for fooling around. This is the last-chance saloon.

# 12

# RAPIDLY DEVELOPING NATIONS

Tackling climate change will require the cooperation of the entire world, but some countries will play a greater role than others. In particular, the most important changes will need to come from two sets of players: the industrialised world, which has the richest economies and bears the greatest historical responsibility for the emissions to date; and the handful of most rapidly developing countries which are likely to contribute the most to future rises in emissions as they play catch-up.

Perhaps it's human nature to forget what's gone before and focus on what's to come, or perhaps it's a convenient get-out for those of us who live in industrialised countries. Either way, the latest fashion in the industrialised world is to declare that there is no point in reducing emissions since any reductions will be swamped by the vast increases to come in rapidly developing countries such as China and India. Because of this, we have decided to start with the five countries that are currently developing most rapidly.

That doesn't mean we believe these countries are 'the problem'. It's true that they are responsible for most of the recent spurt in greenhouse gas emissions, and also make up a substantial proportion of the global total. However, most of them are also acutely aware of the dangers likely to come from climate change. In fact, these countries are already going to great lengths to deal with their emissions, often under very difficult circumstances.

Moreover, and most importantly, these countries tend to produce only very small amounts of greenhouse gas per individual citizen, and have been responsible for very little of the current concentration of greenhouse gases in the atmosphere. They also have this in common: their development needs tend to swamp all other political and economic considerations.

Nonetheless, the five most rapidly developing nations that we describe here will be vital to any future agreement. If any one of them stays outside the agreement, that country could then become a hothouse manufacturer, producing the goods – and the greenhouse emissions – that the other nations weren't allowed to, so that there would be no net savings in global emissions.

The numbers given for emissions for each country come from a report commissioned by the British government from a German consulting firm called Ecofys.[1] Different sources can give confusingly different figures, which are further confounded when some figures are only for carbon, some only for carbon dioxide and some for all greenhouse gases calculated either as carbon equivalents or as carbon dioxide equivalents. The figures given here for emissions are for all greenhouse gases, calculated as a carbon dioxide equivalent. Emissions per capita and total emissions are for the year 2004. Historical emissions are average annual values from 1900 to 2004, per head of the present population.

# China

Per capita: 5.0 tonnes/person
Historical: 1.2 tonnes/person
Total: 6,467 megatonnes
Change in emissions since 1990: +72.7 per cent
Ratified Kyoto? Yes

China has become the latest, greatest bogeyman for climate change sceptics, so it's appropriate to start here. The pace of development in China is extraordinary. A year or so ago, China was building a new coal-fired power station every week. Now it's more like two a week and counting. China has no oil reserves and very little gas. But it does have coal, and plenty of it. And that coal is firing the surge in China's economy.

It has become fashionable to quote the figures for China's new power stations, and to use them to argue that there's no point in western countries doing anything to halt carbon emissions. These new power stations are especially bad news from a climate perspective because coal is the dirtiest of all the fossil fuels, producing not just smoke and smog in the cities, but also much more carbon dioxide for every unit of energy than either oil or gas.

Moreover, although the figures given here from 2004 show China's total output lagging slightly behind that of the USA, by one measure China has now outstripped the US to take the uncoveted position of the world's biggest greenhouse polluter.[2]

Is it fair, then, to say that China is the biggest greenhouse problem? Not exactly. For one thing, many of the countries in the western world have dodged their own carbon dioxide emissions by exporting their manufacturing to . . . China.

Next time you buy something with 'Made in China' stamped on it, ask yourself who was responsible for the emissions that created it.

Even more importantly, China is one of the smallest emitters when you calculate emissions per head of population, especially compared to industrialised nations, and its relative historical contribution to the problem is truly tiny. China can say, with justice, that unlike the industrialised West it has done almost nothing to create the climate problem, and that its citizens play on average a very meagre part in perpetuating it.

The Chinese government's biggest priority is the massive disparity in wealth between the rich citizens of Beijing and Shanghai, and the 700 million or so people living on less than $2 per day. Bridging this gap to bring at least a decent standard of living to China's vast population, which is what's behind the plethora of power stations, is surely a reasonable goal in anyone's book.

However, unless China finds a way to develop without massively increasing its greenhouse emissions, the efforts of the rest of the world will count for very little. For the new international agreement on emissions to stand any chance of success, China has to be on board. (The same, by the way, also applies to the USA – see below.)

The good news is that the Chinese government is at least as aware as any other country of the dangers of global warming. Unlike most other governments, fully two-thirds of the members of its politburo are highly qualified scientists and engineers. These are people who fully understand the climate problem.

They are aware, for instance, that China itself would be hard hit by unreconstructed climate change. There is already a shortage of irrigated land in the interior, and this will only be made worse as the Tibetan glaciers shrink, and the rivers they feed dry up. And Shanghai – the country's economic powerhouse – is one of the world's major cities most vulnerable to flooding both from inland rivers and the rising sea. The Chinese government has already signed an agreement with the UK to investigate ways to improve Shanghai's flood defences, but unless climate change is held in check it will be a real struggle to keep the city above water by the end of the century.

When it comes to a new agreement, China will need to be allowed some expansion of emissions, perhaps through a contraction and convergence approach, along with financial investments from industrial nations through some kind of Clean Development Mechanism. For instance, since the coal-fired power stations are inevitable, it's vital to find a way to capture the carbon dioxide emissions and store them away from the air. The EU has recently agreed to joint funding of a Chinese pilot programme for Carbon Capture and Storage, and the UK has also agreed a project to map potential Chinese sites for burying the carbon. This is especially urgent because retrofitting those two new power stations a week will be much more expensive than building the design in from the start.

But the most important factor in bringing the Chinese into any agreement will be participation by America. As long as the US refuses to agree to targets for itself, the Chinese will be able to cry 'hypocrite'. Nor can the world afford to let these two nations get into an 'I won't till you do' stand-off. China will come on board when the USA does, and using the most reasonable measures of carbon emissions responsibility – historical and per capita emissions – China definitely holds the moral high ground.

## Brazil

Per capita: 5.3 tonnes/person (plus approx. 7 tonnes/person from deforestation)
Historical: 1.6 tonnes/person
Total: 983 megatonnes (plus approx. 1100 megatonnes from deforestation)
Change in emissions since 1990: +40.7 per cent
Ratified Kyoto? Yes

Brazil needs no persuading of the gravity of the climate change problem. Back in 1992 it offered Rio as the venue for the first International Earth Summit, which launched the process that led to the Kyoto Protocol. The government is extremely keen to involve developing nations in the solution. It is also highly aware of the potential threat that climate change poses to Brazil, especially reduced food yield, forced changes in land use and loss of forest. As for India, Brazil's agriculture depends critically on the weather and is highly sensitive to changes in temperature and rainfall. Brazil also has excellent climate scientists to whom the present government clearly listens.

Despite a relatively high state of development, especially in the south of the country, Brazil still has a low figure for its greenhouse emissions per capita. One reason is that it uses hydropower for much of its electricity, meaning that it has one of the world's lowest power emissions rates. Also, after the 1970s oil crisis Brazil began developing the use of sugar cane to make alcohol for vehicle transport. It is now the acknowledged world leader in use of biofuels, meaning that its transport emissions are also extremely low: just 0.74 tonnes of carbon dioxide equivalent per head, compared to 2.24 for the UK and

6.36 for the USA. Overall renewable resources account for a full 40 per cent of its energy supply.

However deforestation in the Amazonian north and the Atlantic north-east of the country still produces huge amounts of carbon dioxide. Most sets of greenhouse figures count only emissions from the use of fossil fuels, and in Brazil's case adding in the figure from deforestation makes a huge difference. Brazil's government is very aware of this and in the past few years has taken significant steps to expand the range of protected areas and prevent illegal logging. More than 40 per cent of the Brazilian Amazon is now under some form of protection.[3]

The problem is that there is currently virtually no economic incentive to prevent deforestation. Under the Kyoto Protocol, industrialised countries can pay Brazil to *reforest* land to balance their own excess emissions. But stopping deforestation was considered too problematic and stayed out of the Clean Development Mechanism. Any future proposal would need to make forest protection a part of the mix.

Considering the rest of Brazil's emissions, contraction and convergence would require slowing the rate of emissions growth by 2020 and reducing overall emissions by 2050. The multi-stage approach would allow a little more short-term breathing space, and the sectoral approach would be especially good for Brazil since its electricity emissions are already so low.

## South Africa

Per capita: 11.1 tonnes/person
Historical: 3.6 tonnes/person
Total: 505 megatonnes
Change in emissions since 1990: +29.7 per cent
Ratified Kyoto? Yes

For a developing country, South Africa has an unusually high level of per capita greenhouse emissions. Like China, its economy is heavily dependent on coal, but the country is considerably more developed. The mining industry – for gold, diamonds, platinum and uranium – is a major part of the economy and is very energy intensive. As the gold has begun to run out, the country has been taking on manufacturing commissions from developed countries. For instance, all BMW 3-series cars are now assembled at Pretoria's Rosslyn plant.

South Africa thus has a large amount of energy-intensive industry, and that looks set to continue. It will also continue to be a mining economy for the foreseeable future. As we mentioned in Chapter 9, the country is investing in the development of Pebble Bed Nuclear Reactors, but this is likely to be for export rather than signalling a major nuclear strategy in South Africa.

The country also has a well-developed sugar cane industry, and ample technological skills for converting a proportion of this to biofuels – although it would be hard to expand the current areas and grow more. It is also still wrestling with the aftermath of apartheid, as well as the ever-present trauma of AIDS.

However, the current government is nonetheless progressive on the issue of climate change, and keen to talk at least at the level of energy and environment ministers (though less so at the level of heads of state). Overall, the government is extremely keen to be a responsible international player. If the terms for developing countries were right, and allowed the country to deal with its myriad social and developmental issues, South Africa would be in.

## Mexico

Per capita: 5.0 tonnes/person
Historical: 1.3 tonnes/person
Total: 520 megatonnes
Change in emissions since 1990: +38.6 per cent
Ratified Kyoto? Yes

As with the other rapidly developing countries, Mexico's first priority is growth. However, the government is also highly aware of the threat of climate change, through desertification, loss of food productivity and coastal flooding from sea-level rise and intensifying tropical storms.

Mexico is already beginning to make some efforts to slow the increase in its greenhouse emissions. The government is also extremely keen to be engaged with the G8 + 5 Gleneagles Dialogue. In 2006 they even hosted the first follow-up meeting of this group after it was initiated the previous year at Gleneagles. If they could be persuaded that their immediate economic growth was not at risk from the new treaty, and if there was a sense of common purpose within the G8 + 5 group, Mexico would be a very good player.

## India

Per capita: 1.6 tonnes/person
Historical: 0.6 tonnes/person
Total: 1,744 megatonnes
Change in emissions since 1990: +57.5 per cent
Ratified Kyoto? Yes

India is probably the most distracted of the rapidly developing countries from the point of view of climate. It has by far the lowest per capita emissions level of the group, and also by far the most pressing developmental problems.

However, the subcontinent as a whole stands to suffer dramatically from global warming. Food production is forecast to drop, and the Ganges–Brahmaputra mega delta in Bangladesh is frighteningly vulnerable to flooding from a combination of sea-level rise and more intense tropical storms. And although the models are as yet unsure about exactly how the Asian monsoon will change with increasing temperatures, nobody expects it to stay as it is.

Indian scientists are certainly well aware of this – the chairman of the IPCC, Rajendra 'Pachy' Pachauri, is based in Delhi, and the Indian National Academy of Sciences has signed three successive global statements calling for action on climate change. India has also already installed a huge amount of wind power, and an Indian company (Suzlon) is one of the world's leading manufacturers of wind turbines.

Given its relatively low state of development but high rate of growth, India is one of the most fruitful sources of opportunities for projects involving the Clean Development Mechanism. Moreover, an encouraging sign came in 2007 from Kapil Siba, the Minister for Science and Engineering, when he requested a meeting with one of us (David King), specifically to propose that India set up an Energy Technologies Institute to develop new, low-carbon energy sources in parallel with the British one. That was the first official thawing of the Indian government's position on climate change. More good news came on June 30 2008 when Prime Minister Manmohan Singh released a National Action Plan on Climate Change, which created eight core 'national missions' running through 2017 and directed ministries to submit detailed implementation plans to the Prime Minister's Council on Climate Change by the end of 2008. The missions cover solar power; energy efficiency; sustainable habitat; water; sustaining the Himalayan Ecosystem; afforestation; sustainable agriculture and improved understanding of climate change. The plan points out that these national measures would be more successful with assistance from developed countries, and promises that India's per capita greenhouse gas emissions 'will at no point exceed that of developed countries even as we pursue our development objectives'.

Launching this plan, Prime Minister Singh said that the science of climate change was now unequivocal, and that 'there is a high value placed in our culture to the concept of living in harmony with Nature . . . India is prepared to play its role as a responsible member of the international community . . . in the multilateral negotiations taking place under the UN Framework Convention on Climate Change.'

If the new agreement allows India to continue its urgent development needs, and potentially profit from international investment via some means similar to the Clean Development Mechanism (through which it already receives major international investment), it is very likely to get on board. Since it is starting from such a very low emissions rate per capita, contraction and convergence would allow India to keep its emissions growing more or less without interference over the coming decade, while bringing financial benefits from the sales of emissions allowances. Prime Minister Singh acknowledged this in his speech, saying that 'long term convergence of per capita emissions is [. . . .] the only equitable basis for a global compact on climate change'.

# 13

# INDUSTRIALISED NATIONS

The world's major industrialised countries will clearly need to take the lead in tackling climate change. Together they have been responsible for almost all the current climate problem; they gained their wealth and advanced state of development largely by exploiting cheap fossil fuels at an early stage. These are the countries that both bear the brunt of the collective responsibility for climate change and have the economic resources to be able to tackle it. All have embraced this responsibility in principle. Most, but not all, have also begun to act.

(Recall that the figures given here for emissions are for all greenhouse gases, calculated as a carbon dioxide equivalent. Emissions per capita and total emissions are for the year 2004. Historical emissions are average annual values from 1900 to 2004, per head of the present population.)

## USA

Per capita: 24.0 tonnes/person
Historical: 12.7 tonnes/person

Total: 7,065 megatonnes
Change in emissions since 1990: +15.7 per cent
Ratified Kyoto? No
Kyoto target for 2012: -7 per cent (not adopted)

America stands head and shoulders above the rest of the world in both its wealth and its greenhouse gas emissions. Though according to one report it has recently ceded its title as top overall emitter to China, the US still emits vastly more per person than almost every other country. It also bears very significant historical responsibility for the greenhouse gases already in the air.

Until relatively recently, America was also a world leader on tackling climate change. American scientists have long pioneered the study of climate change and were among the first to alert the rest of the world to the problem. The US chaired the working group that gave rise to the first global climate treaty, the UNFCCC. And throughout the 1990s, US administrations were very open to finding ways to limit emissions, under the strong advocacy of Vice-President Al Gore.[1]

But in recent years, America has also, famously, pushed the issue of climate change to the sidelines (despite the best efforts of former British Prime Minister Tony Blair to persuade the President otherwise) and refused to ratify the Kyoto Protocol.

The seeds of the American problem with Kyoto lay, as we mentioned in Chapter 11, in the date set by the treaty as a baseline for emissions. By 1998, when the US signed the treaty, American emissions had sky-rocketed compared to their 1990 level, so that any agreement using 1990 as the baseline had become very much harder to achieve. This led to jitters among politicians who were afraid of damaging an increasingly fragile economy. The US Senate – Republicans and Democrats alike – had already voted unanimously for the so-called Byrd–Hagel Resolution, which declared that the US should sign no protocol that 'would result in serious harm to the economy of the United States'. The resolution also criticised the lack of commitments in Kyoto by developing countries. Thus the Clinton/Gore administration did not submit Kyoto to the Senate for ratification.

But the real blow came with the advent to power of President Bush and his fiercely partisan advisers. Now the issue of climate change suffered politically from its close association with the Democrats, especially Vice-President Gore. Moves to change the composition of the scientists on the Intergovernmental Panel on Climate Change (IPCC), for instance, began almost immediately, with any that were considered too closely in tune with the previous administration viewed with suspicion. Shortly after the Republicans came to power, a notorious leaked memo sent from oil company ExxonMobil to the incoming administration had as its chief recommendation: 'Restructure the US attendance at upcoming IPCC meetings to assure *none of the Clinton/Gore proponents are involved in any decisional activities* [their emphasis].'[2] The same memo also called specifically for World Bank Chief Scientist Bob Watson (whose scientific credentials were impeccable, but who had previously worked with the Clinton/Gore administration) to be removed from the chairmanship of the panel. This subsequently occurred.

It probably didn't help that many of Bush's cabinet were closely associated with the fossil-fuel industry. Before their appointments, Dick Cheney had been CEO and Chairman of Halliburton; Bush's first commerce secretary, Donald Evans, had been chief executive of a leading oil and gas exploration company; and Condoleezza Rice was a director of Chevron.[3]

Efforts to halt climate change also suffered from their association with the environmental movement. To many conservative Republicans, environmentalists were scarcely better than communists for their apparent love of regulating industry and restricting economic growth. One of George Bush's first acts as President was to declare that America would not ratify Kyoto and Rice famously added, 'Kyoto is dead'. (Reports of its death, as Mark Twain remarked on reading his own premature obituary, turned out to be greatly exaggerated. Though Bush succeeded in persuading Australia to hold off ratifying, Russia's eventual ratification took the number of countries over the required threshold, and Kyoto has been fully operating – alive and well – since February 2005.)[4]

After that the story of climate change in America was a woeful one, as legions of top-notch American scientists called loudly for action and the Bush Administration sometimes ignored, sometimes – infamously – attempted to suppress these calls. (The attempts at suppression led to widespread condemnation by US scientists[5] and scathing hearings in March 2007 before the Congressional Committee on Oversight and Government Reform.[6]) Jack Marburger, President Bush's chief science adviser, had a tough time of it. In spite of the overwhelming evidence showing that dangerous climate change is already here, he waited until towards the end of 2007 before being prepared to acknowledge in public that climate change is a real and human-made problem.

The oil industry in the US long marched in step with the Bush Administration's position – especially ExxonMobil, which funded a host of think-tanks dedicated to rubbishing the science of global warming. One such think-tank offered $10,000 each to scientists who would write an essay criticising the findings of the IPCC report. Another – the Competitive Enterprise Institute – put out an infamous, country-wide series of TV commercials suggesting that carbon dioxide was an unalloyed benefit for humankind, and had been unfairly besmirched. The scientist whose findings were quoted in the commercials later angrily accused the makers of selective reporting and described the result as 'a deliberate effort to confuse and mislead the public about the global warming debate'.[7] (As we explained in Chapter 1, carbon dioxide is indeed necessary for life, but the science of global warming shows unequivocally that you can have too much of a good thing.)

To quell the climate protagonists, and to satisfy his requirement that developing countries be involved in any agreement, President Bush set up what was widely perceived as a rival to the Kyoto Protocol: the Asia-Pacific Partnership on Clean Development and Climate, involving Australia, the USA, South Korea, China, India and Japan. Like Kyoto, the partnership is at least outwardly dedicated to solving the climate problem. Unlike Kyoto, however, it sets no mandatory targets or specific mechanisms to achieve the voluntary targets put forward by its members. (Since the targets are not mandatory, there is also no sanction for failure to achieve them.)

The partnership centres around the transfer of low-carbon technology from developed to developing nations, with a very heavy focus on carbon capture and storage – the as yet untested method by which the carbon dioxide from coal-fired power stations can be captured and stored underground instead of being released into the atmosphere. This is likely to be a vital tool in reducing emissions from countries like China, India and South Africa, which depend very heavily on coal for their current energy sources. But on its own, it's not enough.

In April 2006, the Climate Institute of Australia issued a progress report on the Asia–Pacific Partnership, which said that even in the most optimistic scenarios the agreement would lead to a global *doubling* of greenhouse gas emissions from present levels by 2050, rather than the drastic reductions that are needed to quell climate change. It also said that the amount of money invested in developing the new technologies so far is much too low to have any serious impact – just 1.1 per cent of the value invested in global carbon markets as a result of the Kyoto Protocol, and a vanishingly small fraction of the amount of money the International Energy Authority says will be invested in energy over the next twenty-five years.[8] Republican Senator John McCain summed up the thoughts of many when he said that the partnership was 'nothing more than a nice little public-relations ploy'.[9]

However, the tide began to turn – in the rest of the United States if not in Washington. Whether or not Hurricane Katrina can be attributed directly to global warming, it certainly served as a wake-up call for how dramatically Nature can bite back even within a 'safe' urban environment, and how foolish it can be to ignore the warning signs.

Meanwhile, Al Gore's passionate association with the cause of climate change switched from being Republican anathema to major asset after his phenomenal success with the book and the movie *An Inconvenient Truth*, and his award of the Nobel Peace Prize in 2007, jointly with the IPCC. Another significant driving force is the state of California, which has a proud record of dealing efficiently with environmental problems – especially the once smog-choked cities of Los Angeles and San Francisco – by briskly applying laws and encouraging the development of new technologies. There was nothing sentimentally green about California's action to bring catalytic converters to the exhausts of its cars, nor did it harm the economy. Every new squeeze on the regulatory system for car exhausts met opposition from the motor industry – but they never stopped selling cars. The car-exhaust catalysts championed by California are now standard issue throughout the industrialised world, and are the main reason why so many cities are much pleasanter places to live in.

California, under the perhaps unlikely figure of its 'Governator', Arnold Schwarzenegger, began to tackle the climate problem with the same brisk efficiency. At a meeting of West Coast governors in 2005, Schwarzenegger invited David King to give a speech outlining the UK's position on climate change. 'When I said that the UK had committed unilaterally to reducing its emissions by 60 per cent by 2050, Schwarzenegger's response was "we'll reduce by 80 per cent". That's the sort of bidding war we should all be getting into.'

The state has begun putting its money where its mouth is. In 2006, California passed the Global Warming Solutions Act[10] which commits the state to return to 1990 emissions levels by 2020 (which means an effective cut of 25 per cent). The Act also instigated a state-wide emissions trading scheme, and Schwarzenegger himself has taken to driving a hybrid Hummer.

Nine north-eastern and mid-Atlantic states have set up their own trading scheme, known as the Regional Greenhouse Gas Initiative (or, more affectionately, as ReGGIe).[11] And hundreds of mayors hailing from cities in every single US state have signed the US Conference of Mayors' Climate Protection

Agreement, which pledges their home cities to reduce carbon dioxide emissions to 7 per cent below 1990 levels by 2012.[12]

The climate for change looked more promising still when Democrats regained control of both the House of Representatives and the Senate in fall 2006. The outgoing Republican chair of the Senate's influential Environment and Public Works Committee was Senator James Inhofe, who once declared that global warming was the 'greatest hoax ever perpetrated on the American people'. The incoming Democratic chair of the same committee has openly welcomed the arrival of a slew of bills aimed at encouraging nationwide emissions reductions.

However, that's not to say that climate change has remained a partisan issue. Most of the new bills have both Democrats and Republicans as sponsors. In April 2007 the otherwise conservative Supreme Court ruled that carbon dioxide and other heat-trapping emissions are 'air pollutants' under the Clean Air Act, and that the Environmental Protection Agency had been wrong in saying that it had no power to curb them. In July 2008 the State of Georgia used this decision to block the building of a new coal-fired power station, which could affect planning for other planned power plants across the country. And the Christian right, once fierce supporters of President Bush's position, have begun to back action on climate change on the basis that we need to act as effective stewards of God's Creation.

The private sector, too, has begun to get in on the climate act. Companies of the stature of Wal-Mart and General Electric have converted to the climate cause and even ExxonMobil has softened its stance. While it is still vehemently opposed to the Kyoto Protocol, it has cancelled the funding of the more egregious lobby groups and begun to discuss what American carbon regulation might ultimately look like.[13]

There is new talk of climate change as a market failure born of unfair fossil-fuel subsidies, and cap and trade schemes as an appropriate capitalist adjustment rather than a tree-hugging regulatory tax. The myriad separate emissions trading schemes that are springing up around the country are encouraging companies to push for a national scheme so that they can plan the future based on a single, consistent set of rules and market conditions, instead of having to work with different schemes in different states. Environmental activist Robert F. Kennedy Jr was moved to write in *Rolling Stone* magazine that, because it encourages efficiency, 'a truly free market is the planet's best friend'.[14] The *New York Times* declared in December 2006 that the colour of the year had been 'green'. And the following January, in his State of the Union Address, President Bush famously declared that a way had to be found to break America's addiction to oil.

There is still, however, a long way to go. Though in the last year or so of his administration President Bush began to change his language about the dangers of climate change, his favoured strategies to counter it were at best doubtful in their efficacy. They include a massive increase in the use of biofuels – which, as we explained in Chapter 8, comes with its own dangers – coupled with an effort to reduce the intensity of carbon emissions per unit GDP by 18 per cent by 2012. This sounds impressive until you discover that the overall emissions would still rise by 13 per cent, which is only a whisker away from the do-nothing 'business as usual' scenario.[15]

Moreover, though President Bush's negotiators agreed to the joint G8 statement issued in Germany in 2007, which accepted the reality of climate change and agreed to work towards reducing global emissions, a fascinating document leaked by Greenpeace showed the extent to which those same negotiators had insisted on watering down the statement's language. For instance, they refused to allow any mention of binding commitments, saying that this approach was 'fundamentally incompatible with the President's approach to climate change'.[16] One lobbyist accused the Bush administration of 'trying to lay landmines under a post-Kyoto agreement after they leave office'.[17]

Just before the German meeting, President Bush proposed to set up talks, chaired by America, between the world's most polluting nations, to run 'in parallel' with the United Nations efforts. However, this was shouted down by other nations, especially Brazil, who saw it as an attempt to undermine the post-Kyoto process. In Germany President Bush reluctantly assented to the statement put out by German Chancellor Angela Merkel, who was chairing the G8 + 5 meeting, that: 'We have agreed that the UN climate process is the appropriate forum for negotiating future global action on climate change.'

And although President Bush signed up to a further G8 statement in June 2008 in Japan, finally setting a number on the level of emissions cuts necessary – a 50% reduction globally by 2050 – developing countries immediately criticised the statement for setting no intermediate goals, and not specifying that industrialised nations would have to take on the major burden of the reductions.

Given this record of recalcitrance followed by reluctance, it was too much to hope that the Bush administration would fully embrace effective action on climate change. But President Obama is set to take a very different stance. He made climate change a consistent part of his campaign speeches, has appointed top-notch energy advisors such as Yale professor Dan Esty, and proposed a detailed strategy to deal with the climate problem as part of his election manifesto. The 'Biden–Obama New Energy for America Plan' pledges, amongst other things, to invest $150 billion into clean energy technology over the next ten years and to implement a country-wide cap-and-trade programme to reduce greenhouse gas emissions by a full 80% by 2050. This won't come a moment too soon. As the *New York Times* put it on the morning after Obama's election victory: 'Climate change is a global threat, and after years of denial and inaction, this country must take the lead on addressing it'.

The United States is one of the world's largest emitters of greenhouse gases per person, is the second largest emitter overall, bears a very large responsibility for historical emissions and also has the world's most advanced economy. If the new international treaty is to have any chance of success, the US will need to lead from the front.

## Russian Federation

Per capita: 13.5 tonnes/person
Historical: 7.1 tonnes/person
Total: 1,938 megatonnes
Change in emissions since 1990: -35.1 per cent
Ratified Kyoto? Yes
Kyoto target for 2012: 0 per cent

In the run-up to the Kyoto agreement, the Russian government repeatedly declared that climate change is very far from its priorities. President Vladimir Putin nailed his colours to the mast in 2003, when he said: 'Russia is a northern country and if temperatures get warmer by 2 or 3 degrees, it's not such a bad thing. We could spend less on warm coats, and . . . grain harvests would increase.'[18] Whether the grain harvest in Russia would indeed go up with a warming of 3°C remains debatable. But every model agrees that above 3°C the harvest would plummet. And climate change would bring other troubles to Russia which might well outweigh the benefits of fewer fur coats.

By 2070, for instance, the IPCC report predicts significantly increased flooding in northern Russia and more frequent droughts in the south of the country. It also predicts that melting permafrost will not just lead to buckled and broken gas pipelines as the ground falls beneath them, but will also expose vast amounts of drained wetlands in Russia to catastrophic fires similar to the ones that swept Borneo and smothered the country in a fug of orange smoke.[19] The problem with climate change is that it's all or nothing – you can't cherry-pick the blessings and leave aside the curses.

Putin made this speech while he was considering whether to ratify Kyoto. The question was significant because the Protocol was designed not to come into effect until countries responsible for at least 55 per cent of the 1990 carbon dioxide emissions had agreed to go ahead. By 2003, of all the big industrialised polluters only Russia, Australia and the US were yet to ratify. Any one of the three would take the count over the 55 per cent threshold, but if none of them ratified, the Protocol would be doomed.

America had already declared its intention not to ratify, and, after intense pressure from the US, Australia also refused. Meanwhile, the signs from Russia were not good. A bilateral meeting on climate change between the UK and Russian scientists was effectively hijacked when Putin's then chief of staff, Andrey Illarionov, changed the agenda at the last minute to bring in a ragbag of sceptics and attempt to prevent the British scientists from speaking at all.

One of us (David King) was leading the UK delegation. He

had already explained that he would have to leave during the conference for further government meetings at the Kremlin. But when he started to go, Illarionov seized the microphone and began screaming that he was a coward and 'commanding' him to stay put to answer his questions. The British delegation left with this extraordinary outburst still ringing in their ears. The next morning's *Moscow Times* bore the unpromising headline: 'The UK declares war on Russia', which turned out to be a direct quote from Illarionov.

But where scientific arguments cannot sway a government, economic ones sometimes prove more powerful. Russia was eager to join the global trading club, the World Trade Organization. Following David King's report back from Russia, Tony Blair went to the EU leaders to propose a horse-trade. If Russia ratified Kyoto, the EU would support its entry into the WTO. This proved a powerful trump card. On 4 November 2004, and in the teeth of Illarionov's continued opposition, President Putin ratified the Kyoto Protocol.

To Russia, backing Kyoto made little practical difference. For purely economic reasons its emissions had plummeted after 1990, meaning that it could meet its Kyoto obligations with ease. In fact, its emissions had dropped so low that it was holding billions of dollars' worth of permits that, in principle at least, it could sell on the Kyoto trading market. However, it didn't do so – probably because only America could have afforded to buy them, and America remained aloof from Kyoto.

Russia's support for a post-Kyoto treaty remains uncertain. On the one hand, its new isolationism coupled with its considerable natural gas exports suggest that it will want to hold on to a carbon-based economy. But on the other, its potential for selling at least some of its permits might well be tempting enough to keep Russia on board if America is part of the mix. As we explained in Chapter 11, any future agreement, however, would almost certainly have to reset Russia's starting level to a more recent emissions figure than 1990.

## Japan

Per capita: 10.6 tonnes/person
Historical: 4.0 tonnes/person
Total: 1,355 megatonnes
Change in emissions since 1990: +8 per cent
Ratified Kyoto? Yes
Kyoto target for 2012: –6 per cent

Considering its advanced state of industrial development, Japan has relatively low emissions per head mainly because much of its electricity comes from nuclear power, and its industry is one of the most energy efficient in the world. It has also long been committed to tackling climate change, being the host country of the meeting that created the Kyoto Protocol in the first place.

Partly because of this, and also because Japan has no oil reserves of its own, saving energy has been elevated to the status of a national imperative. In 2005 the Japanese government's 'cool biz' campaign encouraged civil servants to set their office air conditioners to no lower than 28°C. Thousands of workers agreed to remove their suit jackets and ties, and switch to short-sleeved shirts for the summer – and this in a conservative and conformist business-orientated culture. In metropolitan Tokyo alone, the campaign saved enough energy to power a city of a quarter of a million people for a month.[20] The campaign has now become an annual event. At the beginning of each summer since then, the Prime Minister has removed his jacket and tie, and his cabinet and an extraordinary proportion of the country have followed suit.

The Japanese government remains nervous about the effects that reducing carbon emissions further may have on the Japanese economy, and the country is focusing on technological innovation. It was one of the founder members of the new international fusion project that we described in Chapter 9. It is also the world's biggest investor in solar photovoltaics, and in techniques to make hydrogen gas from water.

Any future approach based on per capita emissions would be favourable to Japan since this would lend weight to the high level of efficiency it has already achieved.

## Canada

Per capita: 23.7 tonnes/person
Historical: 9.8 tonnes/person
Total: 758 megatonnes
Change in emissions since 1990: +27 per cent
Ratified Kyoto? Yes
Kyoto target for 2012: -6 per cent

Canada ratified Kyoto in 2002, but it is presently very far away from achieving its target of a 6 per cent cut in emissions. In fact, between 1990 and 2004 its emissions increased by 27 per cent, which is proportionally even more than for the United States.

There is a great deal of popular support in the country as a whole for action to deal with climate change, but successive governments have stalled on exactly how to put this into practice. In 2005, the then government published a proposal for reaching the Kyoto target using a combination of mandatory emissions cuts for large factories and power plants, and largely voluntary schemes for other sectors. Environmental groups criticised the plan for relying too heavily on voluntary measures and incentives rather than obligatory cuts, but in any case the government did not implement the plan before it was voted out of office in 2006.

The new Conservative minority government, under Prime Minister Stephen Harper, then declared that Canada's Kyoto target was now impossible and cut the funding for many climate-focused schemes. The government did produce an alternative plan to tackle emissions, but this was muddied since it bracketed greenhouse gases with smog and other more immediate and apparent forms of pollution. Also, the obligatory targets set by the plan for industry to reduce its greenhouse emissions were based on the intensity – that is emissions per unit of production – rather than the overall quantity. (We discussed in the section on the US, above, the ways in which this approach is flawed.)

These events sparked a flurry of political activity, including the passage through Parliament of a private member's bill, 'An Act to ensure that Canada meets its global climate change obligations under the Kyoto Protocol', which was designed to try to force the government to comply with Kyoto. All members of the three opposition parties voted for this bill and it was passed through both Parliament and Senate, becoming law on 22 June 2007.

Among other things, the Act obliges the government to specify the greenhouse gas reductions expected for each year until 2012, showing how these will meet Canada's Kyoto obligations. Stephen Harper's Government repeatedly said that it had no intention of attempting this, and in June 2008 became the first government in the world to be taken to court for failing its commitment to Kyoto. After a snap general election on 14 October 2008, Prime Minister Harper continues to head a minority government, and a spokesman said the Canadian emissions policy would await the actions of US President Obama's new administration.

## Australia

Per capita: 26.2 tonnes/person
Historical: 10.3 tonnes/person
Total: 529 megatonnes
Change in emissions since 1990: +25.9 per cent
Ratified Kyoto? Yes
Kyoto target for 2012: +8 per cent

Australia participated in the Gleneagles Dialogue in Mexico, and the recent droughts have prompted considerable support in the country as a whole for action on climate change. However, when he was Prime Minister, John Howard, steadily refused to ratify the Kyoto Protocol. His critics say that this was mainly to curry favour with America, a view that is supported by the fact that, out of 178 parties to the agreement, only the USA and Australia refused to ratify. Moreover, had Russia not been persuaded to change its position and ratify in 2004, Australia's refusal would have been enough to keep the treaty from coming into force, which was the declared wish of President Bush's administration.

Though Australia's Kyoto target was set at a generous +8 per cent above 1990 levels, its current emissions have risen still further, by nearly 26 per cent. It has one of the highest per capita levels of emissions in the world, higher even than the USA. It also stands to lose heavily from future climate changes including increased droughts and heatwaves, further tropical storm damage and the bleaching of corals on the Great Barrier Reef. (Indeed, the state of Victoria is already reeling after seven successive years of drought, and counting.)

During his time in office, Prime Minister Howard put his faith in the Asia–Pacific Partnership on Clean Development and Climate. This sets no binding emissions targets, focuses on attempting to develop new technologies, and, as we explained in the section on the USA, by itself would lead to a significant global rise in greenhouse emissions rather than the reduction that we need.

However, the federal government was put under increasing pressure to implement stringent measures to tackle climate change. Partly this came from individual state leaders. New South Wales has had an emissions trading scheme in place for electricity since 2003, and in 2004 all the Australian states united to form a task force, called the National Emissions Trading Task Force, to push for a nationwide scheme.[21] There has also been a groundswell of popular support. In one poll fully 80 per cent of respondents said they wanted the government to do more to tackle climate change.

In November 2006, in a remarkable turnaround, former Prime Minister Howard made a speech saying 'Australia will be part of future discussions which are designed to get total international agreement involving all of the major polluters, involving all the nations of the world' and mentioned, at least, 'talking about an effective worldwide emissions trading system'.[22]

However, partly because of his unpopular stance on climate change, Howard lost the general election in November 2007 and one of the first acts of his successor, Kevin Rudd, was to ratify Kyoto.

## European Union

The EU is second only to the US in its share of historical responsibility for the greenhouse problem.[23] However, its attitude has been very different. Rather than ducking the problem, the European Union has placed climate change squarely at the top of its agenda for most of the past decade.

The EU committed itself as a bloc to a Kyoto target of reducing emissions by 8 per cent from 1990 values by 2012 – a target that looks very likely to be met,[24] though it will probably require some contribution from Clean Development Projects overseas.

The EU also pioneered a Continent-wide carbon cap and trade scheme, which began in 2005, and which, despite the teething troubles we mentioned in Chapter 10, is responsible for almost all the global market in carbon emissions. And it has set out a comprehensive plan for how the Continent will need to adapt to the changes that are already inevitable.[25]

Perhaps most importantly, the European Union's official policy is now to try to avoid the worst consequences of climate change by restricting temperature rises to no more than 2°C above the pre-industrial level. As we showed in Chapter 6, this may not now be achievable, even with a stabilisation level of 450 ppm $CO_2$eq.

In May 2007, the Spring Council meeting of the European Union reaffirmed this stance, which had been set out in two earlier recommendation documents.[26] It called for developed countries to reduce their emissions levels by 30 per cent above 1990 levels by 2020, aiming for a 60–80 per cent cut in 2050. According to this plan, many developing countries would also need to cut their emissions in later decades, while being encouraged on to a low-carbon path through investments from the developed world.[27] Emissions levels would reach a peak in the next two decades before falling to a global level 50 per cent below where it is today by 2050.

Thus, the EU has already made its negotiating position for a new global agreement very clear. It has also committed 'without prejudice' to a unilateral Continent-wide cut of at least 20 per cent by 2020, explicitly to show leadership, and to set the international ball rolling.

This had an effect on wider groupings. The G8 summit in Germany in June 2007 issued an extraordinary statement jointly with the EU and the five most rapidly developing nations that said: 'We noted with concern the recent IPCC report and its findings. We are convinced that urgent and concerted action is needed and accept our responsibility to show leadership in tackling climate change. In setting a global goal for emissions reductions in the process we have agreed in Heiligendamm involving all major emitters, we will consider seriously the decisions made by the European Union, Canada and Japan which include at least a halving of global emissions by 2050.'

This statement was criticised for its lack of binding targets, which had been summarily blocked by the US. But it was the first document that the world's top economies had put their signature to that even mentioned the need for a cut as large as this and on such a timescale. (Many commentators seemed not to notice that the desired target in this statement was for a reduction of *global* emissions by 50 per cent by 2050, which, as we've already pointed out, would mean a cut of up to 80 per cent for the G8 nations that signed.) Further tireless lobbying from the UK, Germany, and France led to an even stronger statement at the G8 Summit in Japan in June 2008, which committed G8 nations to 'consider and adopt the goal of achieving at least 50% reduction of global emissions by 2050'.

Although this was criticised by developing nations for not specifying interim goals, it was the first time that the US Government had signed up to any document bearing a clear target for emissions cuts.

In January 2008 the EU also upped its climate ante, promising that by 2020, the EU would have cut its greenhouse emissions by 20%, would be producing 20% of its energy from renewable sources, and would have increased energy efficiency by 20% – a strategy that commission President Jose Manuel Barroso called '20:20:20 by 2020', and described as 'the most far-reaching set of legislative proposals to be made by the European Commission for many years.'

## France

Per capita: 9.0 tonnes/person
Historical: 6.6 tonnes/person
Total: 563 megatonnes
Change in emissions since 1990: -0.4 per cent
Ratified Kyoto? Yes
Kyoto target for 2012: 0 per cent

France shut down its last coal mine in 2004 and now generates some 80 per cent of its electricity from nuclear power. While the nuclear option is anathema to many environmental groups it has ensured that France has one of the lowest per capita emissions rates in the industrialised world. Thanks to its nuclear plants, France is responsible for barely a fifth of the average European emissions per unit of electricity generated, though the values from its transport, industrial and domestic heating are much higher than this.

The French government supported international efforts to curb emissions from early on in the negotiations. In 2002 the then President, Jacques Chirac, declared, 'Our house is burning and we are looking the other way', and added that climate change was threatening 'a planetary tragedy'.[28] France suffered especially from the following year's heatwave, which did much to raise consciousness of the dangers of climate change among its citizens.

In March 2005, an Environmental Charter was incorporated into the French Constitution saying that 'the choices designed to meet the needs of the present generation should not jeopardise the ability of future generations and other peoples to meet their own needs'. That same year, an energy bill set out the aim of decreasing energy use by 2 per cent per year, continuing to support nuclear power, and to put particular effort into developing new, low-emissions energy sources.

In parallel with the EU proposals, the French energy bill also set out an ambitious long-term strategy to reduce the country's emissions below 1990 levels by 75 per cent by 2050. Under the terms of the bill, the government is required to do its utmost to achieve this target, although it is not yet obligatory.

When the new President Nicolas Sarkozy was elected in 2007, he also upped the status of the environment in his government by creating a new 'super-ministry', which covers the environment, energy, transport, natural habitats and land planning. Its head, Jean-Louis Borloo, is also Sarkozy's number two.

To achieve its cuts, France is focusing on new technologies, especially biofuels in the transport sector, and strategies to make big improvements in efficiency. For instance, many efficiency improvements in individual homes – such as buying the new, more efficient boilers – now earn considerable tax breaks.

France also has relationships with many African countries involved in Clean Development Mechanism projects.

## Germany

Per capita: 12.3 tonnes/person
Historical: 9.0 tonnes/person
Total: 1,015 megatonnes
Change in emissions since 1990: -17.5 per cent
Ratified Kyoto? Yes
Kyoto target for 2012: -21.0 per cent

Germany has a long and illustrious record of fighting environmental causes in general, and climate change in particular. It was one of the first countries in Europe to make very widespread deployments of wind and solar power. Thanks to its 1999 '100,000 roofs' programme, which offered favourable loans to households installing solar panels, Germany now has the world's largest installed capacity of solar energy. It is also a world leader in manufacturing and exporting renewable energy devices. By one estimate, one in two turbines and one in three solar cells are made in Germany, and some economists have predicted that renewable energy could outstrip car manufacture as the country's most important export industry.

The impetus for domestic action slowed somewhat in recent years, in part because of economic and political problems associated with the reunification of Germany. However, as Chancellor, Angela Merkel has brought new energy to Germany's fight against climate change. A scientist by training, she understands the problem very well and has made it one of the priorities of her administration.

One of the problems faced by Germany in tackling climate change – and one of the reasons for its relatively high per capita emissions – is the country's extensive coal deposits. In spite of the wide take-up of 'green' energy sources, half the country's electricity still comes from coal, which is the most polluting of all the fossil fuels (and much of that is now in the form of brown coal, which is less efficient and more polluting still). In March 2007, a pilot plant began operating in Brandenburg to attempt to capture carbon dioxide from a power plant and convert it to a storable form. So far, the attempt has been modest – the plant is a mere 50 MW and it's not yet clear where the captured $CO_2$ can be stored. But if it is successful, the Swedish company operating it plans to increase the scale.

Because of the economic downturn in the former East Germany after the fall of the Berlin Wall, the emissions of Germany as a whole have fallen significantly since 1990, a fact which is reflected in their Kyoto target. But Merkel wants to go still further. In September 2007, she put forward a list of twenty-nine measures by which Germany could make deeper emissions cuts. These include all the usual suspects that we discussed in Part II. By putting them together, Merkel's government plans to reduce Germany's emissions by an extraordinary 40 per cent by 2020 – the world's most ambitious goal to date.

Merkel has also brought new energy to Germany's role at the forefront of international action. Like Tony Blair, Merkel made climate change one of the key pillars of the German G8 presidency, and it is largely thanks to the intense pressure applied by both these leaders and by President Sarkozy of France that the G8 + 5 meeting in Heiligendamm in June 2007 was able to issue the extraordinary joint statement on climate change that we mention above.

Chancellor Merkel has also now formalised the Gleneagles Dialogue between the G8 and the five most rapidly developing nations, which will continue to try to establish the basis for an international agreement among the world's most polluting economies. This in turn could well be the basis for the fully global agreement on climate change that we urgently need.

## UK

Per capita: 11.0 tonnes/person
Historical: 11.2 tonnes/person
Total: 656 megatonnes
Change in emissions since 1990: -14.2 per cent
Ratified Kyoto? Yes
Kyoto target for 2012: -12.5 per cent

Perhaps appropriately, since the Industrial Revolution started there, the UK has been one of the world's most proactive countries both in implementing national measures and in driving the international process.

When the Labour Party came to power in 1997 they inherited a steep drop in greenhouse emissions since 1990, mainly because of the switching of much of the UK's power supply from oil to natural gas. Deputy Prime Minister John Prescott initially made climate change his mission, and was one of the driving forces at the 1997 Kyoto meeting, which led to the Kyoto Protocol. In 1998 Chancellor of the Exchequer Gordon Brown imposed the so-called Climate Change Levy on $CO_2$-producing energy sources (and also, curiously, on nuclear power). Much of the proceeds from this levy went to set up and run the Carbon Trust and the Energy Savings Trust, two bodies set at arm's length from government, with the brief to raise the public profile of climate change, and also to work with businesses on reducing emissions by improving their efficiency.

In April 2002 the government introduced a scheme whereby utility companies were obliged to generate a certain proportion of their electricity from renewable resources (10 per cent by 2010, and 20 per cent by 2020, not including nuclear power), or to trade their way out of trouble by buying permits from other companies.

The UK also set up the world's first national carbon trading scheme in 2004, which has since been folded into the European scheme. Being first has its advantages. The London stock exchange has certainly captured the carbon trade market, vying for global prominence only with Chicago's Climate Exchange, which has been operating since 2003 in spite of the lack of a nationwide trading scheme in the US.

Since 1997, the UK's overall greenhouse emissions have continued to fall, mainly because of serious efforts to cut the emissions of methane from landfills – which have reduced the emissions of this powerful greenhouse gas by 55 per cent. The UK will therefore have no problem meeting its Kyoto obligations.

In 2003 the UK unilaterally declared that it would reduce its carbon dioxide emissions by 60 per cent by 2050, and challenged other countries to do the same. A White Paper published that year set out a rough sketch of how this could be achieved, and set out the interim target of reducing emissions by 20 per cent by 2010, a level more stringent than the Kyoto one.

However, carbon dioxide emissions have been creeping up in spite of the above national measures, mainly because of the gradual retiring of Britain's aged nuclear power plants. There are also disadvantages in being first. The UK built the world's first commercial nuclear power station, some sixty years ago. But its current generation of power plants are now coming to the end of their life. Fifteen years ago 30 per cent of the UK's electricity came from nuclear. Today that figure is 19 per cent and, unless new plants are built, by 2020 it will be down to 7–8 per cent. Every time a nuclear power plant is replaced by one driven by fossil fuels, the UK's emissions rise inexorably. It is now highly unlikely that the UK will reach its own 2010 target.

Thus in 2007, the government published a new White Paper, giving much more detail on how to reach the 2050 target using a slew of energy efficiency measures as well as bringing in new renewable technologies.[29]

One controversial aspect of the White Paper is the proposal to replace the retiring nuclear power stations with new ones, confirmed in January 2008 when the Government gave the green light to new nuclear stations. Critics have concerns about safety and the disposal of nuclear waste. It's worth noting, though, that the new generation of nuclear power stations have made immense progress in both these regards. As we described in Chapter 9, there are now stations with 'passive safety systems' so that if something does go wrong you can walk away and leave the plant to shut down by itself. And the new generation is so much more efficient than the old that if every nuclear power station in the UK was replaced by a new one, and those then operated for a full forty years, they would still produce only a tenth of the waste that the country already has.

Critics of nuclear power claim that other low-carbon sources could be used both to fill the nuclear gap and reduce the UK's emissions still further. However, we need to use every weapon we can in the fight against climate change, and there aren't many proven technologies out there. Even the relatively established ones have their problems. Wind farms could be contributing 11 GW of power to the national grid right now, but 9.5 GW of that is mired in contested planning permissions.

To address the gap in current low-carbon technologies, David King, working closely with the (then) Chancellor of the Exchequer, Gordon Brown, brokered the establishment of a public–private partnership called the Energy Technologies Institute to develop new, low-carbon technologies. It will receive funding of £100 million per year for ten years, half to come from industry and half from the government. On the board already are motor companies, utilities and oil companies, and negotiations are currently underway to fill the remaining available seats.

It's disappointing, certainly, that the 2010 target is now unlikely to be met. However, we have learned our lesson. To ensure that we do better in future, the UK has also taken steps to enshrine the reduction commitments in law, with the Climate Change Bill. This created an independent Committee on Climate Change, chaired by former CBI chief Lord Adair Turner, which works at arm's length from the government after the model of the Bank of England, and is allowed to use a whole raft of measures to ensure that emissions fall as required.

The Bill also set an initial target of reducing $CO_2$ emissions by 60% by 2050. However, in October 2008 the Committee on Climate Change recommended that the target be significantly increased. It's worth saying a word here about the nature of that 60 per cent target. It was chosen before the EU set out its plan, and on the recommendation of the Royal Commission on Environmental Pollution whose 2003 report[30] said that this level of reduction would be enough to keep global levels of carbon dioxide below 550 ppm, and thus keep temperatures from rising more than 2°C above pre-industrial levels. This was based, among other things, on the third IPCC report, published in 2001, which was rather more optimistic about required levels than the most recent one. Still, at the time, back in 2003, 60 per cent seemed a huge, even preposterous, figure to achieve.

Now, however, it is looking like the very least that we will need. As we explained in Chapter 6, the science has moved on, and to have a good chance of remaining below 2°C we will need to halt *all* greenhouse gases at an *equivalent* carbon dioxide level of 450 ppm. As set out in the EU plan, this would mean cuts to UK emissions of 70–80 per cent in all greenhouse gases, not just carbon dioxide. Thus, following the recommendations of the Committee on Climate Change, the Bill now commits the UK to reduce its emissions by a full 80%, and in all greenhouse gases rather than just carbon dioxide. The Government also committed to include shipping and aviation emissions in this target, although it remains to be determined how the UK's contribution to these sectors will be calculated. The UK can be justly proud of its climate change programme. It is the first country in the world to make such a long-term target legally binding. But though the existing strategy is both impressive and unilateral, it will still need to do more.

On the international stage, the UK has been a crucial player, in many cases stepping into the vacuum of leadership left by America's having turned its back (temporarily, one hopes) on climate change. As well as its avid participation in the Kyoto process, and its role in setting up the European Trading Scheme, the UK has taken considerable steps to unite the world under a climate change banner. In 2005, Tony Blair made climate change one of the two main pillars of the UK's G8 presidency. He invited the five most rapidly developing nations to the G8 meeting in Gleneagles, as well as other major industrial emitters. The result was the beginning of the Gleneagles Dialogue which was followed by a further meeting between these countries in Mexico specifically to try to establish the grounds for a new international agreement.

The process was formalised in Germany in 2007, and – for its capacity to put pressure on the US as well as draw the key developing countries into the debate – looks likely to be a key step in breaking international deadlock. The Prime Minister also put personal pressure on President Bush to agree to the joint G8 statement on climate change issued in Germany in 2007.

When we finally manage to get a good agreement in force, individual nations will then need to implement it. Each will choose its own way, but there will be some common factors. In particular each nation will need to:

- Set in place adaptation strategies to cope with the changes in the decades to come (see Chapter 4).
- Switch to existing low-carbon technologies and (especially in the case of richer nations with more established science bases) fund research and development for new technologies (see Chapters 8 and 9).
- Increase efficiencies and reduce power demand (see Chapter 7).
- Engage in a combination of motivating factors that could include: tax incentives and penalties, nationwide or international emissions permit trading schemes (see Chapter 10).

- Find a way to tap the rising tide of consumer desire for action. For instance, governments will need to empower consumers with knowledge about how best to act, by encouraging accurate labelling of products to reveal their associated carbon dioxide emissions throughout their entire production process, and setting regulatory standards for offsetting schemes (see Chapter 14).

As should be clear from this chapter and the previous one, governments will also need to maintain pressure on all participants to come on board. Somehow, the nations that are already convinced of the dangers of climate change will need to convey this to the rest. It's easy to forget how vulnerable we are. Those of us who live in the richest nations are like the aeroplane passengers up in first class with the flat beds and the complimentary champagne. As climate change will come first to the world's most vulnerable citizens, the rest of us might lie back, relax and think that there's no need to worry. But if the wings of the plane fall off, we all end up just as dead.

# 14

# HOW YOU CAN
# CHANGE THE WORLD

It's easy to believe that global warming is somebody else's
problem – other people will suffer and other people will come
up with the solution. However, this is far from the truth.
There's a clue in the name: 'global warming' is a truly global
problem. None of us is safe from its effects (although some of us
have a better chance of adapting to them). We are all part of the
problem, and each of us will need to be part of the solution.

Today there are more than six billion human beings on
Earth. By the middle of the century there will be nine and a
half billion. Even without the problem of climate change we
would be finding our resources running thin. With it, the
population boom becomes even graver.

Thinking this way presents the human race as one massive
blob. But in fact it's as individuals that we live our lives and
make our choices. Every time each of us switches on a light,
reaches for something in a supermarket, gets into a car or bus,
chooses what clothes to buy or which movie to see, we have all
made a difference to the way the economy works. Choices like
these have driven the world's economies ever upwards in the
twentieth century. They have also led to spiralling greenhouse

gas emissions. Now we will all have to adapt our choices to the new realities of the twenty-first century.

The previous few chapters have shown how much of the answer to the problem of climate change will need to come from the top down, from governments, industries and big international agreements. But none of this will ever happen unless we, the people, push from below. Through the choices we make about more or less every aspect of our personal lives, we need to drive producers and manufacturers along sustainable pathways. Through the choices we make in the ballot box, and through the pressure we put on our local representatives and communities, we need to drive politicians to set our countries on the right paths. We are the ones who have the power to change.

Below, we outline how each of us should start to tackle climate change in our own lives, and why this matters. This is the culmination of almost everything we've already written about. In particular, much of this material has already shown up in Chapters 7 ('More From Less') and 8 ('Planes, Trains and Automobiles'). But we also describe how to put pressure on politicians to ensure that they set the right national goals, and reach the right international agreements.

Some of these points might seem familiar, but others may surprise you. And together these choices add up to something momentous. They will bring about nothing less than a global change in culture. As we've already mentioned, until now we have all treated energy as something that is almost free, and infinitely available. We have wasted resources and ignored the perils of digging ever deeper into our planet's capital. To pull ourselves out of this mess we all need to change our attitude, and realise how precious our energy resources really are.

*

Before we launch into specifics, here are a few words on two particularly contentious issues: carbon offsetting and food miles.

## Going carbon neutral

There is much talk lately of 'going carbon neutral'. Since it's currently impossible to exist in the developed world without causing at least some greenhouse emissions, the only way to do this is to dip into the controversial waters of carbon offsetting.

In principle, it's a good idea, akin to the Clean Development Mechanism of the Kyoto Protocol that we described in Chapter 10. Simply put, when you buy a carbon offset you're compensating for, say, one tonne of your own emissions by paying someone else to reduce theirs by the same amount. Since the air doesn't care where the greenhouse gas comes from, the result is a balance. You've 'offset' your own emissions.

Usually, the 'somewhere else' is a developing country, because that's where the cheapest and easiest opportunities are to make a difference. For instance, if a hospital in India is using kerosene for lighting, your offsetting money can fund the switch to solar panels. This could help India to 'leapfrog' to the latest, cleanest technologies without having to pass through the various intermediate (and highly polluting) steps that we western countries did.

Hardline environmentalists object to this idea in principle. They complain that offsetting lets people off the hook – and even discourages them from changing their own ways. Environmental journalist George Monbiot has, very wittily, compared carbon offsets to the medieval practice of the Church selling indulgences – pieces of paper saying that a particular sin was forgiven, so that you could do it without feeling guilty.

There is some strength in this argument, and carbon off-setting certainly shouldn't be your first recourse. There are plenty of other ways to try to cut down your emissions, including many that we list later in this chapter. Friends of the Earth, Greenpeace and the WWF put out a joint statement about carbon offsetting in which they say that 'we would encourage individuals, business and governments to first do all they can to cut down or avoid emissions of greenhouse gases before considering the purchase of offsets'.[1]

But there are some levels beyond which you can't drop, and some forms of emitting (such as long-haul flying) for which there are no alternatives apart from not making the journey in the first place. In these cases, and as long as you're also making every effort to cut down in other ways, it makes sense to consider offsetting your emissions.

The next problem with offsets, however, is being sure that they actually do what they say. Offsetting companies are mushrooming, and there is currently little or no regulation. Your nice certificate saying that you have offset 10 tonnes of greenhouse gases might not be worth the paper it's written on.

The problems here are the same ones that we mention in Chapter 10 for the Clean Development Mechanism. How can you be sure that the offset you're buying will (1) really happen; (2) really take up as much greenhouse gas as you think; and (3) not have happened anyway, even without your money?

For instance, in the early days plenty of companies offered to plant trees on your behalf. But trees take a long time to soak up carbon dioxide, and if they are burned either deliberately or accidentally during that period, the $CO_2$ goes right back into the air. Also, it's tremendously hard to calculate exactly how much carbon dioxide a tree will take up in its lifetime. Another problem is that, away from the tropics, planting trees where there were none before can actually make things worse by changing the reflectivity of the land and encouraging it to soak up more sunlight.[2] And there's also the danger that people can claim carbon credit for plantations that they were planning to grow anyway.[3]

Without some kind of reliable benchmark, the carbon offsetting industry will always be vulnerable to deliberate fraud, but even well-meaning attempts to provide reliable emissions cuts can fall flat.[4] Various NGOs have therefore clubbed together to create an independent standard for offsetting projects – the Gold Standard.[5] This is awarded only to renewable energy and efficiency projects, specifically because these encourage changes in behaviour rather than just allowing the world to continue its reliance on fossil fuels. The projects are also rigorously and conservatively tested for whether they are truly additional (i.e. they wouldn't have happened anyway) and whether they will give rise to the reduction in emissions they claim.

Thus if you do decide to offset any or all of your emissions, we recommend that you go only for projects that bear this standard. Anything else might just turn out to be snake oil.

## Food miles

As climate concepts go, this one seems to be as simple as it gets. Food has to travel a certain distance from farm to plate. The further it goes, the more transport emissions it causes. Hence it should be best, from a climate perspective, to buy food that has come the shortest distance and hence has the lowest associated 'food miles'.

However, the true picture is more complex. For one thing, it makes a big difference how the food has travelled. Planes are worst of all in emissions terms, followed by cars and heavy goods vehicles (HGVs), though if HGVs are fully loaded they can be relatively efficient, emissions-wise.[6]

More surprisingly, even when you've factored in the mode of transport, the simple idea of food miles can lead you in the wrong direction. It's important to look at the entire greenhouse emissions a particular foodstuff has caused, and not just on the road. For instance, growing tomatoes in greenhouses in the UK, with all the heating and lighting that takes, can cause more overall emissions than growing them in sunny Spain and then transporting them to Britain.[7] And a study in 2006 by the Agribusiness and Economics Research Unit at Lincoln University in Christchurch, New Zealand, concluded that dairy products made in New Zealand and then exported to the European Union were twice as energy efficient as those made locally, and sheep meat four times as efficient.[8]

Partly, such anomalies reflect our increasing desire for food that's out of season locally, or food that could never be grown in the local climate. But they serve to illustrate that looking at how far something has travelled doesn't necessarily help you decide where the lowest emissions lie. Confusions like this would be solved if national governments insisted that products be fully labelled with their cradle-to-grave emissions, which is a policy we should all be pushing for.

In the meantime, a good rule of thumb is that if something is in season, and grown locally, it's likely to have produced fewer emissions than something similar that has come from far away. If a food is out of season, on the other hand, it's harder to tell.

But there's another sting in the food miles tail: the issue of sustainable development. The International Institute for Environment and Development published a report in 2006 saying that the importation of fruit, vegetables and flowers into the UK from sub-Saharan Africa was a vital part of the economy of the countries involved, and supported up to one and a half million livelihoods in some of the poorest countries on Earth. The report also points out that, even though most of the produce is air-freighted, because of lack of infrastructure in the home countries and the danger of perishing en route, the imports still contribute less than 0.1 per cent to the UK's overall greenhouse emissions. Emissions from buildings, personal transport, agriculture and even road miles for transporting food within the United Kingdom all contribute much, much more to the problem. Though Kenyan green beans and fresh-cut flowers have become the unwitting poster child for wasteful food miles, they aren't necessarily the first place we should look for reducing our carbon counts.[9]

## Calculate your carbon footprint

A good start when setting out to reduce your own carbon emissions is to find out what they are. There are now many calculators available on the internet that will help you work out how much greenhouse gas emissions you are personally responsible for. Until now we have all been suffering from a climate version of attention deficit disorder, or perhaps it should be called information deficit disorder. Most of us have no idea how much greenhouse gas we are responsible for, or even which areas of our life produce the most or are most amenable to change.

## At home, work or school

### Switch off at the wall

One of the simplest and most effective things you can do to combat climate change is to switch electrical devices off when you've finished using them. And that means switching them all the way off – at the socket if necessary – rather than just leaving them on standby. It's extraordinary to think that we have learned to be so profligate with energy that the devices we use are actually designed to need power even when they're doing nothing. And it really does make a difference. The International Energy Authority estimates that devices on standby cost the world a full 1 per cent of our greenhouse gas emissions – which is nearly as much as the entire aviation industry.

The UK's Energy Saving Trust has published a report with the jaunty title 'The Ampere Strikes Back' which highlights exactly how much electricity the new gadgets of the electronic age actually draw, even when you think you're not using them.[10] And that means wasting money as well as emissions. By leaving things on standby, a typical gadget-lover is pouring £200 a year down the drain.

### Stay warm, stay cool

It makes clear climate sense to ensure that your home is as well protected from the elements as it can possibly be. Any heat that escapes in winter, or cool air in summer, means that you'll have to waste more emissions. If you live in a house, make sure the insulation in the loft is as good as it can be. Seal off draughts around windows and consider lining curtains. And, yes, turn down the thermostat by a few degrees. Most of our homes are overheated. Since 1970 the interior temperatures of UK buildings have risen by about 5°C.[11] If you're moving home, ask the landlord or vendor how energy efficient the new house is, and don't be afraid to demand changes – such as better insulation – that will make it more efficient. If you're staying put in the UK, the Energy Saving Trust will perform a free check to help you work out how efficient your home is, and how to make it more so.[12]

## Change your light bulbs

It's time that the old, wasteful, incandescent light bulbs were consigned to the scrapheap of history. New, low-energy light bulbs now work brilliantly, and for a fraction of the electricity (and hence emissions). They cost more to buy – though that might change – but they pay for themselves many times over in energy savings. It's really worth changing every light bulb you have.

## Buy the most energy-efficient appliances that you can

Most white goods, such as fridges, washing machines and so on, have been getting more efficient with each new design. Manufacturers have done this expressly because governments have insisted that machines have to tell you how much energy they use, and customers have voted with their wallets. It really does make sense to get the very latest and most efficient machines each time you need new ones. It also makes sense to wash your clothes at the coolest temperature possible.

The Energy Saving Trust points out that electronic gadgets, meanwhile, have been going in the opposite direction –

getting hungrier for energy with each new design. Digital radios, for instance, draw much more energy than their analogue counterparts, and plasma TVs are monster power-users. If you want to buy a flat TV, go instead for an LCD screen, which is much less energy intensive. It's good general practice to minimise your gadgets as much as possible, and always to ask for the most energy efficient. This isn't about being penny-pinching. It's all about treating energy as the precious resource that it actually is. Also, as with white goods, the more customers seek energy efficient gadgets, the more pressure there will be on manufacturers to meet the demand.

## Recycle and reuse

It's a climate cliché but it really does help to reuse plastic bags, minimise packaging and recycle as much as you can, especially aluminium cans. Anything that saves energy is good for cutting greenhouse emissions and reusing a plastic bag even just once means reducing the energy needed to make more. The same principle applies to all the packaging guff that supermarkets try to sell you. Also, much of the stuff you throw away ends up in landfills, where it creates methane – an even more potent greenhouse gas than carbon dioxide.

## Watch exactly how much electricity you're using

If you can, it's a great idea to get a 'smart meter'. This is a simple device that shows you up front, in your living room or kitchen, exactly how much electricity you're using. Some will also show you how this compares to last week, or last year. Research shows strongly that people who know how much electricity they're using tend to cut down on it. It's also satisfying to see how your efforts to cut emissions are being rewarded.

## Switch to a 'green' supplier

See whether you can switch your energy supplier to a company that provides only renewable or low-carbon energy. In most countries there isn't enough of this on the grid to go round for everybody, but the more people push for it, the greater the pressure will be on electricity companies to find alternatives.

## Do-it-yourself

Technologies already exist for installing wind turbines and solar panels on buildings, though they are currently expensive. Prices will start to drop as more people take them up, and planning permission should gradually become easier as public attitudes change. Also watch out for the home-size combined heat and power units that will soon be coming on the market. These will allow you to burn gas to make electricity, and also to make direct use of the heat this generates.

# Travel

## Cut down on your car

Road vehicles account for a staggering 10 per cent of all global greenhouse emissions. What's more, an astonishing proportion of car journeys are for very short distances. Consider walking, or cycling. Try and pool your journeys, or catch a bus or train if you can. For longer distances, trains can be fantastic, low-hassle ways to travel and they also have a tenth of the emissions per passenger of a typical car.

If you live in a town or city, take advantage of the public transport whenever you can. If you live in the countryside, try to persuade your local administration to set up an on-demand bus service, such as the UK's 'Wigglybus', which has flexible routes and can be booked by individuals even after it has set off.

If you replace your car, consider getting a hybrid, or one that will run on biodiesel. Go for models that are more efficient. Consider taking an eco-driving course to learn how to make the most of each precious drop of petrol. And always make sure your tyres are properly inflated.

## Fly less – and if you do fly, offset

It's not entirely just to point an accusing finger at flying and say that it's the major climate villain. In fact, three-quarters of the world's transport emissions come from road vehicles, and flying accounts for only a few per cent of the global total for greenhouse gases.

However, flying certainly adds a hefty weight to an individual's carbon footprint. There are some developments in improved efficiency of planes, and new attempts to find a low-carbon alternative to current jet fuel. But new fuels are unlikely to be available for at least the next few decades, and efficiency improvements look set to be overwhelmed by the sheer increasing weight of passenger numbers.

Thus, it's definitely a good idea to try to fly less. If you do fly, try to choose an airline with a relatively young, and hence energy efficient, fleet. If it's a short-haul flight, check that a train wouldn't do just as well. Consider offsetting the emissions from your flight, and, if you do this, make sure you choose a reliable company with projects that adhere to the Gold Standard.

# Have an influence

## Stay informed

The climate story – scientific, technological and especially political – is developing every day. It can be hard to see your way through the blizzard of information but it does pay to stay informed. At the back of this book we list some good websites and sources of information to trust. (As with everything else in life, when you're deciding who to trust, one of the best ways is to look at what they have to gain.) We'll also do our best to keep our own website, www.thehottopic.net, abreast of the latest developments.

## Be open-minded

You can make a big difference by being prepared to consider some of the more controversial solutions to the problem. For instance, the siting of new wind farms is often bogged down in local planning permissions, and nuclear power has a vocal set of opponents who often aren't prepared to consider the pros as well as the cons. Keep your mind as open as you can; consider all the arguments in the light of the serious threat of climate change. And remember that any kind of change – especially a shift in culture of the magnitude we need – also requires difficult choices. We human beings are deeply conservative in principle, but in practice we have used our flexibility and ingenuity to great effect in the world. These are the qualities that we all need to use for the good of the climate.

It will also be important to be receptive to imaginative new ideas to help us tackle the problem. One intriguing suggestion is that of personal carbon allowances, often advanced in the form of a 'carbon credit card'. This would work like a top-up card for a mobile phone. Each adult would receive an allowance of carbon emissions, to be used against, say, electricity, heating and personal transport. Every purchase in one of these areas would require a swipe of the credit card. If you need more than your allowance, you pay to top your card back up again. If you need less, you can sell your surplus for money. The system for paying extra or receiving money could be as simple as a bank cash machine.

Most versions of this idea assume it will apply only within one nation. But there are some interesting potential variations. For instance, we could each have a personal allowance for our domestic emissions, but any international travel would need carbon credits from a Gold Standard accredited project overseas.

One major advantage of an approach like this is that it would focus our attention on exactly what emissions we are responsible for and encourage us specifically to do something about it. The British government commissioned a preliminary report to study the scope of the different schemes proposed to date, and it makes fascinating reading.[13]

## Vote with your ballot, your wallet and your feet

When you vote, check exactly where the candidates stand on climate issues and put pressure on them to take global warming seriously. There are plenty of websites that will tell you what your representative has said on the subject, and we list some of these at the end of the book. Even if an election is a long way off, lobby your local representatives by e-mail or letter. Chapter 11 explains what sort of international climate agreement they should be pushing for. Tell them they need to seek a global accord to keep greenhouse gases below 450 ppm $CO_2$eq. Ask them to push for important national policies, especially labelling all products according to their greenhouse impacts so that you, the consumer, can make informed choices.

As we've outlined above, even without full information about cradle-to-grave emissions, you can still make a difference by what you buy and how you travel. It's worth keeping the climate in mind with every financial decision you make.

## Act local to change global

The evidence is growing around the world that pressure from local organisations, city councils and states can sway national policies on climate change. We described in Chapter 13 how the former Australian Prime Minister John Howard's hand was forced into backing a national emissions trading scheme by intense pressure from Australia's individual state governments; and how action in the US by local city mayors, and by California and the north-eastern states, has cast President Bush's stance in an increasingly untenable light. In fact, the world over, individual cities, towns and communities are not waiting for governments to act; instead they are taking the issue of climate change into their own hands.

In the UK, for example, the city of Newcastle has ambitions to be the first in the world to go fully carbon neutral. It has put in place a host of policies, starting with the local council itself, but then reaching further to encourage both local businesses and individual citizens to change their climate ways without harming their lifestyles. The initiative is hugely popular and now local politicians there have to vie with one another to show their commitment to tackling climate change.[14]

Woking Borough Council in Surrey has had a similar strategy in place since 2003.[15] And local initiatives abound. In July 2003 a second giant wind turbine was installed to tower over the small town of Swaffham in Norfolk. The first had been in place since 1999 and by the time questionnaires went round to local residents asking whether a second would be acceptable almost 90 per cent voted yes. Together the turbines provide three-quarters of Swaffham's domestic electricity, and the residents are intensely proud of their action.

Elsewhere in the world, many other local cities and regions are working to reduce their own greenhouse emissions. It will probably come as no surprise to hear that Heidelberg in Germany has long been a pioneer of local action on climate change. But what about Austin, Texas? The city of Austin, which lies in the heart of oil country in one of the most conservative states in the USA, is also one of the most progressive when it comes to dealing with climate change. Their Austin Climate Protection Plan is so comprehensive it should shame any government into action.[16] They plan to make every aspect of the city's operations carbon neutral by 2020, to implement 'the most aggressive utility greenhouse gas reduction plan in the nation', make the city's building codes the most energy efficient in America and encourage all businesses and individuals to reduce their carbon footprint to zero.

Western Cape province in South Africa is likely to suffer greatly from future changes in climate, and the inhabitants know it. And so, instead of sitting back and waiting for developed nations to do their part, the regional government has decided to take matters into its own hands. In July 2007, it published a detailed strategy document explaining exactly how it plans to improve efficiency, switch to renewable energy sources and reduce the overall carbon footprint.[17] The targets are impressive. By 2014, the regional government plans to increase overall energy efficiency for the region by 15 per cent, generate 15 per cent of its electricity from renewable resources and reduce its overall greenhouse emissions by 10 per cent. This is extraordinary news. Such a unilateral step, taken in a developing country, could have political repercussions that matter even more than the actual emissions cuts.

The bottom line of all this is that pushing to change the ways of your school, workplace or local council really can make a difference. As local initiatives spread, and as local politicians get the message that climate policies matter, small seeds can flourish quickly and very effectively. If Newcastle, Austin, and the Western Cape province can do it, so can we all.

## Be positive

Don't be 'greener than thou'. The evidence suggests that making people feel guilty makes them less likely to act, not more. And none of us has the right to be smug, no matter what we are doing to reduce our emissions. Since the day we were born each one of us has been inadvertently contributing to the greenhouse problem, and the wealth we now have has been built on the emissions of previous generations. Anything we do now is still doing no more than paying back a fraction of that old debt. Thinking otherwise is to believe that, once you've bought your Prius, climate change is now somebody else's problem. It's not. We're all responsible, and will continue to be until we've stopped global greenhouse emissions in their tracks.

It is, however, a good idea to admire other people's efforts to cut back. The latest research suggests that people are more likely to act altruistically over climate if they feel it enhances their reputation.[18] Gentle persuasion can also help, as can taking the lead. If you've implemented ways of cutting carbon at home, see if you can set up the same ways at your place of work or school.

Opinion polls differ on exactly how people feel about climate change, and what they currently believe. But there is still a substantial proportion of people who think the problem isn't important, or that it doesn't apply to them.[19] One way to help is to talk the people you meet into taking climate seriously. (Our handy guide to common climate myths should help here.)

It's also important not to fall into the trap of thinking that what you do to change your own life doesn't make a difference. It does. Even if the actual amount of emissions that you've cut is only a tiny proportion of the global total, the only way we will solve the climate problem is to do so together. UK negotiators have already discovered that the country's unilateral decision to cut its emissions by 60 per cent by 2050 meant that developing countries such as China and Brazil immediately took them seriously. And the actions of individuals really can put pressure on the government to respond – as the situation in the US clearly shows.

Above all, don't despair. The climate problem is certainly a hard one, but it's not intractable. If you still need convincing, here's a final image that should cheer you up. When we learn to capture sunlight efficiently, we'll have all the energy we need on our very doorstep. Enough energy to power the entire world's requirements can be collected from the land area contained in the six tiny squares on the next two pages.[20]

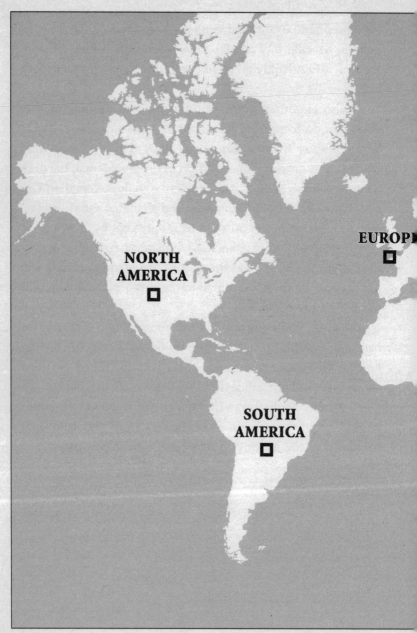

If all the sunlight falling on each of the areas inside these six squares could be completely harvested, that would supply the entire world's energy needs. (Source: Nathan Lewis)

ASIA AND RUSSIA
□

AFRICA
□

AUSTRALASIA
□

# Appendix

## CLIMATE MYTHS, HALF-TRUTHS AND MISCONCEPTIONS

### The science of warming

#### It's not really warming

Yes, it is. The years 1998 and 2005 were the joint hottest on record (that is, in the past 150 years). The years 2002, 2003 and 2004 were, respectively, the third, fourth and fifth warmest on record. In fact, ten of the past eleven years have been in the top eleven. Reconstructions of past temperatures using corals, ice cores and other techniques show that the temperature is hotter now than it has been for at least 1,000 years and probably longer (see Chapter 1).

#### It was warmer during the Middle Ages than it is now

No, it wasn't. Temperatures are higher now than they have been for at least 1,000 years (see Chapter 1).

#### The ice cores show that temperature goes up before $CO_2$ at the end of ice ages, so $CO_2$ can't cause warming

The ice cores do show a time lag between the onset of warming and the rise of $CO_2$ at the end of each ice age.

However, that doesn't mean that carbon dioxide doesn't cause warming. In fact, nobody thinks that carbon dioxide is what causes the ice ages to stop. Instead, a wobble in our planet's orbit changes the distribution of the sunlight we receive. That causes a little warming, which sets in motion other processes to release carbon dioxide. For instance, a warmer ocean holds less carbon dioxide, so more makes it into the atmosphere. Also, a warmer, wetter climate means that less iron-rich dust is blown out on to the sea. In ice ages, this iron probably feeds the growth of plankton that soak up carbon dioxide. Cut off this nutrient source and you have fewer plankton, and more $CO_2$.

The important part is what happens next. That extra carbon dioxide causes warming in its own right, which begets more carbon dioxide which begets more warming. According to the ice cores, the overall warming takes some 5,000 years to complete. The slight shift in sunlight from the Earth's wobble wouldn't be nearly enough to do the job by itself. Instead, most of the warming (after the first few hundred years) comes from feedbacks, including carbon dioxide.

That's a perfectly natural process and is only used by climate scientists to show that carbon dioxide does in fact warm the Earth if it goes up by even just a small amount. The increase at the end of an ice age, by the way, took carbon dioxide levels to a much lower level than they are today (see Chapter 1).

## Temperatures were going down in the middle of the twentieth century even though $CO_2$ was rising, so $CO_2$ can't cause warming

This is a very popular argument put forward by climate sceptics, but it skates over the fact that scientists can explain why temperatures dropped a little in the middle of the twentieth century in the northern hemisphere. In fact, burning dirty fossil fuels produces sulphur-containing particles called aerosols, which reflect sunlight back to space and thus help to cool the planet. They act in a sort of tug-of-war with carbon dioxide, creating cooling that offsets the greenhouse warming.

Researchers now believe that these aerosols were responsible for the slight cooling that took place between about 1940 and the late 1960s. The reason they didn't keep cooling is twofold: we cleaned up our act by banning the fuels that were choking our cities, and carbon dioxide levels rose so high that they won the tug-of-war. Also, the reason this cooling was only seen in the northern hemisphere is that there was neither enough land mass nor enough industry in the southern hemisphere to produce enough aerosols to counteract the effect of carbon dioxide (see Chapter 2).

## Human carbon dioxide emissions are tiny compared with natural sources so they can't be important

It's true that natural sources give off very much more carbon dioxide than humans do, but it's also true that natural sources take up very much more carbon dioxide, too. Roughly speaking, the natural world is in carbon balance. Our own human emissions are what have thrown the world off this balance.

## Carbon dioxide concentrations are tiny compared with the other gases in the atmosphere, so they can't be important

Carbon dioxide does indeed make up a tiny part of the atmosphere; there are just four molecules of $CO_2$ in every 10,000 that the air holds. But carbon dioxide also punches considerably above its weight in the greenhouse effect. The main constituents of air – nitrogen and oxygen – can't trap infrared radiation at all. By contrast, carbon dioxide, even in small quantities, is a very effective trapper of heat. It also triggers feedbacks which enable the air to soak up more water – which is a greenhouse gas in its own right. Thus, changing $CO_2$ and the other greenhouse gases by even a small amount can affect the temperature of the entire atmosphere, just as adding a few drops of ink can change the colour of a bath full of water (see Chapter 1).

## Humans aren't responsible for the warming – it's all down to a natural cycle/changes in the Sun

In fact, the warming over the past few decades has human fingerprints all over it. There's no natural cycle that can explain what we've seen, and the Sun has been going in the wrong direction. (Left to itself, the Sun would have caused a slight cooling.) What's more, models tell us that the increased greenhouse gas concentrations that we have had should cause exactly the changes that we have already seen. There's no more room for doubt in this. Wedunnit (see Chapter 2).

## Impacts of climate change

## The Earth's climate is constantly changing, so why should we worry?

Our planet's climate is certainly very restless, and in times past it has been both very much warmer and very much colder than it is today. But the whole of human civilisation has been built around the climate we have now. For instance, just a few hundred thousand years ago, sea level was several metres higher than it is now, but back then there were no coastal cities waiting to be drowned (see Chapter 1).

## A little warming could be a good thing

There are a few parts of the world where a little warming might indeed be a good thing. For instance, in the middle latitudes – northern Europe, the US and parts of Russia – a temperature rise of about 2°C should actually increase overall crop yields. However, the problem with climate change is that you can't pick and choose its effects. Even for these countries, the increased food production will also come with northward movement of the storm tracks (less rain, more fires and droughts), more intense individual rainstorms (risk of flooding), rising sea level, more intense storms (threats to coastal cities) and more intense heatwaves (mass mortality and threat to crops). In the poorest parts of the world, the effects will be more severe even with a modest rise in temperature. In fact, that's already happening. Even if you didn't want to act on this for the sake of social justice, you'd need to realise that in a fully global economy what brings benefits for some countries will eventually hurt the rest.

The chances are that we are already going to experience the effects of a few degrees warming in any case – that much is too late to stop. But action that we take now could help us avert worse warming, in which even the richest, most northerly countries would suffer (see Chapters 4–5 and Chapter 6).

## If the world warms, fewer people will die from the cold

It's true that there will be fewer extreme cold events in the world, and the reduction in deaths from cold will almost certainly outweigh the increase in deaths from heatwaves.

But that doesn't mean humans will survive better overall. As well as direct deaths from the heat, people will also be more vulnerable to flooding, infectious diseases and starvation. The IPCC report is unequivocal about this. 'Impacts and Adaptations', Working Group II, Chapter 8, says clearly that in terms of numbers of lives these increased dangers far outweigh the reduction in deaths from the cold.

However, many of these deaths are also preventable, as long as we adapt to the changes that are already inevitable (Chapter 3), and reduce greenhouse emissions to stop the changes getting worse (Chapter 6 and following). As German scientist John Schellnhuber put it, we need to 'avoid the uncontrollable and control the unavoidable'.

## 'Climate porn', or disasters that aren't necessarily waiting to happen

### The ocean conveyor belt is about to switch off and plunge the world into an ice age

In fact, though it was a popular disaster scenario in the Hollywood movie *The Day After Tomorrow*, this would be very unlikely to happen at least in this century, even if we didn't act to curb greenhouse gases (see Chapter 5).

### Antarctica is about to slide into the sea

The old, cold eastern part of Antarctica is very unlikely to melt even if temperatures were to rise dramatically. Nobody knows for certain exactly how safe the more vulnerable West Antarctic Ice Sheet is, but we can probably save most of it from melting if we act quickly (see Chapter 5).

### The Amazon rainforest is already doomed

Though one model suggests that large parts of the Amazon could be vulnerable by the middle of the century, most say that the rainforest would be likely to stay intact until the end of the century even if we did nothing to combat greenhouse emissions. If we switch off the chainsaws and divert our attention to cutting down emissions instead, the Amazon rainforest should be around for a very long time to come.[21]

## Misattributions and misconceptions

### The disappearing snows of Kilimanjaro prove/ disprove the existence of global warming

Mount Kilimanjaro is a special case that tells us absolutely nothing about global warming. Its ice cap has certainly existed for some 11,000 years, is currently retreating and may well soon disappear. But we don't yet know exactly why. Because the retreat began in the early nineteenth century, those initial movements can't have been triggered by human-induced climate change (although they might have come from some other human trigger, for instance land-use changes). However, global warming might now be helping to tip it over the edge. The fact that the glacier has survived intact through thousands of years of natural climate fluctuations, and is only now on the point of vanishing completely, supports this idea. But as yet, we simply don't know. Researchers only have a few years of detailed measurements on Kilimanjaro's glacier, and they won't be sure exactly what is causing it to vanish until they have many more years of data.

However, all the fuss about Kilimanjaro is really just a distraction from the bigger picture. Glaciers are retreating the world over, from tropics to poles, and in most of these cases global warming is clearly to blame.

### The war in Darfur/Hurricane Katrina was caused by global warming

In fact, we don't know. Scientists can't reliably attribute any single event to global warming. However, they can say that more strong hurricanes/droughts/floods/famines are on their way as a result of climate change. We can also learn from our past troubles. Whether or not the events in New Orleans and Darfur were 'caused' by global warming, they still show us how devastating climate changes can be if we are not properly prepared (see Chapter 3).

## The power of technology

### Nothing bad will happen for decades, so we should just wait for new technology to come along and solve the problem

We will need new technology to help us out of our climate mess. But as well as developing this, we will also need to start using the technologies and energy-efficiency strategies we've already got (Chapters 7–9). Dangerous climate change is with us, and there will be more to come in the next few decades whatever we do today (see Chapters 3 and 4). Even more importantly, the longer we wait, the harder it will be to avert the worst consequences of future climate change. As we explained in Chapter 6, we need to keep greenhouse gas levels below 450 ppm $CO_2$eq. To achieve that, emissions will have to peak within the next fifteen years and then start to fall. The only option is to act now.

## Economics

### We can't afford to tackle climate change

In fact, tackling climate change turns out to be surprisingly cheap. Many of the strategies we will need to employ to increase efficiency will actually save money where it has previously been wasted (see Chapter 10), and investment in new technologies could well lead to a growth spurt.

## We'd be better off spending the money on aid

This is at best misguided. For one thing, if the money is not used for dealing with climate change, it's very unlikely to go to aid instead. (For instance, the International Energy Agency predicts that more than $20 trillion will need to be invested between now and 2030 to meet the world's growing hunger for power. The choice is whether this is invested in fossil fuels or in low-carbon forms of energy, rather than what else to spend the money on.)

Also, this is not about trying to solve all the troubles in the world – which is just as well since that goal has spectacularly evaded us so far. Instead it's about solving a specific problem faced by all of us, so we can leave behind a climate that our grandchildren will be able to weather.

As we've already said, the next two decades offer our only possible window of opportunity to rein in greenhouse gas levels to one that will achieve this goal. After that, no future generations of humans would be able to keep the greenhouse problem in check. For us, or our children, or our grand-children, it would be too late.

Because of this, we believe it's better to think of the costs of climate change more as an insurance policy against a dangerous future than as a hand-out. And put that way, it becomes a bargain. The amount of money that we would need annually to deal with climate change is barely half the global insurance industry's annual turnover (see Chapter 10).

## Politics

### There's no point in doing anything because China's new power stations will swamp the effects of everywhere else

We will never come up with a global agreement on climate change until everybody takes responsibility for their emissions. Yes, China is the biggest overall emitter, and one of the fastest growing. But it still puts out much less greenhouse gas per head of population than the entire developed world. It has also been responsible for very little of the problem to date. To have any chance of persuading developing countries to join an international agreement the developed countries – to date the main cause of the problem – will need to tackle their own emissions. UK negotiators found that their government's unilateral commitment to reducing its emissions by 60 per cent by 2050 made a big difference to how they were received by the developing world, even though the actual amount involved is only a small proportion of the global total (see Chapters 12 and 13).

### It's already too late, and there's nothing we can do

It *isn't* too late, and there *is* something we can do. Though we can't stop the initial effects of climate change, some of which are already here, we do still have a chance to hold off the very worst things the climate could throw at us. In this book, we have laid out the solutions to the problem: adaptations (Chapter 3), technological (Chapters 6–9), economic (Chapter 10) and political (Chapters 11–13). We have also shown exactly what you can do to make all this happen (Chapter 14). This is neither the time to panic nor the time to bury your head in the sand. It's the time for action.

# Glossary

'**Business as usual**' This phrase is used throughout the IPCC reports and in many other greenhouse analyses to refer to a projected scenario where nothing is done to curb greenhouse emissions in the future.

**Carbon Capture and Storage (CCS)** The idea is to burn fossil fuels in the normal way to generate power, but then to grab the carbon dioxide and bury it before it can escape into the atmosphere. This has the great advantage that it can remove emissions from traditional fossil-fuel plants, thus buying the world some time to develop new low-carbon alternatives. CCS is likely to be especially important for countries like India and China, which are currently exploiting their vast coal reserves at an increasing rate to fuel extremely rapid economic growth. However, it is not yet at a commercial stage and plants using CCS will always be more expensive than those that simply vent their emissions into the atmosphere, so some kind of economic mechanism will be needed to make it viable.

**Clean Development Mechanism (CDM)** A mechanism devised for the Kyoto Protocol in which a (rich) developed country can gain carbon credit by setting up a programme to reduce emissions in a (poorer) developing country, such as India.

**CO$_2$eq** This is shorthand for 'carbon dioxide equivalent' and is a measure of the combined effects of all greenhouse gases: carbon dioxide, nitrous oxide, methane, and the rarer trace greenhouse gases such as chlorofluorocarbons.

It's an important number because different greenhouse gases are more or less effective at causing warming. So to find out how much warming we can expect from all of them, it's not enough just to add their concentrations together. Instead, researchers give a different weight to the concentration of each gas according to its greenhouse potency, using carbon dioxide as the standard.

The resulting number gives the value of pure carbon dioxide that would have the same warming effect as all the greenhouse gases combined. It is a much better measure of the greenhouse effect than simply taking carbon dioxide on its own, and is the one we have used throughout this book.

**IPCC** The Intergovernmental Panel on Climate Change (IPCC) is an international body formed by scientists and government representatives to assess the risk posed by human-induced changes in climate. It was created in 1988 and is open to all members of the United Nations and the World Meteorological Organization. The IPCC doesn't carry out its own research. Instead, it produces reports that synthesise the current state of climate science.

Because the IPCC must reflect the consensus view of all its many contributors, it has a reputation for being conservative. It is also widely considered to be the definitive authority on the science of climate change. It won the Nobel Peace Prize in 2007.

In this book, when we write 'the IPCC report' we are referring to the latest one, the 'Fourth Assessment Report', which was published in November 2007 by Cambridge University Press. The report comprises four volumes: the scientific basis, impacts and adaptations, mitigation of climate change, and an overall synthesis report. It runs to several thousand pages, has taken six years to complete and contains contributions from thousands of scientists and government representatives from more than 130 countries.

**Joint Implementation (JI)** A mechanism devised for the Kyoto Protocol, in which a (rich) developed country can gain carbon credit by setting up a programme to reduce emissions in a (poorer) relatively well-developed country, such as one from the former eastern bloc.

**Kyoto Protocol** The Kyoto Protocol was born out of the UNFCCC (see below) in 1997. It sets out emissions targets for all signatories with the aim of reducing global greenhouse emissions by 5 per cent by 2012. For more explanation of the strengths and weaknesses of the Protocol, and the need for a new international treaty, see Part III, especially Chapters 10 and 11.

**ppm** This stands for 'parts per million' and is the usual measuring unit applied to greenhouse gases, since they exist in relatively small quantities in the atmosphere. One ppm is 0.0001 per cent.

**United Nations Framework Convention on Climate Change (UNFCCC)** This is the world's first international climate treaty. It came into force in 1994 and has since been signed by 189 countries – including the USA. The stated objective of the treaty is to achieve '. . . stabilisation of greenhouse gas concentrations in the atmosphere at a level that would prevent dangerous anthropocentric [human-induced] interference with the climate system'.

# Useful Websites

To calculate your carbon footprint:
http://www.carbonfootprint.com/

To get advice about saving energy/reducing emissions:
http://www.energysavingtrust.org.uk/ (UK)
http://www.carbontrust.co.uk/ (UK)

To offset carbon emissions:
http://www.cdmgoldstandard.org/

To contact your local politicians:
www.theyworkforyou.com (UK)
www.writetothem.com (UK)

To stay informed about the latest climate change science:
www.nature.com/climate/index.html
http://environment.newscientist.com/channel/earth/
    climate-change/
http://www.realclimate.org/ (more technical)

To get accurate answers to frequently asked questions about climate change:

http://gristmill.grist.org/skeptics

http://environment.newscientist.com/channel/earth/dn11462

For more information about international organisations related to climate:

http://www.iea.org/ (International Energy Agency)

http://unfccc.int/2860.php (United Nations Framework Convention on Climate Change)

http://www.ipcc.ch/ (Intergovernmental Panel on Climate Change)

http://www.wmo.ch/pages/index_en.html (World Meteorological Organisation)

# Notes

## Preface

1. D. A. King, *Science*, vol. 303, pp. 176–7, 2004. This article was based on the Zuckerman Lecture 'The Science of Climate Change: Adapt, Mitigate or Ignore?', given by David King in 2002 and available online at www.foundation.org.uk/events/pdf/200210031_King.pdf

## 1. Warming World

1. This is dangerous because even something that seems like a concrete measurement of temperature can turn out to be nothing of the kind. A case in point is the famous 'frost fairs' held on a frozen River Thames in London. Although certain freezing events did take place in the period known as the Little Ice Age, the river has actually frozen over twenty-two times since the thirteenth century, including some periods that were warm elsewhere in the world. The real reason turns out to be local cold snaps, combined with narrow bridge spans that kept the surging tide safely downstream. No complete freezes have happened since 1835, when London Bridge's piers were widened, allowing the tide to flow much further upstream. See P. D. Jones, T. J. Osborn and K. R. Briffa, 'The Evolution of Climate over the Last Millennium', *Science*, vol. 292 (5517), pp. 662–7, 27 April 2001, DOI: 10.1126/science.1059126; and the discussion at http://www.realclimate.org/index.php/archives/2006/03/art-and-climate/
2. It's not quite as simple as it sounds, because growth can be affected by amounts of sunlight, moisture and even how much the tree grew the

year before. But researchers have become expert at assembling all these factors to read the trees' record books.

3. Oxygen comes in different flavours called 'isotopes', each of which has a slightly different atomic weight. Changing temperature alters the ratio in which these isotopes are incorporated from air into the snow.

4. For much more detail about this, see 'Climate Change 2007: The Physical Science Basis' (written by Working Group I and subtitled 'Working Group I Contribution to the Fourth Assessment Report of the IPCC Corporate Author Intergovernmental Panel on Climate Change', and hereafter referred to as IPCC WGI), chapter 6, section 6.6, IPCC reports (Cambridge University Press, 2007), especially figure 6.10c. Full details can be found at: http://www.cambridge.org/browse/browse_highlights.asp?subjectid=710

5. It's hard to tell because there are fewer records from the southern hemisphere – thanks to the lower land mass as well as less overall research – so these conclusions are dominated by northern hemisphere temperatures. See P. D. Jones, T. J. Osborn and K. R. Briffa, 'The Evolution of Climate over the Last Millennium', *Science*, vol. 292 (5517), pp. 662–7, 27 April 2001, DOI: 10.1126/science.1059126; and Timothy Spall et al., 'The Spatial Extent of 20th Century Warmth in the Context of the Past 1200 Years', *Science*, vol. 311, p. 841, 2006, DOI: 10.1126/science.1120514.

6. Quoted in Spencer Weart, *The Discovery of Global Warming* (Cambridge, Mass.: Harvard University Press, 2003), p. 1.

7. See IPCC WGI, chapter 6, especially Figure 6.10c, which shows an assembly of all the different reconstructions of temperature.

8. IPCC WGI, chapter 3.

9. The last ice age was between 3° and 5°C cooler than present; see IPCC WGI, chapter 6. Also note that the temperatures observed to date have been masked by two effects: the cooling effect of particles of air pollution and the time lag caused by the thermal inertia of the ocean.

10. See IPCC WGI, chapter 3. 1996 was the only recent year that stayed relatively cool. Much fuss was made of the news that an adjustment to NASA's records meant that the year of the Oklahoma dust bowl, 1934, was marginally warmer in the US than 1998. While sceptics claimed that this threw the global warming research into disarray, in fact it did no such thing. These two years were long known to be within a few hundredths of a degree of each other in the record of local American temperatures. But averaged over the whole world, 1998 and 2005 remain the joint record holders. Regional records can be interesting, but they don't tell the global story.

11. IPCC WGI, Summary for Policymakers.

12. The most important greenhouse gas in the atmosphere (apart from water vapour) is carbon dioxide, but there are also substantial amounts of methane, nitrous oxide (otherwise known as laughing gas) and small amounts of a set of gases containing chlorine which, as well as being greenhouse gases, also destroy the ozone layer.

13. Water in the atmosphere is extraordinarily dynamic. Between being sucked up from the ocean and rained out again via a cloud, an average water molecule will inhabit the air for just ten days.

14. This so-called 'water vapour feedback' formed the basis for one of the strongest critical arguments against the dangers of climate change. Respected researcher and notable sceptic Richard Lindzen, a professor at MIT, believed that the upper part of the troposphere would dry out as carbon dioxide increased, and this would balance the increased wetness lower down. However, measurements have since proved that argument incorrect. There's more about this in Chapter 2.

15. We don't have space here to go into the history of how the greenhouse effect was discovered, though it's a fascinating story. But if you're interested, you could go to Weart, *The Discovery of Global Warming*, or Gabrielle Walker, *An Ocean of Air* (London: Bloomsbury, 2007), chapter 3.

16. If air is in relatively short supply, some of the carbon will emerge in the form of black soot, which is why when you burn things that used to be alive – like toast – they go black. Some will probably also be emitted as carbon monoxide, the deadly gas that comes out of car exhaust pipes and that people use to commit suicide.

17. For much more on this see the excellent chapter 8, 'Digging Up the Dead', in Tim Flannery, *The Weather Makers* (London: Penguin Books, 2007).

18. Although in principle the process of making food from carbon dioxide, eating it and breathing the carbon dioxide back out again ought to be carbon neutral for humans, agriculture has changed that. Though our hunter-gatherer ancestors were indeed in carbon harmony with their food, the energy we put into farming, and the greenhouse gases this emits, mean that breathing is no longer a carbon-neutral activity. See Chapter 8 for more about the direct emissions from agriculture.

19. It might seem surprising that ice can be different ages in different parts of the continent. But the ice in Antarctica flows constantly, so although the continent has been ice-capped for millions of years, the bottommost ice at some of the thickest points has long since been squeezed out like toothpaste from a tube and has disappeared towards the coast. In some places it has also melted, since the ice at the base of the cap is close to the melting point. The age of the ice that remains

depends on how much snow falls in an average year. More snow falls at Vostok than at Dome C, so for the same thickness of ice sheet the ice at the base is younger.

20. See J-R. Petit et al., 'Climate and Atmospheric History of the Past 420,000 Years from the Vostok Ice Core, Antarctica', *Nature*, vol. 399, pp. 429–36, 1999; and R. Spahni et al., 'Atmospheric Methane and Nitrous Oxide of the late Pleistocene from Antarctic Ice Cores', *Science*, vol. 310, pp. 1317–21, 2005. The ice cores also show very dramatically that higher carbon dioxide (and methane) always goes hand in hand with higher temperature. The two march in impressive lockstep. See section 'Climate Myths, Half-Truths and Misconceptions' for the difference in timing between rising temperature and rising carbon dioxide, and why it isn't relevant to this argument.

21. The curve also shows the carbon dioxide levels snaking up and down a little each year as the air 'breathes'. Because there is more land in the northern hemisphere than the southern, each northern summer carbon dioxide levels drop as plants bind it up into food, and each northern winter levels fall again as the plants slow down or die off.

22. See IPCC WGI, chapter 6, especially Question 6.2.

23. There are also recent signs that methane may be levelling off, although nobody yet knows why, so it's not clear whether this good trend will continue. See I. J. Simpson, F. S. Rowland, S. Meinardi and D. R. Blake, 'Influence of Biomass Burning During Recent Fluctuations in the Slow Growth of Global Tropospheric Methane', *Geophysical Research Letters*, vol. 33, L22808, 2006, DOI:10.1029/2006GL027330.

# 2. Whodunnit?

1. F. Foukal, C. Fröhlich, H. Spruit and T. M. L. Wigley, 'Variations in Solar Luminosity and their Effect on the Earth's Climate', *Nature*, vol. 433, pp. 161–6, 2006.

2. Mike Lockwood and Claus Fröhlich, 'Recent Oppositely Directed Trends in Solar Climate Forcings and the Global Mean Surface Air Temperature', *Proc. R. Soc.* A, 2007, DOI: 10.1098/rspa.2007.1880, available on the web at http://www.pubs.royalsoc.ac.uk/media/proceedings_a/rspa20071880.pdf

3. The effect of clouds on climate isn't quite as straightforward as this. Though low-lying clouds do reduce the temperature in this way, clouds in the upper part of the troposphere can actually warm the climate by reflecting infrared radiation back down to Earth. Also, losing clouds means that more warming gets through during the day,

but less heat is retained at night. Struggling to deal with these issues, and to predict exactly how much cloudiness – and what sort – we can expect in the future, is one reason there is such a wide spread of model predictions for how much temperature increase we can expect, with a given increase in carbon dioxide.

4. These particles can cool the planet in two ways. In the so-called 'direct effect' they bounce sunlight directly back into space. But in the 'indirect effect' they can also help to seed cloud droplets which reflect sunlight. If clouds form around aerosols, they tend to make smaller droplets which live longer in the atmosphere before they grow big enough to fall as rain. Thus aerosols also tend to increase the lifetimes of clouds.

5. See, for instance, the University of East Anglia's Climate Research Unit information sheet at http://www.cru.uea.ac.uk/cru/info/volcano/

6. IPCC WGI, chapter 9, section 9.7.

7. Some of this cooling is because of the disappearing ozone layer, which inhibits the lower stratosphere. Since ozone is also a greenhouse gas, it warms its local stratosphere, and losing it means the stratosphere cools down. However, the loss of ozone isn't enough to explain the whole trend. When the models put in both the known amount of ozone loss and the known amount of carbon dioxide and methane, the stratosphere cools by just the same amount as the instruments have measured. Natural spikes occur in the temperature record from the occasional volcanic eruption but greenhouse gases are nonetheless the drivers of the overall cooling. See, for instance, V. Ramaswamy et al., 'Anthropogenic and Natural Influences in the Evolution of Lower Stratospheric Cooling', *Science*, vol. 311, no. 5764, pp. 1138–41, 24 February 2006, DOI: 10.1126/science.1122587. IPCC WGI, chapter 9, also has more on this.

8. GCM originally stood for 'General Circulation Models', which are the atmosphere-only forerunners of modern climate models.

9. V. Ramanathan et al., 'Warming Trends in Asia Amplified by Brown Cloud Solar Absorption', *Nature*, vol. 448, pp. 575–8, 2 August 2006, DOI: 10.1038/nature 06019.

10. The resumption of major volcanic activity after 1956 probably helped, but it came ten years too late to explain the onset of this cooling.

11. See, for instance, Peter A. Stott et al., 'External Control of 20th-Century Temperature by Natural and Anthropogenic Forcings', *Science*, vol. 290, p. 2133, 2000, DOI: 10.1126/science.290.5499.2133, and the accompanying commentary, Francis W. Zwiers and Andrew J. Weaver, 'The Causes of 20th-Century Warming', *Science*, vol. 290, pp. 2081–3, 2000, DOI: 10.1126/science.290.5499.2081. Also Gerald A. Meehl et al., 'Combinations of Natural and Anthropogenic Forcings in Twentieth-Century Climate', *Journal of Climate*, vol. 17, no. 19, pp. 3721–7, 2004.

12. Brian J. Soden et al., 'The Radiative Signature of Upper Tropospheric Moistening', *Science*, vol. 310, p. 841, 2005, DOI: 10.1126/science.1115602.

## 3. Feeling the Heat

1. David W. Inouye, Billy Barr, Kenneth B. Armitage and Brian D. Inouye, 'Climate Change is Affecting Altitudinal Migrants and Hibernating Species', *Proceedings of the National Academy of Sciences*, vol. 97 (4), pp. 1630–33, 15 February 2000.
2. See 'Climate Change 2007: Impacts and Adaptation' (written by Working Group II and subtitled 'Working Group II Contribution to the Fourth Assessment Report of the IPCC Corporate Author Intergovernmental Panel on Climate Change', and hereafter referred to as IPCC WGII), chapter 1, section 1.3.5.6, IPCC reports (Cambridge: Cambridge University Press, 2007).
3. J. Alan Pounds et al., 'Widespread Amphibian Extinctions from Epidemic Disease Driven by Global Warming', *Nature*, vol. 439, pp. 161–7, 12 January 2006, DOI: 10.1038/nature04246. Other researchers have suggested the decline may be down to climate-related reduction in leaf litter on the ground. See Steven M. Whitfield et al., 'Amphibian and Reptile Declines over 35 Years at La Selva, Costa Rica', *Proceedings of the National Academy of Sciences*, vol. 104, pp. 8352–6, 2007.
4. See IPCC WGII, chapter 4.
5. J. C. Stroeve et al., 'Tracking the Arctic's Shrinking Ice Cover: Another Extreme September Minimum in 2004', *Geophysical Research Letters*, vol. 32, L04501, 2005.
6. Gabrielle Walker, 'The Tipping Point of the Iceberg', *Nature*, vol. 441, pp. 802–5, 2006.
7. J. E. Overland, M. C. Spillane, D. B. Percival, M. Wang and H. O. Mofjeld, 'Seasonal and Regional Variation of Pan-Arctic Surface Air Temperature Over the Instrumental Record', *Journal of Climate*, vol. 17, no. 17, pp. 3263–82, 2004.
8. See Gabrielle Walker, 'The Tipping Point of the Iceberg', *Nature*, vol. 441, pp. 802–5, 2006, and T. C. Johns et al., 'Anthropogenic Climate Change for 1860 to 2100 Simulated with the HadCM3 Model Under Updated Emissions Scenarios', *Climate Dynamics*, vol. 20, pp. 583–612, 2003.
9. IPCC WGII, chapter 4, box 4.3.
10. Open ocean plankton might benefit from the lifting of the ice lid, but the Arctic is poor enough in nutrients that this would probably not be

much compensation. See V. Smetacek and V. and S. Nicol, 'Polar Ocean Ecosystems in a Changing World', *Nature*, vol. 437, pp. 362–8, 2005, DOI: 10.1038/nature04161.

11. 'Ocean acidification due to increasing atmospheric carbon dioxide', Royal Society policy document 12/05 (2005).

12. K. Caldeira and M. E. Wickett, 'Anthropogenic Carbon and Ocean pH', *Nature*, vol. 425, p. 365, 2003.

13. http://www.tos.org/oceanography/issues/issue_archive/issue_pdfs/20_2/20.2_caldeira.pdf

14. See IPCC WGII, Summary for Policymakers.

15. See IPCC WGII, chapter 4, for much more on the specific services that different unmanaged ecosystems provide us with.

16. For this and following, see the discussion in IPCC WGI, chapter 9, section 9.5.4.3.1.

17. Michela Biasutti and Alessandra Giannini, 'Robust Sahel Drying in Response to Late 20th Century Forcings', *Geophysical Research Letters*, vol. 33, L11706, 2006, DOI: 10.1029/2006GL026067.

18. Julian Borger, 'Scorched', *Guardian*, Saturday 28 April 2007.

19. In the past thirty years, total numbers of hurricanes have decreased slightly over that time period in most parts of the tropical ocean. However, there have been unusually large numbers of hurricanes in the North Atlantic in nine of the last eleven years, culminating in the record-breaking 2005 season.

20. T. P. Barnett et al., 'Penetration of Human-Induced Warming into the World's Oceans', *Science*, vol. 309, p. 284, 2005, DOI: 10.1126/science.1112418.

21. K. A. Emanuel, 'Increasing Destructiveness of Tropical Cyclones over the Past 30 Years', *Nature*, vol. 436, pp. 686–8, 2005. See also Emanuel's excellent essay, available at http://wind.mit.edu/~emanuel/anthro2.htm, which gives much more detail about the mechanics of hurricanes, and also points out that the increased damage felt in the US over the past thirty years has as yet more to do with the rush to the coast and flimsy building standards than the impact of the stronger hurricanes. Also note that it's possible that increasing wind strengths high in the atmosphere will help to cut up baby hurricanes before they turn into dangerous adults.

22. Christoph Schär and Gerd Jendritzky, 'Hot News from Summer 2003', *Nature*, vol. 432, pp. 559–60, 2 December 2004.

23. For arguments in favour of the higher figure see http://www.earth-policy.org/Updates/2006/Update56.htm

24. P. A. Stott, D. A. Stone and M. R. Allen, 'Human Contribution to the European Heat Wave of 2003', *Nature*, vol. 432, pp. 610–14, 2 December 2004.

# 4. In the Pipeline

1. See, for instance, Peter A. Stott and J. A. Kettleborough, 'Origins and Estimates of Uncertainty in Predictions of Twenty-First Century Temperature Rise', *Nature*, vol. 416, pp. 723–6, 18 April 2002.
2. Jeffrey A.Yin, 'A Consistent Poleward Shift of the Storm Tracks in Simulations of 21st-Century Climate', *Geophysical Research Letters*, vol. 32, L18701, 2005, DOI: 10.1029/2005GL023684, 2005. There's also a good entry on this subject at http://www.realclimate.org/index.php/archives/2006/12/on-mid-latitude-storms/
3. Nicholas Stern, *The Economics of Climate Change: The Stern Review* (Cambridge: Cambridge University Press, 2007) (hereafter referred to as the *Stern Review*).
4. P. A. Stott, D. A. Stone and M. R. Allen, 'Human Contribution to the European Heat Wave of 2003', *Nature*, vol. 432, pp. 610–14, 2 December 2004.
5. See W. R. Keatinge et al., 'Heat Related Mortality in Warm and Cold Regions of Europe: Observational Study', *British Medical Journal*, vol. 321, pp. 670–73, 2000, available online at http://www.bmj.com/cgi/reprint/321/7262/670
6. *Stern Review*, box 3.5.
7. N. S. Keenlyside et al., 'Advancing Decadal-Scale Climate Prediction in the North Atlantic Sector', *Nature*, vol. 453, p 84–88, 2 May 2008.
8. In 1957/8 it was 0.23 km$^2$ and by 1997 it had grown to 1.65 km$^2$. For this and other details of the Tsho Rolpa adaptation scheme see IPCC WGII, chapter 17, box 17.1.
9. For this and the following, see IPCC WGII, chapter 17, section 17.2.2.
10. W. R. Keatinge et al., 'Heat Related Mortality in Warm and Cold Regions of Europe: Observational Study', *British Medical Journal*, vol. 321, pp. 670–73, 2000, available online at http://www.bmj.com/cgi/reprint/321/7262/670

# 5. Climate Wild Cards

1. The other reason is that northern Europe has a maritime climate – few countries are far from the relative warmth of the sea – whereas central parts of North America are trapped in the middle of a continent.
2. Gabrielle Walker, 'The Tipping Point of the Iceberg', *Nature*, vol. 441, pp. 802–5, 2006, and references therein; see also Stephen Battersby, 'The Great Atlantic Shutdown', *New Scientist*, 15 April 2006.

3. A compensating drop in the sea level in the southern hemisphere would be less severe because it would be spread over a larger area.

4. S. Rahmstorf et al., 'Thermohaline Circulation Hysteresis: A Model Intercomparison', *Geophysical Research Letters*, vol. 32, L23605, 2005, DOI: 10.1029/2005GL023655.

5. Gabrielle Walker, 'The Tipping Point of the Iceberg', *Nature*, vol. 441, pp. 802–5, 2006.

7. C. H. Davis, Y. Li, J. R. McConnell, M. M. Frey and E. Hanna, 'Snowfall-Driven Growth in East Antarctic Ice Sheet Mitigates Recent Sea-Level Rise', *Science*, vol. 308, no. 5730, pp. 1898–1901, 2005, DOI: 10.1126/science.1110662.

8 E. Domack et al., 'Stability of the Larsen B Ice Shelf on the Antarctic Peninsula During the Holocene Epoch', *Nature*, vol. 436, pp. 681–5, 2005, DOI: 10.1038/nature03908.

9. T. A. Scambos, J. A. Bohlander, C. A. Shuman and P. Skyarca, 'Glacier Acceleration and Thinning After Ice Shelf Collapse in the Larsen B Embayment, Antarctica', *Geophysical Research Letters*, vol. 31, L18401, 2004, DOI: 10.1029/2004GL020670.

10. See, for example, Andrew Shepherd et al., 'Inland Thinning of Pine Island Glacier, West Antarctica', *Science*, vol. 291, pp. 862–4, 2 February 2001, DOI: 10.1126/science.291.5505.862.

11. O. M. Johannessen et al., 'Recent Ice-Sheet Growth in the Interior of Greenland', *Science*, vol. 310, pp. 1013–16, 2005, and W. Krabill et al., 'Greenland Ice Sheet: increased coastal thinning', *Geophysical Research Letters*, vol. 31, 2004.

12. E Rignot and P. Kanagaratnam, *Science*, vol. 311, p. 986, 2006.

13. J. M. Gregory and P. Hybrechts, 'Ice-Sheet Contributions to Future Sea-Level Change', *Philosophical Transactions of the Royal Society of London* A, 364, pp. 1709–31, 2006, DOI: 10.1098/rsta.2006.1796.

14. H. Jay Zwally et al., 'Surface Melt-Induced Acceleration of Greenland Ice-Sheet Flow', *Science*, vol. 297, pp. 218–22, 2002.

15. Gabrielle Walker, 'A World Melting from the Top Down', *Nature*, vol. 446, pp. 718–21, 2007, and references therein.

16. V. Romanovsky et al., 'Permafrost Temperature Records: Indicators of Climate Change', *EOS, AGU Transactions*, vol. 83, no, 50, pp. 589–94, 10 December 2002.

17. K. M. Walter et al., 'Methane bubbling from Siberian thaw lakes as a positive feedback to climate warming', *Nature*, vol. 443, pp. 71–5, 7 September 2006, DOI: 10.1038/nature05040.

18. T. Johansson et al., 'Decadal Vegetation Changes in a Northern Peat Land, Greenhouse Gas Fluxes and Net Radiative Forcing', *Global Change Biology*, vol. 12, pp. 1–18, 2006, DOI: 10.1111/j.1365-2486.2006.01267.x.

19. J. E. Hanson, 'Scientific Reticence and Sea-Level Rise', *Environmental Research Letters*, vol. 2:024002, 2007, DOI: 10.1088/1748-9326/2/2/024002.

20. See IPCC WGII, chapter 7.

21. See for instance, Jim Lovelock, *The Revenge of Gaia* (London: Allen Lane, 2006), and Fred Pearce, *The Last Generation: How Will Nature Take Her Revenge for Climate Change?* (Nottingham: Eden Books, 2006).

# 6. What Should We Aim For?

1. These data all come from IPCC WGII, chapter 19, table 19.1, and chapter 20, table 20.7. Note that there's already a danger of confusion when anyone talks about a specific temperature rise because some of these refer to rises above the temperature of pre-industrial times, before global warming had begun to take hold, while others are talking about rises relative to today, when we have already had $0.75°C$ of warming. When anyone mentions a specific temperature rise it's always worth checking the reference point. Throughout this book we will always refer to rises over pre-industrial times, unless we say otherwise.

2. Cited by Michael Oppenheimer and Annie Petsonk in 'Article 2 of the UNFCCC: Historical Origins, Recent Interpretations', *Climatic Change*, vol. 73, pp. 195–226, 2005, DOI: 10.1007/s10584-005-0434-8.

3. 'Climate Protection Strategies for the 21st Century. Kyoto and Beyond', WBGU, 2003, available on the web at http://www.wbgu.de/wbgu_sn2003_engl.html

4. 'Meeting the Climate Challenge', International Climate Change Taskforce, available on the web at http://www.americanprogress.org/kf/climatechallenge.pdf

5. http://register.consilium.europa.eu/pdf/en/05/st07/st07242.en05.pdf

6. Because these values are so uncertain, we have rounded them to the nearest $0.5°C$. These numbers are a combination of the results described in 'Climate Change 2007: Mitigation of Climate Change' (written by Working Group III and subtitled 'Working Group III Contribution to the Fourth Assessment Report of the IPCC Corporate Author Intergovernmental Panel on Climate Change', and hereafter referred to as IPCC WGIII), chapter 3, especially table 3.9 and the discussion in section 3.5 (Cambridge: Cambridge Uni-

versity Press, 2007), and those in G. R. Harris et al., 'Frequency distributions of transient regional climate change from perturbed physics ensembles of general circulation model simulations', *Climate Dynamics*, vol. 27, no. 4, pp. 357–75, 2006, DOI 10.1007/s00382-006-0142-8. The range is for temperatures at an 80 per cent confidence level.

7. *Stern Review*, chapter 7.
8. IPCC WGIII, chapter 1.
9. S. Pacala and R. Socolow, 'Stabilisation Wedges: Solving the Climate Problem for the Next 50 Years with Current Technologies', *Science*, vol. 205, pp. 968–72, 13 August 2004.
10. Fred Pearce describes this well in the appendix to *The Last Generation* (2006).
11. Unlike the wedges, which start at nothing today and increase linearly over the next fifty years, the Virgin prize requires removing a flat billion tonnes per year for at least a decade. If we started doing this in ten years' time and continued for four decades, that would give a total of 40 billion tonnes, which is about half a Socolow wedge.
12. Johannes Lehmann, 'A Handful of Carbon', *Nature*, vol. 447, pp. 143–4, 2007.
13. Oliver Morton, 'Is This What It Takes to Save the World?', *Nature*, vol. 447, pp. 132–6, 2007, DOI: 10.1038/447132a2007.
14. P. J. Crutzen, 'Albedo Enhancement by Stratospheric Sulfur Injections: A Contribution to Resolve a Policy Dilemma?', *Climatic Change*, vol. 77, pp. 211–20, 2006.

# 7. More from Less

1. IPCC WGIII, chapter 6. This figure doesn't include halocarbons which add about 1.5 gigatonnes $CO_2$eq per year, though they are likely to be phased out in any case.
2. http://kim.foresight.gov.uk/horizon_scanning_centre/Energy/Potential_Role_ST/Potential_Role_ST.html
3. http://lab.teriin.org/
4. IPCC WGIII, chapter 6, section 6.4.9.
5. See the IEA fact sheet at http://www.iea.org/textbase/papers/2005/standby_fact.pdf
6. *Stern Review*, box 24.9, page 600.
7. Classic studies carried out by Robert Socolow at Princeton University back in 1978 showed that the energy consumption of identical houses with different occupants could vary by a factor of two.

8. See IPCC WGIII, chapter 6, section 6.4.1.5.

9. http://kim.foresight.gov.uk/horizon_scanning_centre/Energy/Potential_Role_ST/Potential_Role_ST.html

10. Ibid.

11. Ibid.

12. See IPCC WGIII, chapter 8, section 8.3.2.

13. IPCC WGIII, chapter 8.

14. *Stern Review*, chapter 25, figure 25.1. These numbers vary from study to study, and WGIII, chapter 9, of the IPCC report gave a slightly smaller but still very substantial figure of 5.8 gigatonnes $CO_2$ per year 'in the 1990s'. Chapter 3 of the same report gave the figures for emissions from deforestation and soil decomposition after logging as 7–16 per cent of 2004 total greenhouse gas emissions.

15. Selective logging can be done much more sustainably with just a little care. Certification showing the origin of tropical hardwoods and whether they had been harvested in a sustainable way would help to put pressure on loggers to do it right.

16. Planting trees isn't always a climate panacea. There is some suggestion that putting new trees in middle and higher latitudes means replacing bright land with dark tree tops, and hence encourages the Earth to soak up more sunlight – causing further warming. See S. Gibbard, K. Caldeira, G. Bala, T. J. Philips and M. Wickett, 'Climate Effects of Global Land Cover Change', *Geophysical Research Letters*, 32 (23), L23705, 2005. That doesn't, however, apply to the tropics.

17. This is the result of the 'top down' models which start from the varied $CO_2$ levels in different parts of the atmosphere and work backwards to see where they are coming from. The models that calculate from the 'bottom up' using existing land areas find lower values – though they may underestimate the ability of the forests to act as carbon sinks. See IPCC WGIII, chapter 9, for more discussion of this.

18. The extent to which forests are already acting as net carbon sinks is controversial. See, for instance, the recent *Science* paper showing that tropical forests store considerably more carbon than had previously been thought: B. Stephens et al., 'Weak Northern and Strong Tropical Land Carbon Uptake from Vertical Profiles of Atmospheric $CO_2$', *Science*, vol. 316, pp. 1732–5, 2007.

19. *Stern Review*, chapter 25, box 25.2.

20. *Stern Review*, chapter 25, p. 607.

21. See IPCC WGIII, chapter 9, table 9.3.

22. Quoted in IPCC WGIII, chapter 10, section 10.1.

23. For an excellent discussion of these issues, see 'The Population

Problem' by Kerri Smith, *Nature Reports Climate Change*, 15 May 2008, available online (http://www.nature.com/climate/2008/0806/full/climate.2008.44.html).

24. See, for instance, 'The Impact of Women's Education on Fertility In Latin America: Searching for Explanations' by Teresa Castro Martin and Fatima Juarez, *International Family Planning Perspectives*, vol. 21, number 2, June 1995, available online (http://www.guttmacher.org/pubs/journals/2105295.html), and 'Fertility and Infant Mortality Trends in Nicaragua 1964–1993. The Role of Women's Education' by R Pena, J Liljestrand, E Zelaya and LA Persson, *Journal of Epidemiology and Community Health*, vol. 53, pp. 132–137, available online (http://jech.bmj.com/cgi/content/abstract/53/3/132).

25. Kerri Smith, 'The Population Problem', *Nature Reports Climate Change*, 15 May 2008, available online (http://www.nature.com/climate/2008/0806/full/climate.2008.44.html).

# 8. Planes, Trains and Automobiles

1. Emissions were 6.3 billion tonnes $CO_2$eq in 2004, having risen from 1970 by 120 per cent.
2. IPCC WGIII, chapter 1.
3. http://kim.foresight.gov.uk/horizon_scanning_centre/Energy/Potential_Role_ST/Potential_Role_ST.html
4. It also said that rising prices would increase the cost of food imports to developing countries by 9 per cent in 2007. The report is available on the web at http://www.fao.org/docrep/010/ah864e/ah864e00.htm
5. A. E. Farrell et al., 'Ethanol Can Contribute to Energy and Environmental Goals', *Science*, vol. 311, pp. 506–8, 27 January 2006. The numbers in the paper differ slightly from the ones quoted here, but see also the appended erratum.
6. http://www.iea.org/textbase/techno/essentials2.pdf
7. See, for instance, the Friends of the Earth briefing at http://www.foe.co.uk/resource/briefings/palm_oil_biofuel_position.pdf
8. 'Sustainable Bioenergy: A Framework for Decision Makers', available at http://esa.un.org/un-energy/pdf/susdev.Biofuels.FAO.pdf. See also Fred Pearce, 'Fuels Gold: Big Risks of the Biofuel Revolution', *New Scientist*, 25 September 2006, for an excellent overview of the ins and outs of biofuels.
9. Partly because of the potential problems in doing the greenhouse accounting for biofuels, the UN report also concluded that bioenergy could best serve the greenhouse cause if used in place of coal to make

electricity and heat. But it also acknowledged that the dearth of alternative fuels for transport made further research on biofuels very attractive.

10. O Inderwildi, S Jenkins and D A King, *Angewante Chemie* International Edition, vol. 47, pp. 52–53, 2008.
11. *Stern Review*, p. 388, box 15.6.
12. *Stern Review*, p. 388, box 15.6, and IPCC WGIII, chapter 5.
13. See, for instance, the analysis by the UK's Royal Commission on Environmental Pollution: 'The Environmental Effects of Civil Aircraft in Flight', published in 2002 and available on the web at: http://www.rcep.org.uk/avreport.htm
14. IPCC WGIII, chapter 5, section 5.3.3.
15. IPCC WGIII, chapter 5, section 5.3.3, table 5.7. See also an excellent summary of the potential technological developments, along with their possible hazards, in Bennett Daviss, 'Green Sky Thinking', *New Scientist*, 22 February 2007.
16. IPCC WGIII, chapter 5, section 5.4.2.1, and table 5.13.
17. There's an excellent discussion of these issues in a special report for the UK's *Observer* newspaper, Tom Robbins, 'The Big Green Dilemma', 1 July 2007, available on the web at http://www.guardian.co.uk/travel/2007/jul/01/escape.green
18. IPCC WGIII, chapter 5, figure 5.7. Note that this shows the values in terms of carbon, rather than carbon dioxide. To convert you need to multiply by forty-four and divide by twelve. See also V. Eyring et al., 'Emissions from International Shipping: 1. The Last 50 Years', *Journal of Geophysical Research-Atmospheres*, vol. 110 (D17), p. 17305, 15 September 2005, abstract available on the web at http://www.mpg.de/english/researchResults/researchPublications/researchReports/GEO/200541_043.shtml
19. See IPCC WGIII, chapter 5, table 5.4.
20. http://www.railteam.eu/
21. http://www.acea.be/files/463-8.pdf
22. *Stern Review*.
23. Fuel cells could also be used as a storage device to get around the fickle nature of renewable sources such as solar and wind.
24. *Stern Review*, p. 405, box 16.1.

# 9. Power to Change

1. IPCC WGIII, chapter 1, p. 3.
2. IPCC WGIII, chapter 4, table 4.2.

3. IPCC WGIII, chapter 1, p. 13.
4. 'IPCC Special Report on Carbon Capture and Storage', 2005, chapter 1. Available on the web at http://www.ipcc.ch/activity/srccs/index.htm
5. *Stern Review*, p. 400.
6. http://www.worldenergyoutlook.org/press_rel06.asp
7. Unless otherwise specified, the information in the rest of this chapter comes either from IPCC WGIII, chapter 4, or the Foresight Horizon Scanning Technology report at http://kim.foresight.gov.uk/horizon_scanning_centre/Energy/Potential_Role_ST/Potential_Role_ST.html
8. IPCC WGIII, chapter 4, section 4.3.3.1, for the details in this paragraph.
9. IPCC WGIII, chapter 4, table 4.2.
10. IPCC WGIII, chapter 4.
11. IPCC WGIII, chapter 4, table 4.2.
12. *Stern Review*, box 9.2.
13. 'IPCC Special Report on Carbon Capture and Storage', 2005, available on the web at http://www.ipcc.ch/activity/srccs/index.htm
14. *Stern Review*, box 24.7, p. 593.
15. See IPCC WGIII, chapter 4, section 4.3.6.
16. 'IPCC Special Report on Carbon Capture and Storage', 2005, available on the web at http://www.ipcc.ch/activity/srccs/index.htm
17. The fusion process generates a few stray neutrons which will slam into the walls of the reactor and eventually make it radioactive. But the ash itself from the reaction is free of any radioactivity, and the overall waste burden is vastly less than for a fission plant.

## 10. It's the Economy, Stupid

1. Nicholas Stern, *The Economics of Climate Change: The Stern Review* (Cambridge: Cambridge University Press, 2007), chapter 6. The baseline level of costs was 5 per cent of GDP. Including 'non-market' impacts on the environment and human health increased the figure to 11 per cent, including the possibility that the climate may be more sensitive than we think took it up to 14 per cent and considering that the poorer parts of the world would receive a disproportionate share gave a final figure of 20 per cent. Note that these figures mark the eventual impact of business as usual, and as such wouldn't be achieved for several centuries.
2. Put simply, this number accounts for the fact that a percentage drop in

income for someone struggling to survive on £1 per day is much worse than the same percentage drop for someone earning £100 per day. Stern used a figure for this parameter of one, which means that, in this example, a benefit going to the person earning £1 a day would be valued 100 times more than the same percentage benefit going to the person on £100 per day. A figure of two, which is more common, would change the value factor in this example to 10,000.

3. William Nordhaus, 'Critical Assumptions in the Stern Review on Climate Change', *Science*, vol. 317, pp. 201–2, 13 July 2007. There is also a useful editorial in *The Economist*, 'Shots Across the Stern', 13 December 2006.

4. Nicholas Stern and Chris Taylor, 'Climate Change: Risk, Ethics and the Stern Review', *Science*, vol. 317, pp. 203–4, 13 July 2007.

5. See IPCC WGIII, chapter 20, p. 16.

6. Dasgupta wrote, 'To accept it would be to claim that the current generation in the model economy ought literally to starve itself so that future generations are able to enjoy ever-increasing consumption levels.' (In fact, to suppose that eta is 1 is also to suppose that starvation isn't all that painful!) See 'Comments on the Stern Review's Economics of Climate Change by Sir Partha Dasgupta', available on the web at http://www.econ.cam.ac.uk/faculty/dasgupta/STERN.pdf

7. IPCC WGII, chapter 20, p. 16.

8. Partha Dasgupta, 'Discounting Climate Change', *Review of Environmental Economics and Policy*, in the press.

9. IPCC WG III, Summary for Policymakers.

10. Available on the web at: http://www.mckinseyquarterly.com/article_abstract_visitor.aspx?ar=1911&L2=3&L3=0&srid=246 (requires free registration).

11. *Stern Review*, p. xviii.

12. *Stern Review*, p. 386.

13. The Kyoto scheme began operation in February that year, when the Protocol came into force.

14. The UK, Ireland, Spain, Italy, Austria and Greece all had emissions that were higher than their caps. But emissions from the rest of the European Union were lower. See, for instance, A. D. Ellerman and D. K. Buchner, 'The European Union Emissions Trading Scheme: Origins, Allocations and Early Results', *Review of Environmental Economics and Policy*, vol. 1, no. 1, pp. 66–87, Winter 2007.

15. Martin Brough, 'Emission Trading – Can the Carbon Market Drive Investment Decisions?' *Power Engineering International*, available on the web at http://pepei.pennnet.com/display_article/297274/17/ARTCL/none/none/Emission-Trading—Can-the-carbon-market-drive-investment-decisions?

16. For these reasons, economists have already given the experiment a cautious thumbs up. See, for example, the set of papers in *Review of Environmental Economics and Policy*, vol. 1, no. 1, Winter 2007.

17. 'State of the Carbon Market 2007', available via the World Bank's carbon website at http://carbonfinance.org/

18. Cameron Hepburn, Michael Grubb, Karsten Neuhoff, Felix Matthes and Maximilien Tse, 'Auctioning of EU ETS Phase II Allowances: How and Why?', *Climate Policy*, vol. 6, p. 137, 2006.

19. See *Stern Review*, chapter 17, for more on this.

20. http://assets.panda.org/downloads/emission_impossible__final_.pdf

21. M. Wara, 'Is the Global Carbon Market Working?' *Nature*, vol. 445, pp. 595-596, 18 February 2007.

22. Nick Davies, 'Abuse and Incompetence in Fight Against Global Warming', *Guardian*, 2 June 2007.

23. www.cdmgoldstandard.org

24. Michael Wara, 'Is the carbon market working?', *Nature*, vol. 445, pp. 595–6, 8 February 2007.

25. *Stern Review*, p. 610.

26. See http://unfccc.int/methods_and_science/lulucf/items/3757.php. For more discussion of this issue, see Raymond E. Gullison et al., 'Tropical Forests and Climate Policy', *Science*, vol. 316, pp. 985–6, 18 May 2007, published online 10 May 2007, DOI: 10.1126/science.1136163; and M. Santilli et al., 'Tropical Deforestation and the Kyoto Protocol', *Climatic Change*, vol. 71, no. 3, pp. 267–76 (10), August 2005.

27. *Stern Review*, p. 616, box 25.5.

28. *Stern Review*, p. 626, box 26.1.

29. *Stern Review*, p. 628, box 26.2.

30. There's an excellent summary of the business state of play in Kurt Kleiner, 'The Corporate Race to Cut Carbon', *Nature Reports Climate Change*, DOI:10.1038/climate.2007.31), available on the web at: http://www.nature.com/climate/2007/0708/full/climate.2007.31.html

31. http://www.pewclimate.org/docUploads/PEW_CorpStrategies.pdf

## 11. The Road from Kyoto

1. The Nuclear Non-Proliferation Treaty is one of the few that comes close.

2. http://unfccc.int/files/kyoto_protocol/background/status_of_ratification/application/pdf/kp_ratifcation.pdf

3. M. R. Rapauch et al., 'Global and Regional Drivers of Accelerating

$CO_2$ Emissions', *Proceedings of the National Academy of Sciences*, vol. 104, no. 24, pp. 10288–93, 12 June 2007.

4. Ibid.
5. See Ecofys report, 'Factors Underpinning Future Action', p. 13 (hereafter referred to as 'Ecofys report'), available at http://www.defra.gov.uk/science/project_data/DocumentLibrary/GA01093/GA01093_4191_FRP.pdf, for much more detail on this and how it depends on the means of distributing national targets.
6. Evidence from Friends of the Earth to the UK's Environmental Audit Committee, July 2007. See the full report at: http://www.publications.parliament.uk/pa/cm200607/cmselect/cmenvaud/460/460.pdf
7. John Vidal and David Adam, 'China overtakes US as world's biggest $CO_2$ emitter', *The Guardian*, 2 June 2007.
8. Ecofys report fact sheets.
9. ' "Contraction and Convergence" (C&C) is the science-based, global climate-policy framework proposed to the UN since 1990 by the Global Commons Institute (GCI).' www.gci.org.uk
10. Ecofys report, p. 13. Note that the exact figures depend on population scenarios, and would probably have to be adapted to reflect actual population figures, as time passed.
11. Ecofys report, p. 16.
12. Ecofys report.
13. *Stern Review*, p. 527.

## 12. Rapidly Developing Nations

1. The Ecofys report contains much more information about the data sources and their reliability.
2. See http://www.mnp.nl/en/dossiers/Climatechange/moreinfo/Chinanowno1inCO2emissionsUSAinsecondposition.html
3. See the World Resource Institute's report at http://www.wri.org/biodiv/topic_content.cfm?cid=4218

## 13. Industrialised Nations

1. Cited by Michael Oppenheimer and Annie Petsonk in 'Article 2 of the UNFCCC: Historical Origins, Recent Interpretations', *Climatic Change*, vol. 73, pp. 195–226, 2005, DOI: 10.1007/s10584-005-0434-8.

2. http://www.nrdc.org/media/docs/020403.pdf

3. All resigned their posts in order to join the government, and the oil tanker that Chevron named after Rice in tribute to her contribution to the company was subsequently rechristened after an outcry.

4. Clinton later said, of the Bush administration: 'I signed Kyoto and they got out of it.' http://www.washingtonpost.com/wp-dyn/content/article/2005/07/13/AR2005071302350.html

5. See, for instance, the report 'Atmosphere of Pressure' by the Union of Concerned Scientists and Government Accountability Project, February 2007, which documents many of these instances. It's available at http://www.ucsusa.org/assets/documents/scientific_integrity/Atmosphere-of-Pressure.pdf

6. See http://oversight.house.gov/story.asp?ID=1214

7. https://cf.iats.missouri.edu/news/NewsBureauSingleNews.cfm?-newsid=9842

8. http://www.climateinstitute.org.au/cia1/downloads/AP6_Report.pdf

9. http://dir.salon.com/story/opinion/feature/2005/08/06/muckraker/index.html

10. Also known as Assembly Bill 32, or AB32.

11. See http://www.rggi.org/about.htm

12. http://www.usmayors.org/climateprotection/

13. http://www.post-gazette.com/pg/07011/753072-28.stm

14. http://www.rollingstone.com/politics/story/15051506/global_warming_a_real_solution

15. See this account from the American Council for an Energy Efficient Economy: http://www.aceee.org/press/0302carbongap.htm

16. A fascinating insight into this process can be had by reading the heavily red-lined and highlighted document, later leaked by Greenpeace, that bears the US comments on the draft proposal in Germany. See http://weblog.greenpeace.org/makingwaves/G8%20Summit%20Declaration%20-%20US%20comments%20May%2014-1.pdf

17. http://news.bbc.co.uk/1/hi/sci/tech/6651295.stm

18. Greg Walters, 'President Has Not Decided on Kyoto', *Moscow Times*, 20 September 2003, available to subscribers at http://www.themoscowtimes.com/stories/2003/09/30/001.html. Putin did go on in the same speech to acknowledge that certain parts of the country could be hit by floods and droughts.

19. IPCC WGII, chapter 12.

20. See, for instance, Anthony Faiola, 'Japanese Putting All Their Energy into Saving Fuel', *Washington Post*, Thursday 16 February 2006.

21. http://www.emissionstrading.nsw.gov.au/

22. http://www.pm.gov.au/media/Speech/2006/speech2218.cfm

23. M. R. Rapauch et al., 'Global and Regional Drivers of Accelerating $CO_2$ Emissions', *Proceedings of the National Academy of Sciences*, 2007, vol. 104, no. 24, pp. 10288–93, fig. 5, 12 June 2007. The US has produced about 29 per cent of the historical emissions, and the EU about 26 per cent.

24. To divide up the reductions among its members, the EU used the infant triptych approach (see chapter 12), which gave very wide results to reflect the diversity of countries. Luxembourg, for instance, agreed to a hefty cut of -28 per cent whereas Greece was allowed to grow by +25 per cent and Portugal +27 per cent. An agreement modelled on this approach might now form part of the basis for a new fully international agreement.

25. http://ec.europa.eu/environment/climat/adaptation/index_en.htm

26. http://www.consilium.europa.eu/ueDocs/cms_Data/docs/pressData/en/ec/93135.pdf

27. The idea is to do this via some mechanism akin to the Kyoto Protocol's Clean Development Mechanism. The same document also stated that CDM projects would continue to be linked to the European Trading Scheme even after their creator, the Kyoto Protocol, became defunct in 2012.

28. He made this statement at the global summit on sustainable development in Johannesburg in August 2002.

29. The White Paper, 'Meeting the Energy Challenge', is available for downloading at http://www.dtistats.net/ewp/

30. http://www.rcep.org.uk/newenergy.htm

# 14. How You Can Change the World

1. http://www.foe.co.uk/resource/briefings/carbon_offsetting.pdf

2. S. G. Gibbard et al., 'Climate Effects of Global Land Cover Change', *Geophysical Research Letters*, vol. 32 (23), L23705, 2005.

3. George Monbiot wrote an extremely articulate explanation as to why planting trees is a bad way to compensate for carbon emissions, and why offsets themselves can make us dangerously complacent. His article, 'Buying Complacency', was published in the *Guardian* on 17 January 2006 and is available on the web at http://www.monbiot.com/archives/2006/01/17/buying-complacency/

4. See, for instance, Nick Davies, 'The Inconvenient Truth About the Carbon Offset Industry', *Guardian*, Saturday 16 June 2007, http://www.guardian.co.uk/environment/2007/jun/16/climatechange.climatechange

5.  http://www.cdmgoldstandard.org/
6.  'The Validity of Food Miles as an Indicator of Sustainable Development', DEFRA, 2005, available on the web at http://statistics.defra.gov.uk/esg/reports/foodmiles/final.pdf
7.  Ibid.
8.  Caroline Saunders, Andrew Barber and Greg Taylor, 'Food Miles – Comparative Energy/Emissions Performance of New Zealand's Agriculture Industry', *AERU Research Report*, no. 285, July 2006. Available on the web at http://www.lincoln.ac.nz/story_images/2328_rr285_s9760.pdf
9.  James MacGregor and Bill Vorley, 'Fair Miles? The Concept of "Food Miles" Through a Sustainable Development Lens', International Institute for Environment and Development, 2006, available on the web at http://www.iied.org/pubs/pdf/full/11064IIED.pdf
10. http://www.energysavingtrust.org.uk/aboutest/news/ampere/
11. http://kim.foresight.gov.uk/horizon_scanning_centre/Energy/Potential_Role_ST/Potential_Role_ST.html
12. See   http://www.energysavingtrust.org.uk/proxy/view/full/165/homeenergycheck or call 0800 512012.
13. http://www.defra.gov.uk/environment/climatechange/uk/individual/pca/pdf/pca-scopingstudy.pdf
14. See http://www.carbonneutralnewcastle.com/home/
15. See http://www.woking.gov.uk/environment/climatechangestrategy
16. Available    at:    http://www.ci.austin.tx.us/council/downloads/mw_acpp_points.pdf
17. See http://www.capegateway.gov.za/Text/2007/7/ses_july07.pdf
18. Manfred Milinski et al., 'Stabilizing the Earth's Climate Is Not a Losing Game: Supporting Evidence from Public Goods Experiments', *Proceedings of the National Academy of Sciences*, vol. 103, pp. 3994–8, 14 March 2006.
19. In 2007 the *New Statesman* published an excellent article discussing the ramifications of this. See Lois Rogers, 'Climate Change: Why We Don't Believe It', 23 April 2007, available on line at http://www.newstatesman.com/200704230025
20. For more about this, and the new technologies that might help us achieve it, see Oliver Morton's excellent *Eating the Sun* (London: Fourth Estate, 2007).
21. For more on this see the excellent review 'Climate Change, Deforestation, and the Fate of the Amazon', by Yadvinder Malti et al., *Science*, vol. 319, pp. 169–72, 11 January 2008.

# Acknowledgements

The authors would like to thank the following people:

For inspiration and advice especially on the subject of climate change:
Richard Alley, Michael Bender, Henry Derwent, Laura Garwin, John Houghton, Geoff Jenkins, Ralph Keeling, Oliver Morton, Robert Napier, Fred Pearce, John Pyle, Dan Schrag, Jeremy Webb and David Warrilow

For reading and commenting on all or part of the manuscript:
Fred Barron, David Bodanis, Partha Dasgupta, Michael Evans, Tim Flannery, Jim Lovelock, Rosa Malloy, Oliver Morton, Nick Rowley and Bob Watson

For support especially during writing:
Fred Barron, Stephen Battersby, Yann Golzio, Ben King, Toby King, Emily King and Zach King, Jane Lichtenstein, Rosa Malloy, Damian Malloy, Dominick McIntyre, Philippe Mottin, Christine Nesme, Jean-Chris Sinardet, Helene Sinardet, Sammy and Minnie Sinardet, Simon and Anita Singh, Karen Southwell, Helen, Ed and Christian Southworth, Jayne Thomas and John Vandecar

Special thanks to our editors Bill Swainson and Emily Sweet at Bloomsbury and Andrea Schulz at Harcourt, and to our agents Michael Carlisle and Susan Hobson at Inkwell. And extra special thanks to Michael Evans and Hubert Sinardet, without whom this book could not have been written.

# Index